DISCRIMINATION LAW

DISCRIMINATION LAW

A PRACTICAL GUIDE FOR MANAGEMENT

Michael Malone

KOGAN PAGE

First published in 1993

Apart from any fair dealing for the purposes of research or private study, or criticism or review, as permitted under the Copyright, Designs and Patents Act, 1988, this publication may only be reproduced, stored or transmitted, in any form or by any means, with the prior permission in writing of the publishers, or in the case of reprographic reproduction in accordance with the terms of licences issued by the Copyright Licensing Agency. Enquiries concerning reproduction outside those terms should be sent to the publishers at the undermentioned address:

Kogan Page Limited
120 Pentonville Road
London N1 9JN

© Michael Malone, 1993

British Library Cataloguing in Publication Data
A CIP record for this book is available from the British Library.
ISBN 0 7494 0824 3

Typeset by Books Unlimited (Nottm) – Sutton in Ashfield, NG17 1AL
Printed and bound in Great Britain by Biddles Ltd, Guildford and Kings Lynn

Contents

Acknowledgements 9
Introduction 10

Part 1 The requirements of UK and EC Law

1 General principles 15
The definitions of discrimination 15
When is discrimination unlawful? 20
The laws against discrimination 24
The legal consequences of discrimination 25
Summary 28

2 Direct discrimination 29
Direct sex discrimination 29
Marriage discrimination 29
Direct racial discrimination 31
Features of racial, sex and marriage discrimination 32
Causes of direct discrimination 33
Problem areas 36
Practical advice 38
Summary 42

3 Indirect discrimination 43
The social background 43
The legal approach 44
Words and phrases 46
Problem areas 49
Practical advice 52
Summary 58

4 Victimisation 60
The legal approach 60
Practical advice 64
Summary 67

5 When is discrimination unlawful? 68
Duties of employers 68
Duties of employees 75
Practical advice 77
Summary 77

6 Discrimination in filling vacancies, promotion and training 79
The law 79
Identifying and proving discrimination 87
Practical advice 92
Summary 95

7 Genuine occupational qualifications and other exceptions 97
Exceptions which no longer apply 97
Statutory and official discrimination 98
Other general exceptions 102
Genuine occupational qualifications 104
Practical advice 110
Summary 111

8 Positive action 112
The legal exceptions 112
Practical advice 121
Summary 125

9 Sexual and racial harassment 127
The legal approach to harassment 128
Practical advice 134
Summary 139

10 Benefits, detriment and dismissal 140
Terms of employment 140
Benefits, facilities or services 142
Detrimental treatment 143
Dismissal 145
Practical advice 148
Summary 151

11 Pregnancy related discrimination 152
The law and pregnancy 152
Other legal issues 156
Practical advice 158
Summary 159

12 Unlawful advertising and pressure to discriminate 160
Discriminatory practices 160
Advertisements 161
Pressure to discriminate 163
Practical advice 165
Summary 167

13 Equal pay and pensions 168

The Equal Pay Act 168
Pensions 178
Practical advice 180
Summary 182

14 Discrimination outside the employment field 184
Extent and common examples 184
General exceptions 187
Specific exceptions 188
Responsibility for agents and employees 191
Provisions for your benefit 191
Practical advice 192
Summary 192

PART II LEGAL PROCEDURES

15 Dealing with complaints by individuals 197
The questionnaire procedure 197
Documents 199
Time limits 200
Compensation 203
Practical advice 205
Summary 206

16 The role of the commissions 207
The positive role 207
The enforcement role 208
Time limits 211
Practical advice 211
Summary 212

PART III EQUAL OPPORTUNITY POLICIES

17 Adopting a policy 215
Reasons for adopting a policy 215
Formulating the policy 217
Responsibility for the policy 219
Communicating the policy 219
Written programmes and procedures 220
Reviewing existing practices 221
Instructions and training 222
Summary 223

18 Making the policy work 224
Monitoring the policy 225
Reviewing the policy 227
Continuing training 228
Policy initiatives 228
Summary 229

19 Some success stories 230
Manufacturing industries 230
The police 231
Financial services 234
Communications 234
Local authorities 235
General conclusions 236

Appendix 1 Key provisions of the Race Relations Act 1976 and the Sex Discrimination Act 1975 238

Appendix 2 The IPM Equal Opportunities Code 250

Appendix 3 Extracts from EC law 262

Further Reading 264

Table of cases 266

Index 269

Acknowledgements

I am very grateful to the many organisations and individuals who have helped me to write this book, particularly those mentioned below.

Pauline Matthews, of the Equal Opportunities Commission, read the first draft of the typescript and Jayne Monkhouse, also of the Commission, read Chapters 17 and 18, on equal opportunity policies. They both made many invaluable suggestions, the great majority of which I adopted, although I do of course accept full responsibility for all the views expressed in the book.

The Institute of Personnel Management and Dianah Worman, IPM's policy adviser for equal opportunities, have kindly given permission for the reproduction of the IPM Equal Opportunities Code, the full text of which is set out in Appendix 2.

All the information contained in Chapter 19 is based on information supplied to me. The organisations (and the individuals in those organisations) who have given the information to me are Shell UK (Chris Marsh), National Power (Jock Simpson), Hotpoint (Mrs J M W Jones), the Police Staff College at Bramshill (Norman Greenhill), the Greater Manchester Police (Chief Inspector Bill Stretton), Midland Bank (Jane Northam), Allied Dunbar (Chris McCormack), the Independent Television Association (Alison Hall), the BBC (Chris Trynka) and Gloucestershire County Council (Sarah Anderton).

To obtain the information used in Chapter 19, I approached only a small proportion of the equal opportunity employers in Great Britain and I was able to make direct use of only a part of the information supplied. Other employers who kindly supplied a large variety of information included Avis, Barclays Bank, British Gas, Bull Information Systems Limited, Calderdale Health Authority, the CIS, Derbyshire County Council, Gallaher, Leeds City Council, London Weekend Television, Manchester City Council, McDonalds, John Menzies, National & Provincial Building Society, National Westminster Bank, North Manchester Hospitals, Oxford City Council, Royal Insurance, South Manchester College, Tesco, TSB, Yorkshire Bank and Yorkshire Television.

Finally, my thanks to Sheila Heyes and Myra Shaw for typing the several drafts of the book, and to Pauline Goodwin and Jennifer Gubbay and their colleagues at Kogan Page for all their editorial support.

Introduction

Is this book for you?

This book is written for you if you are a private or public sector employer in Great Britain; a director, manager or officer of any organisation which has employees; or an adviser on legal or personnel matters.

The objects of the book are:
1. To explain, with examples, the UK and EC law on racial and sex discrimination and equal pay.
2. To give practical advice on dealing with complaints and legal proceedings.
3. To provide guidance on complying with the law and adopting effective equal opportunity policies.

The scope of this book

The first edition of this book was published in 1980. Like that first edition, this edition deals with both racial and sex discrimination and equal pay. It makes little sense, when advising employers on equal opportunities, to limit the approach to sex discrimination only or to racial discrimination only. Many of the important provisions of the laws on these two subjects are in virtually identical terms.

In one respect, however, this edition is more focused than the first edition. This edition is written specifically for employers. It does not contain advice for employees and job applicants and it does not deal at length with discrimination outside the employment field. The latter cannot, however, be ignored completely, because most employers also have obligations outside the employment field. These are dealt with briefly in Chapter 14.

Developments since 1980

Since 1980, much has changed and much has stayed the same.

On the positive side, many tribunal chairmen and members, and judges, now have a great deal of experience in grappling with the complexities of the law. Another very encouraging development has

INTRODUCTION 11

been the increase in the number of employers, including some very large public and private sector employers, who have demonstrated a commitment to equal opportunities and put substantial resources behind their equal opportunity policies.

There is, however, no room for complacency. For example:

(a) Unlawful discrimination still takes place on a large scale. It ranges from blatant and crude cases of sexual harassment to more subtle discrimination in appointments to senior management posts.
(b) While appeal decisions have clarified some aspects of the law, other provisions remain very complicated. The absence of legal aid for employment cases means that too many cases are fought without legal representation on both sides.
(c) While EC law has been a major influence in sex discrimination and equal pay cases, it has been clumsily grafted on to UK law.
(d) The equal value regulations are slow and cumbersome in their operation.

Terminology

There is no satisfactory single adjective to describe ethnic minority employees. The word 'coloured', which at one time was generally used, is no longer acceptable. The word 'black' is on occasion used in this book as shorthand for 'ethnic minority', even though it is not apt to describe employees whose place of ethnic or national origin is India, Pakistan, Bangladesh or Sri Lanka.

Chapter summaries

At the end of each chapter there is a summary of the main points explained in the text. These summaries should be useful for quick reference once the reader has digested the text itself.

Territorial extent

The contents of this book are relevant to any business or organisation with employees in England, Wales or Scotland. The laws on discrimination and equal pay also apply to some employees on British ships and aircraft, and on oil platforms and other installations. Northern Ireland has its own laws, which are in important respects different from those which apply to the rest of the United Kingdom (for example, religious discrimination is expressly covered). This question of the territorial extent of the law is covered in more detail in Chapter 5.

Future changes in the law

The law does not stand still. This book explains the law as at 1 January 1993. Inevitably the law will change in the future, as a result of appeal decisions and possibly further UK and EC legislation. This book predicts some of the possible changes, but there will also be others.

Part 1
The requirements of UK and EC law

1
General Principles

Discrimination is sometimes unlawful. This sentence is literally true, but unhelpful. It immediately invites several questions.
1. What does the law mean by discrimination?
2. When is discrimination unlawful?
3. Where are these laws against discrimination to be found?
4. What are the legal consequences of unlawful discrimination?

Questions 1. and 2. need to be asked about every complaint of discrimination. Has discrimination, as defined by law, taken place? If so, has it taken place in circumstances in which the law forbids it? Similar questions have to be asked in order to find out whether some *proposed* act or omission would be unlawful.

The following examples illustrate the distinction between an act which is not covered by any legal definition of discrimination and an act of discrimination which is not forbidden by law:

(a) You turn down a candidate for a post as your personal assistant because she boasts of being fanatically opposed to smoking and drinking. There is no law against discrimination on account of a person's social attitudes.

(b) You are a woman and you buy a business. One of the senior male employees leaves because, he tells you, he cannot bear the idea of working for a woman. His refusal to work for you is an act of sex discrimination against you, but the law does not forbid discrimination by employees against their employers.

The definitions of discrimination

This book is concerned with the laws against racial discrimination and sex/marriage discrimination. Each of these laws contains the following three distinct definitions of discrimination:
1. Direct discrimination, which is explained in Chapter 2.
2. Indirect discrimination, which is explained in Chapter 3.
3. Victimisation, which is explained in Chapter 4.

Direct discrimination

As an employer or manager, you are faced with making decisions which will affect the lives of your employees and job applicants. You can bring pleasure by offering jobs and promotions to a higher grade; you can cause pain by selecting employees for redundancy or dismissing them for misconduct. There is direct discrimination if decisions such as these are based on some factor which the law does not permit you to take into account.

It is inevitable that, when making personnel decisions, you will treat some persons less favourably than other persons are or would be treated. If you interview ten applicants for one vacancy and appoint one of them, you have treated the nine unsuccessful applicants less favourably than the person appointed. If you reject all the applications and re-advertise the post, you have treated all ten applicants less favourably than a hypothetical applicant who would have been acceptable to you. In either case, the law is broken if your decision is affected by one of the forbidden factors.

There is direct racial discrimination if the unfavourable treatment of a person is on racial grounds. These are widely defined to include:

- colour;
- ethnic or national origins;
- race;
- nationality.

There is direct sex discrimination if a person is treated unfavourably:

- because she is a woman;
- because he is a man;
- because he or she is married (in the employment field only).

Indirect discrimination

The elimination of direct racial, sex and marriage discrimination would not in itself lead to equality of opportunity for all employees and job applicants. Many organisations have rigid, often traditional, criteria for filling job vacancies and inflexible rules to be observed by their employees. These criteria and rules can have a disparate impact on certain groups. For example, some employers require their employees to sign a mobility clause, under which they can be transferred to a different part of the country, even though in practice the mobility clause is never enforced. This requirement tends to be an obstacle to women rather than men and to married women rather than single women.

The mobility requirement in the above examples could amount to indirect discrimination, unless the employer could justify it objectively.

An important difference between direct discrimination and indirect discrimination is that a finding of indirect discrimination does not lead to an award of compensation, so long as it can be shown that there was no intention to discriminate.

The following examples illustrate the above point and also the distinction between direct and indirect discrimination:

(a) You are recruiting a security guard. A woman telephones you about the job and you reject her application, without even seeing her or asking her any questions. You do so because you regard the job as unsuitable for a woman. This is a clear case of direct sex discrimination. Compensation will be payable.

(b) Advertising this same post, you state a minimum height requirement of 5ft 10ins. The requirement is the same for both men and women and accordingly there is no direct discrimination. However, the requirement will eliminate a large proportion of women and a considerably smaller proportion of men. Your requirement therefore amounts to indirect discrimination, unless you can justify it objectively. This would not be easy, since there is no necessary correlation between height and strength; it is doubtful whether height alone would deter intruders. No compensation will be payable, if you can show that the height requirement was not imposed in order to exclude women.

(c) When your error is pointed out, you amend the height requirement to 5ft 10ins for men and 5ft 6ins for women. This amended requirement will result in direct sex discrimination against men who could comply with the lower requirement of 5ft 6ins but not with the higher requirement of 5ft 10ins. Compensation will be payable.

(d) Having become an enthusiast for height requirements, you stipulate that applicants for a secretarial post must be at most 5ft 6ins tall. This requirement has been imposed for an obvious discriminatory motive, to exclude most men. A man who could not meet the requirement and who took his case to an industrial tribunal would almost inevitably be awarded compensation.

Victimisation

There is an obvious risk that employers and others who face complaints of discrimination may hit back by victimising the complainant and the complainant's witnesses, for example by dismissing them or denying them promotion. The definitions of discrimination therefore include discrimination by way of victimisation.

Other kinds of discrimination

This book is concerned with racial, sex and marriage discrimination. There are also more recent laws relating to discrimination on the grounds of trade union membership or non-membership. Laws of a different kind, outlined later in this chapter, relate to the disabled. However, other kinds of discrimination, although equally indefensible morally, are not explicitly prohibited. For example:

(a) The local authority of which you are personnel director has a policy of appointing as chief officers only those candidates who

share the political views of the controlling party. This policy, while it may amount to maladministration (and be unlawful on that account) does not offend against any discrimination law.
(b) You are a strict moralist and you will not employ any man or woman who refuses to assure you that he or she is heterosexual. This practice of yours is not direct discrimination as currently defined.

So why does the law concern itself with racial, sex and marriage discrimination and not, for example, with discrimination in relation to political beliefs and sexual orientation? The answer is that the laws relating to racial and sex/marriage discrimination were a response to specific social and political pressures.

Racial discrimination—the social background

Laws relating to racial discrimination in Great Britain were passed in 1965 and 1968 and then replaced by the current Act in 1976.

At that time, hundreds of thousands of British citizens, many of them born in Britain, were being denied equal opportunity and fair treatment simply because they had black or brown skins. Their job applications were rejected out of hand; houses, flats and lodgings suddenly ceased to be available when they appeared on the doorstep or in the agent's office: they were turned away from pubs and dance halls. Politicians of all parties came to recognise that open and widespread discrimination of this kind was not only an intolerable affront to the individuals affected; it was also a recipe for social and political unrest. There was also the factor that laws relating to racial discrimination were seen by some politicians as something of a 'trade-off' for laws restricting new immigration.

The laws against racial discrimination are not, however, concerned only with discrimination on grounds of colour and indirect discrimination against black workers. Most of the men and women who live and work in Great Britain and who have black or brown skins are readily identifiable (and could face discrimination) by reference to the ethnic group (or 'race', so far as that concept has any meaning) to which they belong, or to the country from which they or their parents or grandparents came. A few of them have foreign nationalities. Accordingly, the definition of direct discrimination includes discrimination on the grounds not only of colour but also of race, nationality or ethnic or national origins. A side-effect of this very broad definition of racial discrimination is that it includes discrimination against individuals who in practice rarely if ever experience discrimination against them (eg Scots living and working in England).

Sex discrimination—the social background

The current UK legislation relating to sex and marriage discrimination was passed in 1975 (although there have been some amendments since). At that time women, although not a minority group, were still second-class citizens in many respects. Women were increasingly choosing (or being compelled by economic necessity) to have careers and to manage their own affairs. They were expected, however, to conform to traditional career and social patterns. Many employers were prejudiced against the idea of employing women as managers, engineers or labourers. Women tended to be employed in jobs with low pay, low status and few prospects. They were frequently treated as appendages of their husbands when they applied for mortgages or consumer credit (and had their applications rejected if they had no husbands). Attitudes were changing, but the pace of change was slow. Domestic pressures for legislation were reinforced by similar movements in other parts of western Europe and by the American example.

The laws relating to sex discrimination are not concerned only with discrimination against women. Although the widespread and unacceptable discrimination against women was the reason for the legislation, discrimination against men existed (and still exists) on a significant scale. It was therefore decided that the definition of discrimination should include sex discrimination against men (for example, where a man wishes to do secretarial work or some other job traditionally regarded as 'women's work').

Moreover, some employers are particularly prejudiced against married women as opposed to men or unmarried women. They fear that a married woman's job will take second place to her domestic responsibilities. Moreover, some strict requirements, for example relating to mobility and full-time working, are more likely to affect married women than unmarried women. The definition of discrimination, but in the employment field only, therefore includes discrimination against married workers of either sex.

Religious discrimination

England, Wales and Scotland, unlike Northern Ireland, do not currently have any laws which expressly include religious discrimination in the definition of discrimination. The reason is that religious discrimination outside Northern Ireland is not perceived to be a sufficiently serious and widespread problem to justify legislation. There can, however, be an overlap between racial and religious discrimination because of the way in which indirect discrimination is defined (as explained in Chapter 3). For example:

(a) Your company does not allow sales representatives to grow beards, because you regard them as untidy. Because of this rule, a Sikh is unable to accept an appointment as a sales representative; his religious views would prevent him from shaving off his beard. Although there are no discrimination laws expressly referring to religious discrimination, the Sikhs have been held to be an ethnic as well as a religious group. Accordingly, by applying your strict rule to the potential employee, you have indirectly discriminated against him.

(b) You belong to a fundamentalist sect and you refuse to employ any Catholics. A Catholic Irishman living in England applies for a job and is turned down. He could succeed in a claim of indirect racial discrimination against you. The reason is that the proportion of Irish workers in Great Britain who are non-Catholic is much smaller than the proportion of non-Irish workers who are non-Catholic.

Age discrimination

Similarly, there are at present no discrimination laws expressly dealing with age discrimination, in spite of the increasing concerns about able and experienced men and women who are thrown on to the scrapheap in their forties and early fifties. However, for reasons which will be explained in Chapter 3, age discrimination can in certain circumstances amount to indirect sex discrimination (and also indirect racial discrimination).

Sexual orientation

As already mentioned, the law does not include discrimination relating to sexual orientation within the definition of discrimination. However, there would be direct sex discrimination if you enquired about the sexual orientation of male job applicants and rejected applications from homosexuals, but failed to make similar enquiries about the sexual orientation of female job applicants.

'Lookism'

Similarly, although employers are entitled if they wish to surround themselves with beautiful people, they must not thereby discriminate on grounds of sex. For example, when recruiting office staff, you reject job applications from women who are not slim and attractive, but you frequently appoint men who are fat and ugly. This is direct sex discrimination against the female applicants who are rejected on account of their looks, although in practice few women would contemplate proceedings.

When is discrimination unlawful?

The law forbids discrimination only in specified circumstances. It seeks to strike a balance between achieving the necessary objectives and interfering as little as possible with the way in which individuals choose to run their lives.

The main objectives to be achieved by the law are equality of opportunity in relation to employment, housing, education and access to goods and services. Most businesses, of whatever size, have obligations both to their employees and to their customers. Local authorities have a variety of roles and must not discriminate as employers, landlords, providers of recreation and cultural facilities or as education authorities.

As explained in Chapter 5, the laws against discrimination apply to almost every employer in Great Britain.

Virtually every act of discrimination (as defined by law) against a job applicant or employee is forbidden. The detailed obligations of employers are explained in Chapters 6, 9, 10 and 11. There are, however, some very limited exceptions, mainly relating to job vacancies, which are explained in Chapters 7 and 8. Unlawful advertising and instructions to discriminate are dealt with in Chapter 12. Differences in pay and other contract terms, as between men and women, are dealt with not as discrimination but under the quite different provisions relating to equal pay, as explained in Chapter 13. The obligations which businesses, public bodies and others have to their customers and to the public are outlined in Chapter 14.

Prejudice and discrimination

Although direct racial or sex discrimination is usually the result of prejudice, the law does not forbid the prejudice itself or the expression of that prejudice. If you are prejudiced against women at work or against ethnic minorities, you may freely express your prejudices to your family and friends, so long as you do not infringe public order legislation, for example by incitement to racial hatred. The laws against discrimination are not intended to circumscribe the activities of the saloon bar bore. It can be a different matter, however, as explained in Chapter 6, if as an employer or manager you express your views at work or while interviewing job applicants.

Furthermore, the criminal offence of incitement to racial hatred is one of which you as a manager should be aware. If inflammatory material is circulated to your employees or if they are harangued at the factory gate (either during an election or at any other time) you may then be left to cope with the industrial relations consequences and you may wish to ask the police to take action if an offence has been committed.

The offence can be committed in one of the following ways:

(a) The publication or distribution of a pamphlet or some other 'written matter' which is threatening, abusive or insulting (the expression 'written matter' does not necessarily involve words; it includes, for example, a photograph or cartoon).
(b) Using threatening, abusive or insulting words at a public meeting or in a public place.

There is then a further essential ingredient of the offence. The prosecution must be able to show that, having regard to all the circumstances, the likely effect of the words or written matter was to stir up hatred against any racial group in Great Britain.

If, therefore, racial harmony in your work place is threatened by activities of this kind, you should report the facts to the police so that they can investigate and, in an appropriate case, seek the consent of the Attorney General to bring a criminal prosecution.

Social and domestic activities

Even if you act on your prejudices, discrimination in the social and domestic context is not generally forbidden. The current legislation on sex discrimination was preceded by a 1974 white paper, *Equality For Women*, which stated that 'in general the Government does not and should not seek to intervene in the private relationships of citizens'. If you are a domestic tyrant, whose every word is law to your wife and daughters, that is a matter between you and them; the law is not concerned. If you choose to limit your circle of friends to those who share your skin colour as well as your tastes in beer and sport, then that too is your own affair.

Even if you do not employ anyone or run any kind of business, you may nevertheless become subject to the discrimination laws if you do something which involves dealing with the public. For example:

(a) Once a year you open your garden to the public for charity. You personally receive no payment. Because you are racially prejudiced, you allow white visitors but not a black visitor to shelter in the house when it starts raining. This racial discrimination is unlawful.

(b) You are negotiating to sell your house to a white colleague at work. The sale has not been advertised in any way. A black colleague makes a much higher offer and you refuse the offer because you are racially prejudiced. The law does not forbid this act of racial discrimination. However, once you involve the public, by instructing an estate agent or by advertising the sale in any way (even by a notice in the window), you then become subject to the laws against discrimination.

Clubs

One of the most controversial subjects, when the present legislation went through Parliament, was that of clubs. A club which is genuinely private is still entitled to discriminate by not admitting women as members. The only penalty facing men who choose to belong to a club which excludes women is boredom. For racial discrimination purposes, however, the line was drawn differently. Even a genuinely private club (if it has at least 25 members) is not permitted to discriminate on grounds of colour and may discriminate on other racial grounds only in strictly defined circumstances.

Private households and small businesses

A similar attempt was made in the employment field to strike a balance between extending equality of opportunity over as wide an area as possible, while at the same time not forcing people to disregard their prejudices even in a domestic or similar setting. The approach was stated in the white paper *Equality For Women* in the following terms:

As the Street Committee observed, the law should not attempt to deal with relationships which are so personal or intimate that legal intervention is either likely to be ineffective, or is politically or socially unacceptable.

On this basis, the legislation, as originally enacted, did not cover employment for the purposes of a private household, except where the kind of discrimination complained of was victimisation. It was, however, unlawful to cause offence by placing advertisements indicating an intention to discriminate on racial grounds. This remains the position so far as racial discrimination is concerned, but the exception for domestic employment so far as sex discrimination is concerned has now been whittled down, as explained in Chapter 5.

When laws against racial discrimination and sex discrimination were first brought in, in the 1960s and 1970s respectively, there were also exceptions for very small businesses (with fewer than six employees). In effect, these small businesses were treated in the same way as domestic employment. However, the total number of people employed in small businesses is very substantial and these exceptions have been removed.

Discrimination by employees

In general, the duty not to discriminate in a particular relationship is a one-way duty, as mentioned in the second example at the beginning of this chapter. There must be no racial or sex discrimination in the way in which you as an employer recruit your staff; you yourself, however, have no redress if a person with key skills, whom you are keen to employ, refuses to work for you because you are a woman or because you are black. There is no moral distinction between the two cases; it is simply that discrimination by workers against employers or potential employers is not a major problem in practice. Moreover, laws to prohibit discrimination in these circumstances would be very difficult to enforce and politically unacceptable.

Individual employees do have certain obligations towards their fellow employees and the customers of the business, as explained in more detail in Chapter 5. The main circumstances in which one of your employees is at risk of facing proceedings (either as well as you or occasionally independently) are:

(a) where the employee is alleged to be guilty of racial or sexual harassment (these are the most common examples);
(b) where the employee is a manager or officer making recruitment and other personnel decisions;
(c) where the employee is dealing directly with the public (for example, a doorman or bouncer deciding who should be allowed into a dance hall or night club);
(d) where the employee puts pressure on you to discriminate unlawfully, for example by threatening industrial action if you appoint a black or female supervisor.

The laws against discrimination

This book is concerned with racial, sex and marriage discrimination and the related subject of equal pay. There are two kinds of discrimination law which affect employers in England, Scotland and Wales. There are several Acts of Parliament and Regulations made under those Acts; there is also the law of the European Community of which the United Kingdom is a member.

UK legislation

The main Acts of Parliament are the Sex Discrimination Act 1975 (the SDA) and the Race Relations Act 1976 (the RRA). A few of the key sections of the RRA and the SDA are set out in Appendix 1. These are the sections which most commonly crop up in discrimination complaints against employers. It will be seen that the two Acts are in many important respects in virtually identical terms. The RRA was to a large extent based on the SDA; it also amended the SDA in certain respects.

There had been earlier, more limited, Race Relations Acts in 1965 and 1968; these are no longer in force. There has also been a further Sex Discrimination Act, that of 1986. This Act amended the SDA; the sections of the latter which are set out in the appendix are shown as amended.

There is a separate Act relating to equal pay as between men and women, the Equal Pay Act 1970 (the EPA). Although passed in 1970, the EPA did not come into force until the end of 1975, at the same time as the SDA. The EPA, which is dealt with in Chapter 13, was substantially amended by the SDA even before it came into force.

Community law

All these Acts are, however, subordinate to the law of the European Community. They are liable to be affected (and the SDA and the EPA have been affected) by community law in the following ways:

(a) Community Directives and decisions of the European Court can require the amendment of UK legislation. An important example is the amendment of the EPA by the 1983 Regulations which introduced the principle of equal pay for work of equal value.

(b) Community Directives can also be used in certain circumstances as a guide to the meaning of the UK legislation, where the latter is unclear or ambiguous.

(c) Directives can also, where they are sufficiently clear in their terms, create directly enforceable rights against public sector employers. Under the SDA, in its original form, employers could openly discriminate between men and women by having one compulsory retirement age for men and a different age for women, eg 65 for men and 60 for women. The law was changed by the SDA 1986, as a result of a decision of the European Court

that employees in the public sector could rely on a Directive in order to bring proceedings about discrimination of this kind.
(d) Some provisions of community law, particularly Articles of the Treaty itself, give directly enforceable rights to both private and public sector employees. The effect is to override gaps and exemptions in the UK legislation. The most important example to date has been Article 119 of the EC Treaty, which lays down the principle of equal pay for work of equal value. The implications of Article 119 are considered in Chapter 13.

The legal consequences of discrimination

For many years there has been a law intended to give disabled workers a reasonable opportunity of obtaining employment. If you employ a lift or car park attendant, you should appoint someone who is registered disabled. Furthermore, 3 per cent of other jobs (if you have more than 20 employees) should be reserved for those who are registered disabled. If, for example, you have a car park attendant, a lift attendant and 300 other employees, then you should employ at least 11 men and women who are registered disabled. It is an offence not to comply with these provisions, but employers are very rarely prosecuted.

There are three differences between the above provisions and those for enforcing the laws against racial and sex discrimination. These differences are as follows:

1. You are not required to meet a racial quota or to have equal numbers of women employees or women managers. You are simply required not to discriminate in making recruitment, promotion and other personnel decisions.
2. Racial or sex discrimination is not a crime; it is a civil wrong, giving rise to a liability to pay compensation.
3. Proceedings in respect of racial and sex discrimination are generally brought not by a public or statutory body but by the individual victim of the discrimination.

Industrial tribunals and county courts

If a complaint is brought against you as an employer, it will be heard by an industrial tribunal, like unfair dismissal, redundancy and other employment complaints. If proceedings are brought against you in respect of discrimination outside the employment field (for example, by a customer), then these proceedings will be heard in the county court. Chapter 15 outlines the procedure and contains practical advice on dealing with complaints. The following are the main differences between employment and non-employment cases:

(a) The time limit for making a complaint in an employment case is only three months; outside the employment field the time limit is six months.

(b) The job applicant, employee or former employee who brings an industrial tribunal complaint against you will not be able to obtain legal aid (although assistance may be obtainable from elsewhere, such as one of the statutory commissions mentioned below or from a trade union); legal aid is available for county court proceedings.
(c) You will not normally be awarded costs if you successfully defend an industrial tribunal application (or be ordered to pay costs if you lose); costs are normally awarded to the successful party in the county court.
(d) There is a limit (currently £10,000) on the compensation which can be awarded by an industrial tribunal for racial or sex discrimination (although a greater sum can be awarded if the complainant has also been unfairly dismissed); there is no limit on the amount of the compensation or damages which can be awarded by the county court.

Tribunals and community law

The industrial tribunals were established by Parliament to deal with complaints under various Acts of Parliament under which rights have been given to employees and job applicants (including the RRA, the SDA and the EPA). Technically, they have not been given express jurisdiction to deal with claims under community law. However, in practice, the various rights enjoyed under community law are treated as if they had been created by the relevant Act of Parliament and as if they were subject to the same time limits and the same maximum amount of compensation.

Appeals

The unsuccessful party in any industrial tribunal case can appeal on a point of law to the Employment Appeal Tribunal (the EAT), with further appeals (in each case if leave to appeal is granted) to the Court of Appeal (CA) and then the House of Lords (HL). Appeals from the county court go direct to the Court of Appeal. There is no right to bring proceedings in the European Court of Justice (ECJ), but the UK Courts and Tribunals can refer a case to the ECJ for a ruling on community law. Many of the decisions of the EAT, the Court of Appeal, the House of Lords and the European Court of Justice have been reported, either in the general law reports or in the specialist law reports on employment law, such as the Industrial Relations Law Reports (IRLR) and the Industrial Cases Report (ICR). Many of these reported decisions are essential guides to the meaning and effect of the laws against discrimination and are referred to in this book. There is a table of case references at the end of the book.

The commissions

There are two statutory commissions, the Equal Opportunities Commission (EOC) and the Commission for Racial Equality (CRE). The

EOC is concerned with the SDA and the EPA; the CRE is concerned with the RRA.

Although the legal action which most commonly results from unlawful discrimination is a complaint by the aggrieved individual, both the CRE and the EOC have powers to carry out formal investigations and also to bring proceedings in their own names. Their functions and powers in relation to unlawful advertising and pressure to discriminate are explained in Chapter 12 and their other powers are dealt with in Chapter 16. The purpose of proceedings by the EOC or the CRE is not to punish the offender, but to obtain a finding which can ultimately lead to an injunction to prevent further unlawful acts.

Both the EOC and the CRE have the power to assist complainants in discrimination cases, either financially or by providing legal representation. Both commissions will also give advice, including advice to employers who wish to comply with their legal obligations or adopt an equal opportunity policy. The addresses and telephone numbers of the main offices of the two commissions are given in Chapter 16.

The codes of practice

An important function given to both commissions was to prepare codes of practice. The code of practice issued by the CRE (for the employment field) came into force in 1984 and that issued by the EOC came into force in 1985, in each case after the codes had been approved by the Secretary of State.

If as an employer you disregard the provisions of one of these codes, that is not an offence in itself. However, the provisions of the relevant code can be taken into account in any proceedings. This rule is particularly important in relation to indirect discrimination, as explained in Chapter 3.

This book contains numerous references to the two codes and there is information near the end of the book (under the heading *Further Reading*) on where to obtain copies of the Codes.

The IPM Equal Opportunities Code is set out in Appendix 2. This code is a non-statutory code, but it contains useful practical guidance on equal opportunity (including fair treatment of the disabled and avoidance of age discrimination). This code is likely to be revised when the Trade Union Reform and Employment Rights Bill has become law, but most of the guidance given in the code will probably be unaffected.

Equal opportunity policies

There is nothing in the SDA or the RRA which directly requires employers to adopt equal opportunity policies. However, it will be seen in Chapter 5 that you as an employer can be held responsible for acts of discrimination by your employees, even if these acts have not been authorised by you; indeed, you can be held accountable even if you have expressly forbidden the acts in question. There is a defence if you have taken all reasonably practicable steps to prevent the act of discrimination or acts of that kind; however, you will find it difficult to make out this defence if you have not taken effective steps to adopt and implement an equal opportunity policy. Chapters 17 and 18 contain advice on preparing and implementing equal opportunity policies, while Chapter 19 gives examples of major employers who have adopted successful policies.

Summary

1. There are two questions to be asked in order to determine whether an unlawful act has taken place or whether a proposed act would be unlawful:
   (a) Does this act amount to discrimination, as defined by law?
   (b) Does the law declare it to be unlawful to discriminate in these circumstances?
2. Racial discrimination is widely defined; the laws relating to sex discrimination also cover discrimination against married persons, but only in the employment field. The definitions of discrimination include direct and indirect discrimination and also victimisation.
3. The law prohibits almost every act of discrimination, as defined by law, by employers against job applicants and employees. The law also covers discrimination in relation to housing, education and the supply of goods, facilities or services to the public or a section of the public.
4. Employers in Great Britain are subject to EC law as well as domestic legislation. Community law has been particularly important in relation to equal pay and sex discrimination.
5. Unlawful discrimination has civil, not criminal, consequences. The usual remedy is a complaint to an industrial tribunal (or to a county court, in non-employment cases) leading, if successful, to an award of compensation.

2
Direct Discrimination

If you are an employer or a manager, you may often need to make choices or decisions affecting employees and job applicants. Out of several applicants for a job, who is to be appointed? Which employees should be promoted or sent on management courses? How should a particular employee be disciplined for misconduct? Which employees are to be selected for redundancy?

If any choice or decision is directly affected by the sex or marital status of the employee or job applicant, then there is direct sex discrimination against that person. If the choice or decision is directly affected by factors such as colour, ethnic or national origin, or nationality, then there is direct racial discrimination.

Direct sex discrimination

The definition of direct discrimination against a woman is contained in Section 1(1)(a) of the SDA. The full wording of the definition is set out in Part I of Appendix 1 to this book. There is direct discrimination if she is treated less favourably than a man is or would be treated and if this less favourable treatment is on the grounds of her sex. The effect of Section 2(1) is that the definition also applies to discrimination against a man.

Marriage discrimination

Despite its name, the SDA is not concerned only with sex discrimination. The definition of discrimination also includes unfavourable treatment of a person on the ground of his or her marital status. The relevant definition is in Section 3(1)(a) of the SDA. This wording is also set out in Part I of Appendix 1.

It should be noted that marriage discrimination is within the statutory definition of discrimination only in the employment field. If you discriminate against married customers this is outside the Act.

Under the definition, a married woman complaining of marriage discrimination has to compare her case with the way in which an unmarried woman is or would be treated; for a married man, the comparison is with the way in which an unmarried man is or would be treated. There can be an overlap between sex discrimination and marriage discrimination.

The following examples illustrate how these provisions can work in practice:

(a) Your company provides a creche for the children of women employees only. You are directly discriminating against male employees, who are denied the opportunity of bringing their children to the creche.

(b) There is a change of policy. The creche is not large enough to take the children of all the employees who would like to use it, but you make it available to the children of all unmarried employees, of both sexes, on the ground that single parents are the employees most likely to need the facility. You are directly discriminating against married men, who are being treated less favourably than unmarried men, and against married women, who are being treated less favourably than unmarried women.

(c) You extend the creche to include the children of employees who are married women. There is now both sex discrimination and marriage discrimination against married male employees. They are being treated less favourably than married women and they are also being treated less favourably than unmarried men.

(d) There is a further change of policy. The new chairman of the company is a strict moralist and he decrees that the creche should be made available only to the children of married employees, of both sexes. There is now no discrimination as defined by the SDA.

There would also, of course, be no direct discrimination if the creche were made available to the children of all employees; or if no creche at all were to be provided; or if places were allocated on the basis of personal circumstances, irrespective of sex or marital status.

Discrimination against unmarried persons

The definition of discrimination contained in the SDA 1975 does not include unfavourable treatment of a person on the ground that he or she is unmarried. There would, for example, be no discrimination, as defined by the Act, in the following circumstances:

(a) The applicants for a job as your personal secretary include a married woman, with grown up children, and an unmarried woman. Even though the latter has better qualifications and experience, you appoint the married woman because you believe that the unmarried woman is more likely to move away.

(b) You appoint a married man rather than an unmarried man as cashier of your company because you believe that a married man is more likely to be responsible, careful and trustworthy.

(c) You appoint a married man rather than an unmarried man as housemaster at a boys' public school, because the school will then also have the unpaid services of his wife.

(d) Your company expects sales executives to be married, so that they and their spouses can jointly entertain major customers.

The failure to cover discrimination against unmarried persons was no doubt because such discrimination was thought to be less widespread and less serious than discrimination against married persons.

Direct racial discrimination

The definition of direct racial discrimination is contained in Section 1(1)(a) of the RRA. The full wording of the definition is set out in Part I of Appendix 1. It will be seen from this definition that there is direct discrimination if a person is treated unfavourably 'on racial grounds'. The latter expression is defined in Section 3(1), which is also to be found in Part I of the appendix. The expression is a very broad one and covers not only unfavourable treatment on the ground of colour but also unfavourable treatment on the ground of nationality, race (whatever that means), or national or ethnic origins.

Nationality and national origins

The following examples illustrate the distinction between nationality and national origins:

(a) You are an officer of a local authority which, because of the high rate of unemployment, gives priority to job applicants who are nationals of the UK or other EC countries. A job applicant who is a national of, say, a Commonwealth country could complain of discrimination on the ground of nationality.

(b) Two women, both British citizens, apply for the job of cook in your staff canteen. One of them was born in France and the other was born in England. Without investigating the qualities of the two individuals you appoint the woman born in France because you love French cooking. This is direct discrimination on the ground of national origins.

It was said by Lord Simon of Glaisdale, in *London Borough of Ealing v Race Relations Board*, that for the purposes of national origin England, Wales and Scotland are separate nations. There would, for example, be direct racial discrimination if an Englishman, living in Wales, is turned down for a job with your company in Wales because you have a policy of giving priority to candidates of Welsh origin.

Racial grounds

In order to prove that someone has been treated unfavourably on racial grounds it is not necessary to show that the belief which has been formed about his or her ethnic or national origins is a true one. For example, Michael Malone applies in writing for a job with your company. You reject the application out of hand because you believe from his name that he is Irish. This is direct racial discrimination on your part. It is immaterial that your belief is incorrect.

Racial segregation

The RRA expressly provides, in Section 1(2), that racial segregation falls within the definition of direct racial discrimination. For example, your factory has a good many workers of Asian origin. Some, but by no means all, have language difficulties. All the workers of Asian origin are employed on one particular shift and even those employees who speak perfect English are not allowed to transfer to other shifts. These employees have been the victims of direct racial discrimination, even if they have not lost any money or suffered any other tangible detriment through not being able to transfer.

Features of racial, sex and marriage discrimination

In many cases of racial and sex discrimination, it is possible to point to a person of a different sex, marital status or racial group who has been treated more favourably than the complainant. If the less favourable treatment is on the ground of the difference in sex or marital status, or on racial grounds, then there is direct sex or racial discrimination. On the other hand, there is of course no discrimination if the less favourable treatment has nothing to do with any of these grounds. For example:

(a) There are two candidates for a job, one white and one black. The white candidate is appointed because he or she has better qualifications than the black candidate and for no other reason. The black candidate has been treated less favourably than the white candidate, through not having been appointed to the post, but this less favourable treatment is not on racial grounds and there is therefore no direct discrimination.

(b) There are two candidates for promotion in your company, a woman and a man. The woman is better qualified but the man is your son. You promote him not because of his sex but because of the family relationship. There is no direct sex discrimination.

Hypothetical comparisons

There can, however, be direct discrimination even if there is no actual person who is treated more favourably than the complainant. For example:

(a) There are several candidates for a vacancy, but only one has suitable qualifications. This candidate is black. Because of his colour you are not prepared to appoint him and the vacancy is therefore left unfilled. There has been direct racial discrimination against the candidate. Even though you treated him in the same way as the unqualified white candidates, you treated him

less favourably than you would have treated a qualified white candidate if there had been one.
(b) There are two candidates for promotion, both married women. The better qualified candidate has children; the other does not. You promote the childless candidate; if the other candidate had been a married man with children then you would certainly have promoted him. There has been direct sex discrimination against the unsuccessful candidate; you have treated her less favourably than you would have treated a man in the same circumstances.

More than one ground

What is the position where the unfavourable treatment is partly on grounds which have nothing to do with sex, marital status or race? The law is that there is direct discrimination in these circumstances if the sex or marital status of the complainant, or racial grounds, played an important part in the decision complained of. In *Owen and Briggs v James*: a black woman applied for a post as a secretary with a firm of solicitors. Her application was turned down partly because she was black and partly for other reasons. It was held by the Court of Appeal that there was direct discrimination against her in these circumstances.

Causes of direct discrimination

Direct discrimination by an employer or manager is usually caused by his or her own prejudice. Discriminatory attitudes and motives are not, however, essential elements of the definitions of direct discrimination, which can arise because:

(a) you are concerned that other people may be prejudiced;
(b) you give way to pressure to discriminate;
(c) the discrimination seems a good idea at the time;
(d) you are motivated by misplaced benevolence;
(e) the discrimination is unintentional.

Concerns about other people

It is very easy to persuade yourself that you are entirely free from prejudice but that appointing a particular person to a job would expose him or her to ridicule or humiliation, because other people are prejudiced. There would be direct discrimination in the following cases:

(a) A man applies for a vacancy in the typing pool. Although he is well qualified for the post, you turn down his application because you do not wish to upset your existing typists, who are all women, or to have to sort out the problem if they make life difficult for him.
(b) Your receptionist leaves and you would normally promote your

office junior, who has on several occasions stood in for the receptionist very successfully. However, you decide not to appoint her because she is black and you do not want to risk offending any customers who may happen to be racially prejudiced.

If the law were to permit employers to pander to the real or supposed prejudices of their employees or customers, it would be very difficult for the law to have any impact. Most employers will tend to play safe rather than risk offending a customer. It is different if the choice is between a real risk of legal proceedings and a more remote possibility of the customer's being unhappy.

Pressure to discriminate

The law recognises no legal excuse for giving way to pressure to discriminate unlawfully. It does not matter whether the pressure comes from existing employees or from customers. For example:

(a) There is a vacancy for a supervisor and the best qualified candidate is a woman. Some of the men on the shop floor tell you that they will go on strike if they have to take orders from a woman. You back down and fail to promote the woman. You have directly discriminated against her, even though personally you wished to promote her.

(b) You tell a major customer that you have seen several candidates for a post as a sales executive, dealing with that particular customer's account, and that you are proposing to appoint an outstanding black candidate. The customer says that he insists on dealing with a white person. You therefore appoint one of the other candidates. This is direct racial discrimination.

Most shop-floor pressure to discriminate will crumble if faced with firm management. No union would be likely to give support to its members in such circumstances.

Furthermore, a person who puts pressure on you to discriminate is himself acting unlawfully. If you report the facts to the EOC or the CRE (as the case may be), the commission will then be able to take action against the offender, as explained in Chapter 12.

It seemed a good idea

An act does not cease to be one of discrimination simply because you acted to avoid a real problem or from motives of chivalry. For example:

(a) You have a number of employees who were born in a country which is currently at war with a neighbouring country. You have a job application from someone born in that neighbouring country. You turn the applicant down, in order to avoid possible racial conflict within the factory. This is direct racial discrimination on your part.

(b) You are a senior police officer. You will not allow women officers to patrol at night, unless accompanied by a male colleague, or to take part in riot control. Your purpose is to protect the women, but your actions amount to direct sex discrimination. You could face a complaint either from a male officer, who is required to perform more than his share of the dangerous duties, or, more probably, from a female officer, who is denied the opportunity to play a full part in the work of the force and to prove that she is as good as the men.

Misplaced benevolence

A benevolent motive does not affect the definition of discrimination. For example:

(a) The local authority for which you work is concerned that ethnic minority unemployment in the area is higher than the average. It therefore decides to give priority to ethnic minority applicants for certain jobs. This is no less an act of direct racial discrimination than it would have been if the authority had decided to give priority to white applicants.

(b) A woman is promoted to departmental head, in preference to a better qualified male colleague, because your company has no women as departmental heads. There has been direct sex discrimination by your company against the male employee.

Unintentional discrimination

Conduct can fall within the definition of direct discrimination even if there is no express intention to discriminate on racial grounds, or on grounds of sex or marital status. This principle was firmly established by the House of Lords in the case of *James v Eastleigh Borough Council*. In this case Mr and Mrs James both used their local swimming pool. They were both the same age, 61. This meant that she, being over 60, was a pensioner; he, being under 65, was not. The local authority allowed pensioners in free of charge. Mrs James, being a pensioner, was allowed in free; her husband had to pay.

Mr James complained that there had been direct discrimination against him on the ground of his sex. The council argued that there was no discrimination because there was no intention to discriminate on grounds of sex. He had been made to pay not because he was a man but because he was not yet a pensioner. A woman who was not yet receiving the pension would have been treated in exactly the same way.

This argument was rejected by the House of Lords. If Mr James had been a woman aged 61 he would have been allowed in free; accordingly, it was on the ground of his sex that he was being made to pay.

This was, of course, a case outside the employment field, but the principle applies in employment cases as well. The question to be asked is whether the employee or job applicant would have been treated differently *but for* his or her sex, marital status, colour or ethnic origin, etc.

This 'but for' test is particularly important in cases where the effects of past discrimination are still being felt. The following cases are two actual examples.

In *Barclays Bank plc v James*, Mrs James had joined the bank in 1969. She had the same compulsory retirement age, 60, as men in her grade who had joined after 1 April 1973. However, any man who had joined the bank at the same time as Mrs James would have had a retirement age of 65.

The case was heard by the EAT before the decision of the House of Lords in *James v Eastleigh*, and it was ruled by the EAT that there had been no unlawful discrimination. It was because of her grade, not because of her sex, that Mrs James had the retirement age of 60. It was immaterial that her grade was in itself determined by the discrimination which had occurred before 1973. However, Mrs James lodged an appeal and in the light of the decision in *James v Eastleigh*, the bank did not oppose the appeal. Mrs James would have had the different grade, and therefore the different retirement age, *but for* her sex.

The case of *Steel v The Post Office* was dealt with some years ago as a case of indirect discrimination. Mrs Steel was a postwoman. Because a rule which was directly discriminatory against women was not abolished until 1975, her seniority dated back only to that year. If she had been a man, her seniority would have dated back at least to 1969. She applied for a transfer to a vacant walk, but on the basis of seniority the walk was allotted to a man whose seniority dated from 1973. (By a coincidence, these dates, 1969 and 1973, are the same as in the case of *Barclays Bank plc v James*.)

Mrs Steel succeeded in a claim of indirect discrimination. Under the law as now laid down by the House of Lords in *James v Eastleigh* her claim would have been one of direct discrimination. She would have been appointed to the vacant walk *but for* her sex.

Problem areas

The major problem area, where the law is still uncertain, is that of the treatment of pregnant employees and job applicants. For example, does the dismissal of an employee because she is pregnant fall within the definition of direct discrimination? The whole question of discrimination in relation to pregnant employees and job applicants is considered in Chapter 11.

The following are two further areas where the law is uncertain or unsatisfactory:

(a) discrimination against one of a married couple;
(b) discrimination on account of marriage plans.

Married couples

Is it direct discrimination to treat a person unfavourably not because he or she is married but because he or she is married to some particular person? For example, your company has a policy of not employing any husband and wife in the same department. Two employees marry and the wife is transferred against her will. Does this amount to direct discrimination?

If the wife has been singled out for the transfer because she is a woman, then there has plainly been direct sex discrimination against her. If, on the other hand, the policy is to transfer the more junior employee and the wife is more junior in this particular case, then there has been no direct sex discrimination.

So far as marriage discrimination is concerned, one question to be considered is whether the same action would have been taken if the couple had been living together but not married. If not, then it would appear that the wife has been transferred on the ground of her marital status and that there has therefore been direct discrimination against her.

The following actual case also illustrates the point. In *Coleman v Skyrail Oceanics Limited*, Mrs Coleman, who was newly married, and her husband were employed by rival travel agents. The two companies had discussed the situation and agreed that one of the couple should be dismissed because of the risk of leakage of confidential information. They agreed that Mrs Coleman should go because her husband was presumably the breadwinner.

It was held by the Court of Appeal that the dismissal amounted to direct sex discrimination because of this assumption about Mr Coleman being the breadwinner. However, the Court of Appeal did not view the case as being one of marriage discrimination. The question whether the employer would have acted in the same way if the couple had been living together without being married does not appear to have been addressed.

Marriage plans

On a strict interpretation, the SDA 1975 does not cover discrimination against a person on the ground that he or she is about to be married. In the 1976 case of *Bick v Royal West of England Residential School for the Deaf*, Miss Parsons was employed as a residential child care officer. She told her employers that she was to be married on 31 January to Mr. Bick. She was dismissed in December, because of her impending marriage.

It was held by an industrial tribunal that there had been no marriage discrimination against Mrs Bick because she was not married at the date of her dismissal. This was not an appeal decision and accordingly it is not binding in future cases. However, the decision would appear to be correct on a strict interpretation of the SDA and it indicates a flaw in the Act.

There would, of course, have been direct sex discrimination against

Miss Parsons if there had been evidence to show that a man who was about to be married would not have been dismissed. However, there was no question of this being the case.

It is impossible for any similar problem to arise under the RRA, because of the way in which racial discrimination is defined. For example, you interview two job applicants, both from the same country in central Europe. One of the applicants is about to acquire British nationality and you appoint him on that ground, even though the other applicant is better qualified. This is direct racial discrimination; you have made your decision on racial grounds. It is immaterial that at the date of the decision both applicants still had the same nationality

Practical advice

The question of marriage discrimination which has just been considered is not the most important of the questions on which practical advice may be required. However, if you do have any rules regarding the employment of married couples (whether generally or in the same department), or the employment of persons married to employees of a competitor, you should consider the following points:

(a) Are your rules really necessary, or could you find some other way of achieving your objectives?
(b) In applying the rules do you avoid discrimination as between men and women?
(c) Do your rules apply only where the relevant employees are married to each other? If so, you should change the rules to cover any close relationship, including one between two unmarried employees.
(d) Have you also considered whether your rules, and the way in which you apply them, could give rise to an unfair dismissal claim?

Definitions in equal opportunity policy

A very important question is how you define discrimination for the purposes of your equal opportunity policy. While you must include all the elements of the statutory definitions contained in the SDA and the RRA, you are not limited to those elements. This question is explored in Chapter 17.

Preventing discrimination

The remaining question is the most important of all. How is direct racial, sex and marriage discrimination within your organisation to be avoided? This is a question to which we will return in later chapters. In particular, Chapter 6 deals with the major question of avoiding discrimination in recruitment and promotion. The first step, however, is that all managers who are called upon to make selection and other personnel decisions (and you personally, if you run your own business) must be made aware of the definitions of direct discrimination and of the prejudices and assumptions which can lead to direct discrimination.

Prejudice

Most acts of direct discrimination are caused by racial prejudice or by prejudice about the employment limitations of men, women or married workers. Managers and officers need to become aware of and face up to their prejudices, in order to ensure that their decisions are not influenced by them. Ideally, the very existence of racial prejudice and of prejudice relating to male, female and married workers should be challenged by reasoned discussion, but in practice not all prejudice can be eliminated in this way. The next best thing is for every manager and officer to become aware of his or her ideological baggage and declare it to himself or herself whenever a personnel decision has to be made. If a person making a personnel decision is aware of his or her prejudices, he or she can then make a conscious effort to put them on one side in order to arrive at a fair and objective decision.

Prejudice about men

While the great majority of complaints of sex discrimination are made by women, it is by no means unusual to find discrimination against men. The following are some of the assumptions which are commonly held and which can lead to direct sex discrimination against male employees or job applicants:

(a) that women are more suitable than men for jobs which demand caring qualities, such as nursing, teaching or looking after young children, and also social or personnel work.
(b) that women are more likely to work uncomplainingly at boring jobs or for low pay.
(c) that women are more likely to have the nimble fingers required for some jobs in manufacturing or packing.
(d) that a man in the typing pool or in a factory of women would be a figure of fun.
(e) that a man would be unsuitable for a post which involved taking orders from a woman, because both he and she would find the relationship unnatural.

Whenever recruitment and other decisions are influenced by this kind of assumption there is direct sex discrimination against the men affected.

Prejudice about women

All the above prejudices have their counterparts in attitudes towards and assumptions about women. For example:

(a) that women do not like to get their hands dirty and are unsuited to jobs as engineers or mechanics;
(b) that a woman is unlikely to display qualities of originality and ambition;
(c) that women do not have the physical strength and stamina for labouring jobs and other jobs which require heavy lifting or prolonged physical effort;
(d) that a woman on a male-dominated shop floor would distract the men and be a disruptive influence;
(e) that a woman would be unable to exercise authority over male colleagues.

It is by no means uncommon for contradictory assumptions to be made about women and for male strengths to become female weaknesses. For example:

(a) Women range from the unpredictable to the bureaucratic, while men are either innovative or well organised.
(b) Women are sometimes strident and sometimes timid, while men are either assertive or modest.
(c) Some women are erratic and some are dull conformists; men make both original thinkers and good team players.

A further prejudice which is widely held about women, and young women in particular, is that they do not make good long-term prospects, particularly for a job which involves training. The theory is that they are likely within a few months to become pregnant and to give up work in order to raise a family. The training will then be wasted.

There is direct discrimination against any job applicant or employee whose adverse treatment is affected by assumptions such as these. The code of practice under the SDA spells out, in paragraph 13(a), that each individual should be assessed according to his or her personal capability to carry out a given job. It should not be assumed that only men will be able to perform some kinds of work and that only women will be able to perform other kinds.

Prejudices about married employees

In practice, the most common form of direct marriage discrimination is against married women. Many employers are prejudiced against married women, as job applicants or promotion candidates, if the job involves:

(a) regular travel, including overnight stays away from home;
(b) working unsocial hours;
(c) attending residential training courses;
(d) moving house every two or three years.

Employers and managers commonly assume, without detailed investigation, that married women, whether or not they already have children, will be prevented by their family commitments from fulfilling the requirements of jobs such as these. Similar assumptions are occasionally made about married men, particularly where the job could involve moving house frequently. The assumption is that a man with a wife (and perhaps children) is less likely than an unmarried man to be willing to uproot himself.

Even where the job is a conventional office or factory job, many employers and managers are prejudiced against married women, particularly young married women, on the ground that they are more likely to need time off to look after sick children. Married men are rarely victims of this prejudice, no doubt because the sharing of responsibility for looking after children is still the exception rather than the norm.

Racial prejudice

The following are some of the common prejudices which can lead to direct racial discrimination against ethnic minority employees or job applicants:

(a) that they are more likely to have difficulty in written or spoken communication;
(b) that they are more likely to need long absences to visit family overseas;
(c) that they are more likely to need time off for religious observance;
(d) that a black supervisor or manager would be unable to exercise effective authority over white employees;
(e) that employing black employees in front-line positions could lead to the loss of clients or customers.

The last two examples are similar to the kind of prejudice which can prevent the appointment of women to posts not in the past commonly held by women, such as works manager or technical sales representative.

Paragraph 1(14)(b) of the CRE code recommends that staff responsible for shortlisting, interviewing and selecting candidates should be given guidance or training on the effects which generalised assumptions and prejudices about race can have on selection decisions.

Pressure to discriminate

It must also be clearly understood by everyone involved in recruitment or any other personnel decision that pressure from other people is not an excuse for racial or sex discrimination. It does not matter whether the pressure comes from customers or from employees; in either case you will be breaking the law if you give in to it.

The code of practice under the SDA recommends, in paragraph 23(a), that personnel staff, line managers and all other employees who may come into contact with job applicants should be trained in the provisions of the SDA, including the fact that it is unlawful to instruct or put pressure on others to discriminate. There is also a recommendation in the code of practice under the RRA, in paragraph 1.30, that guidance should be given to all employees, and particularly those in positions of authority or influence, and that decision makers should be instructed not to give way to pressure to discriminate.

Summary

1. There is direct discrimination if, on grounds of sex:
   (a) a woman is treated less favourably than a man is or would be treated;
   (b) a man is treated less favourably than a woman is or would be treated.
2. There is direct discrimination in the employment field only if, on grounds of marital status:
   (a) a married woman is treated less favourably than an unmarried woman is or would be treated;
   (b) a married man is treated less favourably than an unmarried man is or would be treated.
3. There is direct racial discrimination if a person is treated less favourably than other persons are or would be treated and if this unfavourable treatment is 'on racial grounds'. This expression is broadly defined. It includes colour, race, nationality or ethnic or national origins. Racial segregation always amounts to direct racial discrimination.
4. Discrimination usually results from prejudice of some kind, but prejudice is not a necessary part of the definition. An act does not cease to be discrimination if caused by pressure from other people or by a benevolent motive. Direct discrimination can even, occasionally, be unintentional.
5. The following are important steps in preventing direct discrimination within an organisation:
   (a) Ensure that managers are aware of and on their guard against the common prejudices which can lead to discrimination.
   (b) Instruct managers on the importance of resisting pressure to discriminate.

3
Indirect Discrimination

The purpose of the laws against discrimination is to break down barriers to equal opportunity. Chapter 2 dealt with barriers which are put up directly because of a person's sex, marital status, colour or some other racial factor. This chapter is concerned with cases where there is formal equality of treatment, but also some barrier which indirectly tends to restrict equality of opportunity for men, women, married persons or persons of a particular racial group.

The social background

It is common, and to a great extent legitimate, for employers to adopt firm criteria, rules and policies in order to make decisions or to regulate the activities of their employees.
For example:
(a) It is sensible to narrow the field of applicants for a driving job by excluding automatically any applicant who does not have a driving licence. For some technical jobs, a science or engineering degree or considerable practical experience is essential.
(b) Most organisations have written disciplinary rules and procedures. Indeed, the law relating to unfair dismissal requires such matters to be put in writing and not dreamed up at the whim of the employer or manager.
(c) Similarly, selection for redundancy should be made according to agreed, customary or reasonable criteria. An employer who simply walked into the factory and sacked the first ten workers he saw would have difficulty in resisting complaints of unfair dismissal.

Historical factors

At the time of the current legislation, in the mid-1970s, there were several factors which made women and black workers vulnerable to strict requirements and criteria, particularly in relation to recruitment and promotion. For example:
(a) Many ethnic minority workers had been born overseas and did not speak English as their first language. Written tests and other strict language requirements, even for manual jobs, were bound to restrict job opportunities for many of them.

(b) Excessive educational requirements, such as requiring a degree for an ordinary clerical job, affected both women and black workers. As a result of social and parental attitudes, a comparatively small proportion of women had gone on to higher education; the education of many ethnic minority workers had been disrupted by immigration or handicapped by language difficulties.

The above factors are now less significant. The proportion of ethnic minority workers born and brought up in Great Britain is high, and is increasing. They speak English as their first language and many of them are educational high-fliers. Similarly, education opportunities for women have greatly improved, even though women are still in a small minority on engineering and some science courses.

Current factors

There remain, however, important factors which prevent many women and black workers from complying with certain requirements and conditions.

In spite of some shift in attitudes, women still have the main responsibility for bringing up children. Because of these responsibilities, many women have a break of several years in their careers; others are able only to work part time. The latter are disadvantaged by, for example, rules which limit the level to which part-timers can be promoted or put part-timers first in the queue for redundancy.

Membership of many ethnic groups is linked with religious and cultural factors which impose requirements relating to dress and appearance. There can be a clash between these requirements and the strict rules on dress and appearance adopted by many employers.

These are important aspects of the social background to the indirect discrimination provisions of the law. Many other examples will be touched upon in the course of this chapter.

The legal approach

The legal definitions of indirect discrimination are technical and complicated. They contain several words and phrases which have been repeatedly analysed by the EAT, the Court of Appeal and the House of Lords. Some matters are now well established, but there remain several problem areas.

Indirect sex and marriage discrimination

Indirect discrimination against a woman is defined by Section 1(1)(b) of the SDA.

By reason of Section 2(1) of the SDA, the definition of indirect discrimination against a man is exactly the same, but with all the references to men and women being switched round.

There is then a similar definition of indirect discrimination against a married person, but in the employment field only, in Section 3(1) of the SDA.

All these provisions are set out in Part I of Appendix 1.

The following example illustrates how these definitions can work in a straightforward case.

How the SDA works in practice
Clerks in your organisation are eligible for promotion to the top grade only after ten years' unbroken service. Several male employees have been able to meet this requirement and have been duly promoted; no female employee has the continuous service required. A few women have been employed for a total of more than ten years, but their employment has been interrupted during the years when they were bringing up children; others, because of their family responsibilities, did not start working for you until they were in their thirties or early forties.

Any of the women mentioned in the above example could complain of indirect sex discrimination. The reasoning would be as follows:

(a) You have applied a requirement to her, ie that to be promoted to a higher grade she must have at least ten years' continuous service.
(b) She cannot comply with the requirement.
(c) Her inability to comply is to her detriment; she has been denied the chance of promotion.
(d) The proportion of your female employees who can comply with the requirement is (at nil) considerably smaller than the proportion of the men who can comply with it.
(e) You would have great difficulty in justifying the requirement, particularly bearing in mind that it excludes women with more than ten years' total service, but with a break in the middle.

In many cases, (e) is the key question. The fact that a requirement is indirectly discriminatory in its effect is not conclusive. There is no indirect discrimination, within the legal definition, if you can objectively justify the requirement or condition complained of.

Indirect racial discrimination

The RRA defines indirect discrimination by reference to the term 'racial group'. The definition of indirect discrimination is contained in Section 1(1)(b) and 'racial group' is defined in Section 3(1). Both these provisions are set out in Part I of Appendix 1.

How the RRA works in practice
The following example illustrates the working of these provisions and also makes the point that the ethnic minorities are not always on the receiving end of indirect discrimination (although they usually are).

You are an ardent Welsh Nationalist and own a factory in Wales. An Englishwoman applies to you for a job as a machinist and you turn down her application because she cannot speak Welsh. She would not need to speak Welsh to do the work as a machinist and indeed all the existing shop-floor workers generally converse in English.

In this example you would have no answer to a complaint of indirect racial discrimination because:

(a) You have applied to the applicant the requirement that to be appointed she must be able to speak Welsh.
(b) She could not comply with the requirement.
(c) Her inability to comply was to her detriment, because it caused the rejection of her job application.
(d) The proportion of non-Welsh workers who could comply with the requirement is considerably smaller than the proportion of Welsh workers who could comply.
(e) You would have no chance of justifying the requirement, since it is not related at all to the job for which the woman applied.

Words and phrases

It may seem bizarre for an English worker in Wales to be described as a member of a racial group. The expression is, however, very broadly defined in the RRA. It is one of four key terms to have been clarified by the appeal courts and tribunals. The four are:

1. Racial group.
2. Can comply.
3. Requirement or condition.
4. Justifiable.

The expression 'racial group', of course, appears only in the RRA; the other three expressions are used in both the RRA and the SDA.

Racial group

A racial group can be defined by reference to colour, race, ethnic or national origins, or nationality. In the above example, the racial group of the complainant was defined in a negative way, ie 'non-Welsh' rather than 'English'. This would be the sensible approach in the context of the example. The approach was endorsed by the House of Lords in the case of *Orphanos v Queen Mary College*, in which a Cypriot was refused an educational place because he did not live in the EC. It was ruled that he belonged to three racial groups, Cypriot, non-British and non-EC.

The *Orphanos* case also illustrates the point that a person may belong to more than one racial group, depending on the definition used. That point is in fact expressly made in the RRA itself. A Sikh born in India but having British nationality would belong to at least four racial groups, depending on the definition used: colour, national origin (Indian), nationality (British) or ethnic origins (Sikh).

INDIRECT DISCRIMINATION

Sikhs and Jews

But are the Sikhs an ethnic group? Are they not a religious group, like the Jews?

This question does not need to be answered for direct discrimination purposes. If an employer or manager believes that Jews or Sikhs are a racial group and treats members of the group unfavourably on that account, then he is acting on racial grounds whether or not his belief is correct. The position would be exactly the same if he regarded workers with blue eyes or red hair as separate racial groups and automatically turned down their job applications.

It can, however, be necessary to wrestle with the definition of a racial group in order to apply the indirect discrimination provisions. The question arose in the case of *Mandla v Lee*, a successful claim of indirect discrimination outside the employment field. A headmaster insisted that pupils must wear a uniform and that it would be inappropriate for a young Sikh pupil to wear a turban and other distinctive articles of dress. His motive was to promote good race relations within the school by eliminating ethnic differences where possible. It was held by the House of Lords that 'ethnic' is a very broad term and that Sikhs (and also Jews and gypsies) have sufficient history and customs to be described as an ethnic group.

This decision means that you must be on your guard against strict rules on dress and personal appearance. If you apply to a Sikh applicant or employee a strict rule against turbans or beards, this is indirect racial discrimination, except in the rare case where the rule can be objectively justified. A strict rule against wearing trousers at work could give rise to indirect discrimination against a Muslim woman, where the religion and customs of her ethnic group prevent her from complying with it.

Can comply

The expression 'can comply' was also considered by the House of Lords in the above case of *Mandla v Lee*. In the physical sense, the schoolboy could have complied with the requirement or condition. He *could* have removed his turban, for example. It was held, however, that 'can comply' does not mean 'can physically comply' but 'can in practice comply'.

A similar approach is adopted in cases of indirect sex and marriage discrimination. Any woman with young children could in theory work full time, go off on long residential training courses, travel throughout the country and regularly stay away overnight. In practice, for most women with young children, these options are not available.

Requirement or condition

Several cases have established the principle that the words 'requirement or condition' include any strict rule, practice, policy, test or yardstick, whether or not formally expressed. These cases include the *Holmes* and *Hampson* cases mentioned later in this chapter.

Requirements and preferences

In another sense, however, the term 'requirement or condition' has been given a restrictive meaning. The Court of Appeal has approved a distinction between, on the one hand, a strict requirement or condition and, on the other hand, a factor, criterion or preference to which weight is given but which does not operate as an absolute bar. The case of *Perera v Civil Service Commission* illustrates this point.

Mr. Perera, who was born in Sri Lanka, was able to comply with the formal requirements for a post as a legal assistant in the Civil Service, but he had a lack of relevant experience. This lack of experience did not rule him out of consideration for the post, but it was one of several factors which were taken into account and which meant that he was not appointed. He claimed that there had been indirect racial discrimination against him.

It was held by the Court of Appeal that his claim failed, because experience was not a strict requirement. There was no absolute bar to his appointment. The lack of experience was simply one of the factors taken into account.

If, however, you adopt a strict requirement or condition, you do not improve your legal position by describing it as a preference. For example, you are recruiting for a post as a management trainee. Your advertisement states that preference will be given to science graduates, not because any scientific knowledge is required for the job, but because you believe that a science degree course provides the most rigorous mental training. Although possession of a science degree is referred to only as a preference, in practice you exclude from your short list all the arts graduates with first class degrees and include all the science graduates with third class degrees. The proportion of women who have science degrees (as opposed to arts degrees) is considerably smaller than the number of men. If a woman arts graduate who has applied for the post complains of indirect sex discrimination, she should have little difficulty in proving that you have in practice applied to her the requirement that to be short-listed she must have a science degree.

Justifiable

A key question for employers is whether some existing or proposed requirement, condition, rule or criterion can be objectively justified. If so, it is taken outside the legal definition of indirect discrimination.

Guidance on the meaning of 'justifiable' was given by the Court of Appeal in the case of *Hampson v Department of Education and Science* (the case went on to the House of Lords, where the decision did not affect the Court of Appeal ruling on 'justifiable'). In this case a woman born in Hong Kong was qualified to teach there. She was required by the Department to take an extra qualification in order to teach in the UK. The requirement was held not to be justified in the particular circumstances.

The following principles were clearly established by this case:
(a) The test is an objective one. There is no chance of a requirement or condition which is subjective and eccentric being upheld.
(b) The requirement or condition must serve some real need on the part of the business or other organisation. It cannot be justified simply on the grounds of tradition or administrative convenience.
(c) On the other hand, the requirement or condition does not have to be absolutely essential in the sense that the organisation could not function without it.
(d) A court or tribunal considering a requirement or condition has to strike an objective balance between the discriminatory effect of the requirement or condition and the reasonable needs of the person who applies it.

Another example of a case where the defence of justification failed is *Greater Manchester Police Authority v Lea*. In this case an applicant for a post as an operations room assistant with the police was ruled out because he was in receipt of an occupational pension. He had compulsorily retired on medical grounds from his previous job following a road traffic accident. The Police Authority had a policy of not employing persons who were receiving occupational pensions or who had accepted voluntary redundancy or early retirement. The evidence was that the policy barred a greater proportion of men than of women.

The purpose of the requirement or condition was to prevent employment being offered to those voluntarily unemployed, in a time of very high unemployment. While this was a laudable social objective, it was not related in any way to the needs of the job to be carried out and accordingly the requirement was unjustifiable.

Problem areas

It is possible to identify many requirements and conditions which are potentially discriminatory and against which employers and managers should be on their guard. Practical advice on this subject is given later in this chapter.

There are, however, some respects in which the law is not yet clear. As a result, it may be difficult in a specific case to determine whether the law has been broken or whether you have a technical defence. Some of the problem areas can be described as follows:

- pools and statistics;
- the 'whole job' cases;
- the 'passenger' cases.

Pools and statistics

A complaint of indirect discrimination can succeed only if the requirement or condition complained of has a discriminatory effect on a relevant group to which the complainant belongs. If, for example, a woman job applicant complains about a requirement, she must show that the proportion of women who could comply with the requirement is considerably smaller than the proportion of men who could comply with it. This aspect of the definition raises the following questions:

(a) Proportion of what? Who are these women and men? How widely are the two pools to be drawn? The whole female working population and male working population; or those qualified for the particular job but for the requirement or condition complained of; or some other group?
(b) What does 'considerably smaller' mean? Is it possible to put a figure on it?
(c) Is detailed statistical evidence needed in all cases? Or can the industrial tribunals use their common sense and experience? Can it be assumed, for example, that the proportion of women who can comply with a requirement of full-time working is considerably smaller than the proportion of men?
(d) What happens if the statistics are incomplete? Can the industrial tribunals make assumptions on the basis of the limited statistics available?

It is impossible to give a general answer to questions (b) and (c). The industrial tribunals may adopt whatever approach is reasonable in the context of a specific case. There can be cases in which two different tribunals would quite properly adopt two different approaches. The Court of Appeal has, however, in the 1992 case of *Jones v University of Manchester*, given some guidance on question (a). The pools, in a recruitment case, will normally consist of those qualified for the particular job (or those who would have been qualified but for the requirement or condition complained of).

The answer to question (d), is also clear. An industrial tribunal may base a decision on the statistics put before it, even where those statistics are incomplete (or relate to larger or smaller groups than those with which the tribunal is concerned). Reference has already been made to a case brought by Mr Perera against the Civil Service Commission. He had been successful in an earlier case involving the same parties, *Perera v Civil Service Commission*, in 1982. Mr Perera was an executive officer in a local VAT office and he wished to become an administrative trainee. However, there was an upper age limit of 32, which he could not comply with. At the VAT office where he worked there were 34 white executive officers, of whom 22 were under the age of 32. There were 13 ethnic minority officers, of whom not one was below the age of 32. The only statistical evidence before the tribunal was this evidence and similar evidence relating to two other VAT offices; there were no statistics in respect of the many other offices. It was nevertheless held that the industrial tribunal had been entitled to make a finding of indirect racial discrimination on the evidence before them.

The whole job

Many women who work on a full-time basis are unable to continue doing so, because of their family commitments, and seek the opportunity to work part time or job share. If as an employer you refuse an application of this kind, is it possible, in principle, for your employee to complain of indirect sex discrimination? In other words, have you applied to her the requirement or condition that she must work full time in order to remain in your employ; or can you argue that the only job which exists and which she is employed to do is a full-time job, so that it is inappropriate to speak of a requirement or condition in this context? You have not *required* her to do the whole job; that is simply the job which she has been employed to do.

This question has arisen more than once and has been answered in different ways by the EAT.

In *The Home Office v Holmes*, Mrs Holmes was employed by the Home Office. She wished to be able to spend more time at home with her two small children and she therefore asked if she could work part time. Her request was refused, because of a rule against part-time working at her grade. Her claim of indirect sex discrimination succeeded and the decision was upheld by the EAT.

A different approach was adopted by the EAT, five years later, in 1989, in *Clymo v London Borough of Wandsworth*.

Mrs Clymo was a branch librarian and her husband was a senior assistant librarian at another library in the same district. When she became pregnant, she wished to share her job with her husband. The council was willing to allow job sharing of her husband's post, but not the post of branch librarian. Mrs Clymo complained of indirect sex discrimination.

It was held by the EAT that full-time working was not simply a requirement or condition but was part of the description of the job itself, and that there were therefore no grounds for complaining of indirect discrimination. The judgment said:

> in many working structures, whether in industry or public bodies, Local Government or elsewhere, there will be a grade or position where the job or appointment by its very nature requires full-time attendance.

At one extreme, requiring a cleaner to work full time would be a requirement or condition; at the other, full-time working would be part of the nature of an appointment as managing director. Where to draw the line between these extremes is a managerial decision for the employer, acting reasonably.

In *Briggs v North Eastern Educational Library Board*, the Northern Ireland Court of Appeal preferred the approach adopted in *Holmes* to that adopted in *Clymo*. Since Northern Ireland has its own legal system this decision is not binding on the tribunals in Great Britain, but it is a decision to which persuasive authority could be given. Accordingly, the law is in a state of considerable uncertainty on this question, although the current trend is to follow *Holmes* and *Briggs*, rather than Clymo.

The 'passenger' cases

A further question which has still to be resolved is illustrated by the following example.

You refuse to promote part-time workers above a certain level. You have many women employees who are affected by this rule and who have to work part time because of their family responsibilities. However, a complaint is made by a woman who is not married and has no children. She works part time because she requires dialysis treatment for a kidney disorder. Can she complain that your rule amounts to indirect sex discrimination against her, even though the factors which prevent her from working full time could apply equally well to a male employee?

In one sense it may appear unfair if the woman in the above example were able to bring a successful claim, in effect as a 'passenger', relying on legislation which was not designed for this kind of problem. You could argue that the requirement of full-time working to be eligible for promotion does not have any taint of gender so far as this particular complainant is concerned.

On the other hand, there are strong arguments the other way and the decision in *Jones v University of Manchester* (page 50) suggests that they may prevail. The purpose of the provisions relating to indirect discrimination is not to put money in the pockets of complainants, but to secure the removal of requirements and conditions which have a discriminatory effect. The woman in the above example, if successful in her complaint, would not receive any compensation; you would have no difficulty in showing that there was no discriminatory motive for the requirement. If in consequence you removed the requirement, then other women would benefit as well, including those whose family circumstances prevented them from working full time.

Practical advice

The following steps should be taken to eliminate indirect racial and sex discrimination from your organisation:

1. All managers should be made aware of the requirements, conditions, rules, criteria and practices which are most likely to have an indirectly discriminatory effect. Many of them are identified later in this chapter.
2. It is virtually impossible to predict, either in the codes of practice or in this book, every variety of discriminatory requirement and

condition. For example, when the Police Authority in the *Lea* case (mentioned earlier in this chapter) introduced their rule against employing those who had taken early retirement, etc, they could have had no idea that the rule would be discriminatory. Managers must be made aware of the definition of indirect discrimination and of the test for identifying discriminatory requirements.
3. Indirect discrimination is often thought of mainly in terms of recruitment and promotion. Both the codes of practice, however, make the point that indirect discrimination must also be avoided in relation to other personnel decisions, such as those relating to:
    (a) training (CRE code, paragraph 1.16(d); EOC code paragraph 25(f));
    (b) day release, personal development and career development (EOC code, paragraph 25(c) and (f));
    (c) transfers (CRE code paragraph 1.16(b); EOC code paragraph 25(e));
    (d) selection for redundancy (CRE code paragraph 1.17(b); EOC code paragraph 32(b));
    (e) eligibility for benefits, facilities and services provided to employees (CRE code paragraph 1.20(b)).
4. A flexible approach is to be recommended. It will be recalled that the Court of Appeal, in one of Mr Perera's cases, ruled that giving weight to some particular factor is not the same as applying a requirement or condition. However, simply changing the label serves no purpose. If in reality you have a strict requirement or condition, you will not take away the discriminatory effect simply by describing it as a preference.
5. Whenever you identify a requirement or condition which does have a discriminatory effect, you should not retain that requirement or condition unless you can justify it objectively. You should ask yourself the following questions:
    (a) Is it relevant to the commercial or other needs of your company or organisation?
    (b) Does it serve an important purpose?
    (c) Would it still serve that purpose if you modified it in some way (for example, by raising an upper age limit or by lowering the educational qualifications required)?
    (d) Is there a less discriminatory way of achieving the same purpose?
6. Once you have decided that some requirement or condition is justifiable, you must not then forget all about it. You must regularly examine and review your procedures and criteria and change them once you find that they could have a discriminatory effect and are not justifiable. This advice is given in the CRE code, paragraph 1.4(e).

Common requirements and conditions

There are many discriminatory requirements and conditions which are identified in the codes of practice or which have been the subject of tribunal complaints. Where any of the requirements and conditions mentioned below have been referred to in one of the codes of practice, the paragraph number is given. In the first few cases, the requirement is potentially discriminatory under both the RRA and the SDA.

Experience and seniority

Because of past discrimination, and also educational and social factors, strict requirements of seniority or experience can be discriminatory under both the RRA and the SDA. So far as the RRA is concerned, if experience in the UK is required then this requirement could be discriminatory against those who have obtained their experience overseas. This latter point is made in paragraph 1.6(b) of the CRE code; paragraph 25(c) of the EOC code refers to promotion on the basis of length of service.

Loaded tests and criteria

Both codes refer to selection tests and assessment criteria which contain loaded questions or have a cultural or sex bias.

The CRE code, in paragraph 1.13(d) and (e), advises that test markings should measure the individual's ability to do or train for the job in question and warns against irrelevant questions or exercises on matters which may be unfamiliar to racial minority applicants. For example, general knowledge questions should not be asked about matters more likely to be familiar to applicants born and brought up in the UK.

Similarly, paragraph 21 of the EOC code states that if selection tests are used they should be specifically related to job and/or career requirements. They should be relevant and free from any unjustifiable bias, either in content or in scoring mechanism.

The following would be an extreme example of a test question containing both sex and cultural bias: A test batsman opens six times, carries his bat once and finishes the series two short of a double nelson. What is his average?

Any listener to Test Match Special would immediately answer 44, but the terms of the question would bemuse for example, a recent immigrant from eastern Europe.

The CRE code, in paragraph 1.19(b), and the EOC code, in paragraph 25(a), also recommend that the assessment criteria under any performance appraisal system must be examined to ensure that they are not unlawfully discriminatory.

Educational qualifications

Requiring excessive or inappropriate qualifications (such as a degree for a straightforward clerical job) could be indirect discrimination under both the RRA and the SDA. It is only in recent years that women have begun to gain access in equal numbers to higher education and there are still few women on, for example, engineering courses; some racial groups are also under-represented in terms of GCSE passes and degrees.

The CRE code (in paragraph 1.13(c)) also draws attention to the failure to recognise qualifications obtained overseas. It would be a clear case of indirect discrimination if you were to disregard or treat as inferior an overseas degree, diploma, certificate or other qualification which is comparable with some UK qualification.

Age limits
The possibility that an age limit can in certain circumstances be indirect racial discrimination has been demonstrated by one of Mr Perera's cases, mentioned earlier in this chapter.

An age limit can also be indirect sex discrimination. In *Price v The Civil Service Commission*, a 1977 case, Mrs Price wished to join the Civil Service, but the grade which she wished to join was open only to applicants between the ages 28 and 35. She was over the age of 35 and was therefore ineligible. At the time of her complaint, the immediate reason why she was ineligible was simply that she was over the age of 35. However, her complaint was put in a broader way than this. She said that she could never have complied with the rules, because between the ages 28 and 35 she had the responsibility of bringing up her children and was not available for full-time work. Her claim was upheld.

Paragraph 13(c) of the EOC code states that age limits should be retained only if they are necessary for the job. It points out that an age limit could discriminate against women who (like Mrs Price) have taken time out of employment for child-rearing. Paragraph 25(g) adds that age limits for access to training and promotion should be questioned.

Narrow recruitment practices
There can be indirect discrimination under both the RRA and the SDA if you use recruitment methods which mean that black or female applicants never have the chance of applying for a job.

Paragraph 1.10 of the CRE code highlights the case where employees are recruited, solely or in the first instance, through the recommendations of existing employees or through trade unions. Where the existing labour force or the trade union members are mainly white, then the result of such practices will tend to be the recruitment of new white employees, even where the local labour market is multiracial.

The CRE code points out (in paragraph 1.6(a)) that similar problems could occur if advertisements are unjustifiably confined to particular areas or publications. An example would be advertising a job in a local newspaper with a limited circulation, so that it is read in mainly white residential areas, even though the catchment area also includes multiracial areas.

The CRE code goes on to recommend (in paragraph 1.9) that employers should not confine recruitment unjustifiably to agencies, job centres, careers offices and schools which provide only or mainly applicants of a particular racial group. If, for example, a school in a mainly white residential area has almost exclusively white pupils, it follows that clerks or typists recruited by approaching that school will almost certainly be white, even if there is no element of direct discrimination.

A similar problem is referred to in paragraph 20 of the EOC code. Employers who deal with single sex schools should ensure, where possible, that both boys' and girls' schools are approached.

Paragraph 19 of the EOC code also recommends that:

(a) advertisements should be placed in publications likely to reach both sexes;
(b) promotions and transfers should be published to all eligible employees so as not restrict applications from either sex;
(c) recruitment wholly or mainly by word of mouth should be avoided, if the workforce is mainly of one sex;
(d) if job applicants are supplied through trade unions and the only members to come forward are all of the same sex, the matter should be discussed with the unions and an alternative approach adopted.

Shifts and hours of work
It is necessary for many employers, particularly in manufacturing, to organise work on a shift basis. Matters should, however, where practicable, be arranged so as not to limit job opportunities for women in general, for married women in particular or for members of particular racial groups.

If, for example, you require married women to work on the night shift, a large proportion may be unable to comply because of their responsibilities for children, and your requirement could amount to indirect discrimination, unless justified by the needs of the business. If a woman with young children asks for flexibility in terms of her working hours, a refusal could amount to discrimination if you are refusing on principle and not for some objective business reason.

A rigid and unjustifiable approach towards fixed working hours could also amount to indirect racial discrimination. The CRE code points out, in paragraph 1.24(a), that members of particular racial groups may have needs which conflict with existing work requirements, in terms of observance of prayer times and religious holidays.

Clothing and uniforms
If you have inflexible rules on dress and personal appearance, these rules could amount to indirect racial discrimination against members of particular racial groups, whether applied to job applicants or existing employees.

The CRE code refers, for example, to rules which would prevent a Sikh from wearing a turban or some Asian women from wearing a saree or trousers (paragraph 1.24 of the code).

A Sikh could also be prejudiced by a requirement that employees must not have beards. Such requirements have been upheld in one or two cases where food manufacturers imposed them in order to maintain standards of hygiene, but you would have little chance of justifying such a requirement unless you had first of all investigated all the alternative possibilities (such as arranging for the beard to be covered in some way during working hours).

Language requirements
There are obviously many jobs for which a command of written or spoken English is required. A sales person or receptionist unable to speak and understand English would be of little value to most employers; a clerk or secretary who could not read and write in English would not get very far.

There are, however, a great number of manual jobs which require no ability to read and write, either in English or in any other language, and only a very limited command of spoken English. If you require applicants for jobs such as these to pass a written test, or even fill in an application form, you could be indirectly discriminating against members of some ethnic minority groups.

The CRE code recommends (in paragraph 1.13) that:

(a) you should not require a standard of English higher than that needed for the safe and effective performance of the job;
(b) you should not disqualify applicants who are unable to complete an application form unassisted, unless personal completion of the form is a valid test of the standard of English required for the safe and effective performance of the job.

Residential requirements
Many job applicants from the ethnic minorities have worked and lived overseas. The CRE code recommends (in paragraph 1.6(b)) that you should avoid prescribing requirements such as length of residence or experience in the UK.

Other kinds of requirement can also have a discriminatory effect. In one case, an employer refused to consider job applications from anyone living in a particular district in Liverpool, because of problems which had been experienced in the past with certain employees from that district. It happened that the district had a high percentage of black residents and, accordingly, a black job applicant from that district succeeded in a claim of indirect racial discrimination.

Residential requirements of a different kind can also amount to indirect sex discrimination. Women, and married women in particular, may be unable to comply with a requirement as to *future* residence. Training should not be restricted to employees able to attend residential courses, unless there is no other practicable way of providing the training.

Mobility
There could also be indirect sex discrimination if you have unjustifiable requirements and conditions relating to the mobility of employees. Many married women may be unable to comply with:

(a) a requirement that all employees must sign a contract agreeing to transfer and move house if required;
(b) a rule under which employees promoted to a particular grade must then move to a branch in a different part of the country.

Several major employers with many branches, such as banks, building societies and the Inland Revenue, have addressed themselves to the question of adapting traditional mobility requirements so as not to restrict the career development of married employees.

Part-time workers
One of the most common examples of indirect sex discrimination is giving second-class status to part-time workers who are predominantly women, refusing to promote them beyond a certain level and putting them first in line for redundancies.

The EOC code also makes the point (in paragraph 29) that you should review any arrangements under which part-time workers do not enjoy pro-rata pay or benefits with full-time workers, to ensure that these arrangements are justified. However, any complaint relating to pay and other financial terms of the contract would have to be dealt with under the Equal Pay Act, not the SDA, as explained in Chapter 10.

Physical requirements
There are many labouring and other jobs for which a minimum standard of strength or stamina is required. Excessive and irrelevant requirements could, however, amount to indirect sex discrimination. In many jobs which appear to need a great amount of physical effort, skill and experience are more important than brute strength.

An assumption that a woman would not have the strength for a particular job is direct discrimination, not indirect; so too is a requirement that women but not men should take a test to demonstrate that they are strong enough for the job.

Summary

1. There has been indirect racial or sex discrimination if the answers to the following questions are yes to (a), (b) and (c) and no to (d):
    (a) Have you applied a requirement or condition, as opposed to a mere preference, to a job applicant or other individual?
    (b) Was the requirement or condition detrimental to the person to whom you applied it, because he or she could not comply with it?
    (c) Was the requirement or condition discriminatory in its effect on members of a relevant group to which that person belongs, ie a racial group or one consisting of men, women, married men or married women? In the words of the legislation, was the proportion of the members of the group who

could comply 'considerably smaller' than the proportion of non-members who could comply?
    (d) Was the requirement or condition justifiable at the time you applied it? Did it serve some job related and important purpose, which could not have been achieved in a non-discriminatory or less discriminatory way?
2. The practical steps which you should take include the following:
    (a) Identify potentially discriminatory requirements and conditions, using the guidance contained in the codes of practice.
    (b) Abandon or modify any which cannot be justified.
    (c) Keep under review any which are retained.

4
Victimisation

Many victims of sex or racial discrimination are reluctant to bring proceedings, particularly against their present employers. They fear that they may end up being dismissed, denied promotion or penalised in some other way. For the same reasons, employees hesitate before bringing equal pay claims and tend to be unwilling to give evidence for colleagues who have discrimination or equal pay cases.

Unsuccessful job applicants should generally have less to lose. Even they, however, may fear being branded as troublemakers by other employers, as well as those complained about.

The legal approach

In order to give some reassurance to potential complainants and their witnesses, both the RRA and the SDA contain a definition of victimisation, which is then treated in the same way as direct discrimination.

The definition of victimisation

Victimisation is defined in Section 4 of the SDA and in Section 2 of the RRA. Both these sections are set out in Part I of Appendix 1. It will be seen that the definitions are in almost identical terms, except that the definition in the SDA refers also to the EPA.

On the face of it, the meaning and application of the provisions should be straightforward. For example:

(a) One of your employees believes that he has been denied promotion on racial grounds. He takes his case to an industrial tribunal and a white colleague gives evidence on his behalf. The claim is successful. As a result, these are the only two employees denied a rise in the next pay round. This is a clear case of victimisation under the RRA.

(b) One of your managers is accused by his secretary of having ridiculed an application for a post as a typist, because the application came from a man. Investigation reveals that the accusation was false and that the secretary has a grudge against the manager. Disciplinary action against the secretary would not involve victimisation under the SDA, because her allegation 'was false and not made in good faith'.

The three cases

Unfortunately, the three reported cases on victimisation have all been less straightforward than the above examples.

In *Kirby v Manpower Services Commission* in 1980, a clerk at a job centre reported to the local Council for Community Relations (and others) apparent acts of racial discrimination by two client employers. As a result, the manager of the job centre moved him to a job as a filing clerk where he had no contact with the public. This was not specifically because he had made an allegation by reference to the RRA, but because he had disclosed confidential information to an outside body.

Mr Kirby's complaint of victimisation was unsuccessful. However, this decision cannot be relied on in future cases, because the reasoning adopted by the EAT was rejected by the Court of Appeal in the later case of *Aziz*, which is mentioned below.

The next case was *Cornelius v University of Swansea* in 1987. Mrs Cornelius brought unsuccessful proceedings against the college under the SDA and then appealed against the industrial tribunal decision. She made two complaints of victimisation. The college had refused to allow her complaint to be heard under its grievance procedure, pending the decision of the industrial tribunal; the college also refused to act on her request for a transfer before her appeal had been decided.

The complaint of victimisation was unsuccessful. The university administrators had deferred action on the grievance and the transfer so as not to embarrass the handling of the proceedings or do anything inconsistent with the outcome. It was not specifically because the proceedings related to sex discrimination that they had acted in this way; they would have done the same whatever the nature of the complaint.

The third case was *Aziz v Trinity Street Taxis Limited* in 1988. Mr Aziz, a taxi operator, was a member of a company which promoted the interests of local taxi drivers and operated a radio system for the sole benefit of its members. He objected to being required to pay a fee of £1,000 for a taxi of his to be admitted to the radio system. The possibility of discrimination against him under the RRA began to form in his mind. To obtain evidence he made tape recordings of conversations with several members, who appeared to sympathise with his view. Mr Aziz brought an unsuccessful complaint of racial discrimination with regard to the imposition of the £1,000 fee and another matter. Then one of the drivers whose conversation had been recorded became aware of the recording and raised the matter with the company. The outcome was that Mr Aziz was expelled from the company. He then brought a complaint of victimisation under the RRA.

The three questions

This complaint of victimisation was unsuccessful. The Court of Appeal upheld the decision but rejected the reasoning which had been adopted by the EAT. The three issues and the correct approach to these issues were as follows:

1. Had Mr Aziz done 'a protected act'? It was ruled that making the tapes was a protected act. It was said by Slade, L J, that an act can "properly be said to be done 'by reference to the Act' if it is done by reference to the race relations legislation in the broad sense, even though the doer does not focus his mind specifically on any provision of the Act."
2. Was he treated less favourably than other persons would have been treated in the same circumstances? It was ruled by the Court of Appeal that he was. A person who had not done the protected act (making the tapes) would not have been expelled.
3. Was Mr Aziz expelled *by reason that* he had done a protected act? His claim failed on this issue. He was expelled because the making of the secret recordings was considered to be an underhand action and a breach of trust. He would still have been expelled even if he had made the recordings for some quite different reason, nothing to do with any suspected racial discrimination.

Problems with the approach in Aziz

One obvious difficulty about the approach to issue (3) above is that it could close the door to a complaint of victimisation even where the complainant has acted in an entirely legitimate and conventional way. Consider the following unreported tribunal case.

A female employee who had several years' service complained that she was entitled to the same rate of pay as a male employee. In fact, her claim to equal pay was not well founded, but it was a claim made in good faith. The employer's response to the claim was to dismiss her that same day. He gave a quite different reason for the dismissal, but his explanation was rejected by the industrial tribunal, which upheld complaints of victimisation and unfair dismissal.

Now suppose that in the above case the employer had admitted the reason for dismissal but said that he would have dismissed an employee who had made any kind of claim or threatened any kind of proceedings against him. He would have acted in exactly the same way even if the employee's complaint had been entirely unrelated to the EPA or the SDA. On a strict application of the reasoning in *Aziz*, this defence should succeed; the dismissal was not for doing a protected act. Surely this cannot be right.

The 'but for' test

The answer could be that at some future stage the decision in *Aziz* will have to be reconsidered in the light of the decision of the House of Lords in *James v Eastleigh Borough Council*. This case was explained in Chapter 2. It will be recalled that the effect of the decision of the House of Lords in this case was to establish the 'but for' test in direct discrimination cases; if a woman would have been treated more favourably 'but for' her sex, then it is not necessary to establish a discriminatory motive for the treatment which she complains about.

Similarly, if this approach is adopted in victimisation cases, then the question will be whether the complainant would have been treated more favourably 'but for' having done the protected act. Of the three questions posed by the Court of Appeal in *Aziz*, question (3) will disappear. It will be sufficient if the complainant has done a protected act and has been treated less favourably than a person who had not done a protected act would have been treated.

The effect, however, of reconsidering the decision in *Aziz* in this way would be that future cases such as *Kirby*, *Cornelius* and *Aziz* itself would have to be decided differently. In each of these cases, the complainant would have been treated more favourably *but for* having done the protected act. The implications for a case like *Cornelius* are considered later in this chapter.

Implications of the 'but for' approach
What of cases such as *Kirby* and *Aziz*, where a person employs unconventional means to ventilate a complaint or to obtain evidence? Where is the line to be drawn? For example, a black employee attacks and injures a white fellow employee, having been provoked by the latter's racial harassment at work. Your natural reaction, as an employer or manager, would be to take disciplinary action against both employees, the white employee for the racial harassment and the black employee for the assault. In considering what action to take against the black employee you would of course make due allowance for the provocation which he had received.

Can you, however, lawfully deal with the matter in this way? Could the black employee argue that the assault on his white colleague was carried out 'by reference to' the RRA and was therefore a protected act?

One would not expect a complaint of victimisation to succeed in these circumstances. The correct approach is surely that the black employee would not be able to satisfy test number (1) in *Aziz*. It is one thing to say that recording conversations to obtain evidence of racial discrimination is an act done 'by reference to' the RRA; it would be going a great deal further to say that an assault on a fellow employee can also be done 'by reference to' the RRA or any other legislation. When responding violently to provocation, an employee 'does not focus his mind' on the legislation either in the broad sense or in any specific sense.

Financial penalties and the SDA

The first example given in this chapter was that of two employees being refused a wage increase because of their involvement in a complaint under the RRA. Would you, however, be in breach of the victimisation provisions in the SDA if you were to adopt a similar method of penalising an employee for making a complaint under the SDA or the EPA? Consider the following example.

A woman makes an allegation of sexual harassment against a senior manager. The allegation turns out to be justified. Resolving the matter causes you a considerable headache and as a result, a few months later, the woman receives a lower pay rise than the other women in the department. There are no men doing similar work or work of equal value, so she cannot bring a claim under the EPA. Does she have a good case for claiming victimisation?

The doubt arises because of the way in which the SDA deals with victimisation. The method is to include victimisation in the definitions of discrimination, so that victimisation is then dealt with in the same way as direct discrimination. However, as will be seen in Chapter 10, the SDA does not deal with discrimination in relation to the rate of pay; any such claim has to be brought under the very different provisions contained in the EPA and there are clear provisions in the SDA to prevent an overlap between the two Acts.

It is probable, although not certain, that a victimisation claim in the above example would succeed. The employee would not be complaining about her rate of pay as such; she would be complaining about your single act in giving her a lower increase than her colleagues, in order to penalise her for having made the allegations of sexual harassment. You would have subjected her to a detriment for having done a protected act.

Practical advice

There are four main questions on which advice may be required:

1. What general guidance and instructions should be given to managers?
2. What steps should you take where there is a pending complaint, as in *Cornelius*?
3. How should you prevent victimisation of a successful or unsuccessful complainant or job applicant?
4. What procedure should you have for dealing with complaints of victimisation?

Guidance and instructions for managers

The CRE code recommends (in paragraph 1.32) that guidance on the victimisation provisions should be given to all employees and particularly to those in positions of influence or authority.

You should explain the full definitions of victimisation (under the SDA as well as the RRA) and the full range of personnel decisions and actions in which victimisation must play no part. The CRE code (in paragraph 1.22) gives the example of disciplinary measures being used to victimise an individual who has complained about racial discrimination, or given evidence about such a complaint. Similarly, the EOC code recommends (in paragraph 31(a)), that particular care is taken to ensure that an employee who has taken action in good faith under the SDA or the EPA is not less favourably treated than other employees, for example by being disciplined or dismissed. Managers and supervisors must also be instructed that:

(a) The definition of victimisation includes treating someone unfavourably because they have threatened to make or support a complaint, or because it is suspected that they may do so.
(b) There is victimisation under the SDA if someone is penalised for having made a claim under the EPA or because a claim is threatened or suspected.
(c) The failure of a discrimination or equal pay complaint does not give a green light to victimisation. So long as the complaint was made in good faith, the complainant must not be penalised for having made it.
(d) Victimisation must be avoided in relation not only to disciplinary measures but also to withholding benefits. It is, for example, unlawful to overlook someone for promotion because he or she has (in good faith) complained of racial or sex discrimination, or made an equal pay claim.

Pending complaints

In the *Cornelius* case, mentioned earlier in this chapter, the management took the view that they should put off dealing with the complaint under the internal grievance procedure until the tribunal complaint had been disposed of. This approach is not to be recommended. The EOC code suggests (in paragraph 31(b)) that employees should be advised to use the internal procedures, where appropriate, but without prejudice to their right to apply to an industrial tribunal within the three months time limit.

In a case like *Cornelius*, there should be no real difficulty for most employers. If an employee with a tribunal complaint of discrimination also complains under the internal grievance procedure, what possible disadvantage could there be in dealing immediately with the grievance? At worst, if your investigation shows the complaint to be well founded, you will be able to offer redress immediately and will not incur the publicity of defending a tribunal application unsuccessfully. At best, if you carry out a thorough and objective investigation which shows the complaint to be unfounded, then you will have strengthened your case in the industrial tribunal.

The other aspect of *Cornelius* related to the refusal to consider a request for a transfer, pending the outcome of the appeal from the tribunal decision. It is difficult to see what moral or practical justification there can be for freezing personnel decisions relating to an employee pending the outcome of a tribunal application or appeal. If an employee who is involved in tribunal proceedings against you applies for a transfer or is due a promotion, training or a pay rise, you should make the decision which you would have made if there had been no tribunal proceedings. In particular, you should take the following steps:

(a) Have a meeting with the employee, to make it clear that the matter will be dealt with strictly on its merits, without regard to the tribunal application. The meeting should be attended by any managers who will be involved in the decision and it should be minuted.
(b) If your organisation is large enough, the decision should be made by an officer or manager who is not involved in the tribunal complaint. If possible, an independent person from your personnel department should be involved at all stages.
(c) The reasons for the decision should be put down in writing.

Preventing discrimination

Many complaints of victimisation are brought by employees who continue to be employed after the case is all over. Whatever the outcome of the case, you and your employee then have to work together. This can be very difficult, particularly where the proceedings involve serious allegations on both sides, as in many cases of sexual harassment.

It is unrealistic to imagine that victimisation will be prevented and a normal working atmosphere restored if you simply fail to mention the proceedings and act as if nothing had happened. It is suggested that the following steps be taken:

(a) Always have a meeting with the complainant, in order to reassure him or her that no victimisation of any kind will be tolerated. Explain the procedure for making an internal complaint if any victimisation is suspected.
(b) Instruct the employee's managers and immediate colleagues that the matter is closed and that any victimisation will be dealt with as a serious disciplinary offence.
(c) Carefully monitor any future decisions relating to the employee, for example on applications for promotion, to ensure that the decisions are made fairly and objectively.
(d) Consider involving an independent person, such as a personnel manager from another department, in all such decisions, in order to ensure fair play.
(e) If the complaint of discrimination was upheld, consider carefully the position of any managers and other employees responsible for the act of discrimination. Do they understand where they went wrong and would they act differently in future? Or has any manager involved been shown to be unfit to remain a manager?

Job applicants

A further problem which could occasionally arise is that of a job application being received from a person who has made a complaint of discrimination about the refusal of a previous application. You should have a system which enables you to identify any such application, so that you can then take steps to ensure that the application is dealt with fairly and objectively. In particular, the application should not be dealt with by the person or persons who dealt with the previous application, unless this is absolutely unavoidable.

Procedure for complaints

The EOC code recommends (in paragraph 31(c)) that particular care is taken to deal effectively with all complaints of victimisation. It should not be assumed that they are made by those who are oversensitive.

A senior manager should be identified as the person to whom complaints should be made. What if that manager is himself the subject of a complaint, however? And what happens if there is an urgent complaint and the manager is away on holiday or otherwise unavailable? Where practicable, other senior managers should be named as being available to deal with complaints in cases such as these.

All employees should be made aware of the procedure for making a complaint and the person to whom they should go.

Summary

1. The law deals with victimisation in the same way as with direct discrimination.
2. The definitions of victimisation are very broad. They include treating a person less favourably than other employees or job applicants are or would be treated because that person:
   (a) has complained of discrimination or made a claim under the EPA;
   (b) has given evidence about or otherwise supported some other person's complaint;
   (c) has made an allegation or taken some other steps in relation to a possible complaint;
   (d) has threatened to do any of these things;
   (e) is suspected of being about to do any of these things.
3. If a person is victimised for making or supporting a complaint, it makes no difference if the complaint was withdrawn or was unsuccessful, so long as it was made in good faith.
4. You need clear policies and clear guidance to managers on the following matters:
   (a) Dealing normally with employees or job applicants while their complaints are pending.
   (b) Ensuring that there is no victimisation after the event.
   (c) Providing a grievance procedure and making sure that employees understand how to use it.

5
When is Discrimination Unlawful?

Employers come in all shapes and sizes. You may own a corner shop, workshop or two-room office, employing only one or two people; or you may be responsible for running a multi-national company, local authority or government department, responsible for tens or even hundreds of thousands of employees. The first question considered in this chapter is the general scope of your duty not to discriminate against people who work for you or want to work for you, whether casually or as regular employees.

If your business or organisation is a very large one, then decisions affecting employees and job applicants will be delegated to a large number and variety of managers and other staff. To what extent can the owner of the business, whether an individual, a company, a local authority or the government itself, be held accountable for acts of discrimination by individuals outside the immediate management team? This is the second question considered in this chapter.

Duties of employers

No employer is above or outside the discrimination laws. You have obligations under these laws whether you are:

- an individual running your own business, whether in manufacturing, farming, wholesaling, retailing, the professions, financial services or any other field;
- a partnership;
- a limited company;
- a charity or other organisation;
- a school or university;
- a local authority or health authority;
- a government department or public body.

The Crown is not only subject to the law in the same way as any other employer; the Crown and other public sector employers (including local and health authorities) have additional responsibilities.

WHEN IS DISCRIMINATION UNLAWFUL?

A complaint against a public sector employer can be based on an EC Directive, even where the Directive has not yet been translated into UK legislation. An important example is the *Marshall* case which is described in Chapter 10.

There are some circumstances in which the law permits discrimination in relation to some particular recruitment or training decision (or occasionally decisions of other kinds). These exceptional cases are considered in Chapters 7 and 8. In general, however, you have obligations to every person who works or wishes to work for you, so long as they can meet very broad requirements relating to:

1. The nature of the employment or other working relationship.
2. The kind of establishment where the work is done or is to be done.
3. The location of the establishment or other place of work.

The working relationship

You have obligations to virtually every person engaged in or applying for conventional employment by you, from the most junior clerk or manual worker to the most senior manager.

There is an important difference in this respect between the discrimination laws and the unfair dismissal legislation. Your duty not to discriminate is owed to new employees and job applicants, those who work or wish to work fewer than eight hours a week and those who are above the normal retiring age.

There are also six special cases, where workers who are not employees in the conventional sense may enjoy all or some of the same rights as ordinary employees. These are:

- some self-employed workers;
- contract workers;
- partners;
- some company directors;
- some statutory officers;
- some ministers of religion.

Self-employed workers

There has been an increasing trend in recent years for certain employees to become technically self-employed. The list includes craftsmen and labourers on building sites; sellers, on commission, of life policies, pensions and encyclopaedias; managers who become consultants; taxi drivers; even some shop managers.

The discrimination laws generally apply to all these cases as if you had entered into an ordinary employment contract. The reason is that in both the SDA (Section 82) and the RRA (Section 78), 'employment' is defined to include employment under 'a contract personally to execute any work or labour'. Any person doing or applying to do any work for you personally has the same rights as an ordinary employee or job applicant.

In the case of *Quinnen v Hovells*, a man and two women were engaged as self-employed assistants to sell goods in a department store, on a commission basis, for the 1982 Christmas season. The man complained that he was receiving less money than the two women and his engagement was terminated. It was held by the EAT that the Industrial Tribunal had jurisdiction to deal with his complaints, since he was engaged under a contract to do work personally.

It is different, however, where the work in question is done or is to be done not by the other party in person but by his or her own employees.

The distinction was illustrated by the case of *Mirror Group Newspapers Limited v Gunning* in 1986. In that case, Mrs Gunning's father had had a contract with Mirror Group Newspapers to distribute newspapers for them. He had a good many employees in the business. Mrs Gunning complained that after her father died the newspaper group refused to allow her to take over the contract and that this refusal was because of her sex. It was held by the Court of Appeal that she would not have been 'employed' for the purposes of the SDA. Although the contract would have involved some personal work on her part, the dominant purpose of the contract would have been for her to arrange and organise the work to be done by her own employees.

Contract workers
You may from time to time have to bring into your establishment, particularly if it is an office, workers employed by an outside agency, in order to carry out some specific assignment or, more commonly, fill in for employees who are on holiday or off sick. Section 9 of the SDA and Section 7 of the RRA specify a number of ways in which you must not discriminate against these 'contract workers'. For example:

(a) Your receptionist is off work for a week and you ask an agency to send a 'temp'. When the latter arrives you find that she is black. Because you have some customers who may be prejudiced you ask the temp to work on filing instead and transfer the filing clerk to reception. This is unlawful racial discrimination.

(b) You require a temp for the typing pool and the agency propose to send you a man. You reply that you are not prepared to have a man working in the typing pool. This is unlawful sex discrimination.

Partners
Section 11 of the SDA and Section 10 of the RRA prohibit discrimination against partners or potential partners. The difference between the two Acts in this respect is that the relevant provisions of the RRA apply only to a firm consisting of six or more partners. The exception for firms of fewer than six partners was also originally in the SDA, but was removed by the SDA 1986.

The following would be examples of unlawful discrimination against partners or potential partners:

(a) You fail to offer a partnership to an outstanding candidate, on the ground that he has shown a lack of commitment by remaining an American citizen.

(b) Married women who are offered partnerships in your firm are offered a lower partnership share than the male partners, on the ground that their income is likely to be the second income in the household.

Any claim by a woman partner about salary or other partnership terms has to be brought under the SDA, not the Equal Pay Act.

Company directors
A company director who has a service contract has the same rights as any other employee.

Most non-executive directors, however, do not have service contracts. If such a director is removed from the board on racial grounds or because of his or her sex, is there a remedy under the RRA or the SDA? This question has not yet been determined. The argument against there being a remedy would be that the director is not employed under a contract; his or her statutory and other responsibilities arise from his or her status as a director.

Statutory officers
Although civil servants can present complaints under the discrimination laws, there is one class of Crown servants whose special status denies them that right (except in one special case). These are the holders of statutory offices. A statutory office is simply one created in pursuance of a statute. The holders of statutory offices include:

- ministers of the Crown;
- judges;
- the commissioners appointed to the CRE and EOC;
- Justices of the Peace.

A person who holds or aspires to such an office, whether it is paid or unpaid, is without any remedy at all under domestic legislation if he or she suffers racial or sex discrimination. The possibility of a claim under an EC Directive by a statutory office holder or a person who wishes to become one has not yet been tested.

Although a person who holds or seeks a statutory office has no rights under either the RRA or the SDA, each Act does create certain obligations in relation to statutory offices. Where an appointment is made by a minister of the Crown or a government department, the minister or department must not discriminate either in making the appointment or in the selection process. If a minister or department were to discriminate, any aggrieved individual would have no remedy personally, but the appropriate commission could take action. For instance, the EOC could conduct a formal investigation into the way in which appointments to the commission itself or to the CRE are made by the Home Secretary, and could serve a non-discrimination notice on the minister if it became satisfied that he was discriminating against women (the example is hypothetical).

Police officers
There is one important case where the exception for statutory officers does not apply. The office of constable is a statutory office, but for the purposes of both the SDA and the RRA a police officer (or cadet), or a person applying to join the police force, has the same rights as any ordinary employee or job applicant. A senior officer who discriminates must answer to an industrial tribunal as if he were an employer, but any award against him or costs incurred by him are payable out of the police funds.

There are special provisions under which regulations may permit a limited amount of discrimination in relation to both police and prison officers. Men and women may be treated differently in requirements relating to height, uniform or equipment, or allowances in lieu of uniform or equipment. Accordingly, a man wishing to join the police or prison service cannot complain under the SDA on the ground that the minimum height requirement for men is greater than that for women.

Ministers of Religion
Under the SDA, an employer may discriminate on grounds of sex against a person who wishes to become a minister of religion, if the job is limited to members of one sex:

(a) so as to comply with the doctrines of the religion; or
(b) so as to avoid offending the religious susceptibilities of a significant number of its followers.

There are of course Churches in which women Ministers have the same status as men. At the time of writing, the main obstacle to the ordination of women in the Church of England appears to have been overcome, although attempts are still being made to find a formula which will satisfy the significant number of clerical and lay opponents.

It may not always be possible to identify a contract under which a minister of religion is employed or engaged. However, where there is (or is to be) a contract of some kind, then the law permits no racial discrimination against ministers or candidates.

The kind of establishment

Most employees work in or are based at a shop, factory, office, farm or mine. The law also applies to employees at other establishments, such as oil platforms, so long as they are in British territorial waters.

There are, however, the following special cases:

- private households;
- ships;

■   aircraft and hovercraft.

Private households
You have only very limited obligations under the RRA when recruiting or employing persons for the purposes of a private household. This exception applies to your treatment of the staff who work in your house and garden and drive your private car; it also covers the case where a company or other organisation provides staff for the private use of a senior employee.

The exception would almost certainly not, however, cover any of the following cases:

(a) The provision to an employee of staff for business purposes, such as the driver who takes the employee to meetings or the domestic staff who provide official or business entertaining.
(b) The staffing of accommodation provided for the intermittent use of business customers or official visitors; the establishment would probably not be regarded as a private household.

As mentioned above, however, you do have some limited obligations under the RRA, even where the employment is genuinely for the purposes of a private household. These are as follows:

(a) You are not permitted to advertise your intention to discriminate. It would be unlawful to place an advertisement in the newspaper (or even a poster in the window) stating that you wished to recruit, for example, a chef born in France.
(b) The exception does not apply to the treatment of contract workers. If you arrange for an agency to send along a temporary employee to replace an employee who is off sick or on holiday, it would be unlawful for you to send the temporary employee away or otherwise treat him or her adversely on any racial ground.
(c) The exception does not apply when the discrimination is by way of victimisation. For example, your company owns a house which is occupied by a director and his family. The company employs two gardeners, one white and one black. The latter complains of racial discrimination in the allocation of work to him. In fact this claim is covered by the exception, but he is not aware of this and his claim is made in good faith. Because of his threat to lodge a racial discrimination complaint you dismiss him. This act of discrimination, being victimisation, is not covered by the private household exception.

The SDA originally contained an exception in the same terms as that contained in the RRA. However, the SDA was amended in this respect by the SDA 1986. The general rule now is that there must be no sex discrimination either in recruiting staff for the purposes of a private household or in the way in which staff are treated. There is, however, a very limited exception so far as recruitment is concerned; this is explained in Chapter 7.

Ships

Apart from local fishing vessels and ferries, most ships which sail to or from British ports spend only a comparatively small time in port or in British territorial waters. Are you subject to the RRA and the SDA if you are a shipping company or if you provide staff, such as entertainment staff and croupiers, to work on board ship?

The rules are contained in Section 10 of the SDA and Section 8 of the RRA. The first question to be asked is whether the ship is registered at a port of registry in Great Britain. If it is, then the SDA and the RRA apply except where the employee works *wholly* outside Great Britain. If the ship is not so registered, then the discrimination laws apply only if the employee works at least half the time in Great Britain (ie in port or in British territorial waters).

Sailors recruited overseas

There is a special provision in Section 9 of the RRA under which most sailors recruited overseas fall outside the RRA, even though part of their work is done in British territorial waters. The exception also applies to employees brought to Great Britain with a view to employment on board ship.

Aircraft and hovercraft

The rules which apply to aircraft and hovercraft are similar to those for ships. The first two questions are:

(a) Is the aircraft or hovercraft registered in the UK?
(b) Is it operated by a person (or company) who has his principal place of business in Great Britain or is ordinarily resident in Great Britain?

If both these questions are answered yes, then the discrimination laws apply to the employees on the aircraft or hovercraft (and to any applicants for the work), unless the work is done (or is to be done) wholly outside Great Britain (which would rarely be the case). If the answer to either question is no, then the discrimination laws apply only if at least half the work is done in Great Britain (eg where aircrew or cabin staff work wholly or mainly on internal flights).

The place of work

The question of mobile establishments, ie ships, aircraft and hovercraft, has already been considered. There is then the question of mobile employees, such as long-distance lorry drivers, travel company couriers, overseas sales representatives and managers of overseas branches.

To find out whether the discrimination laws apply to these jobs (or applications for them), you need to ask the following questions:

(a) Is the work done wholly or mainly outside Great Britain? If not (so that at least half the work is done in Great Britain), then the SDA and the RRA do apply and there is no need to ask any further questions.

(b) If work is done wholly or mainly outside Great Britain, is it done at or from some particular establishment? If not, what is the establishment with which the work has the closest connection?
(c) Once the establishment has been identified, is that establishment in Great Britain?

The following examples illustrate the working of these rules:

(a) Your road haulage company employs long-distance lorry drivers who spend most of their working life driving on the Continent. However, your depot is in Kent and your drivers start and finish their journeys there. The discrimination laws apply, because the depot in Kent is the establishment from which their work is done or with which their work has the closest connection.
(b) Your travel company employs couriers who are based permanently at a hotel in Spain, meeting the clients when they arrive at the airport in Spain and reporting to your office in Spain. The discrimination laws would not apply.
(c) Your company, which is based in Great Britain, employs a manager to run a branch in South America. The discrimination laws would not apply to this employment. If, however, the manager then applies for promotion to a senior post at head office, you must comply with the discrimination laws in dealing with this application. The discrimination laws could also apply in the converse case, where an employee at the office in Great Britain applies for a transfer to a post overseas.

These rules do not, of course, apply to employment on a ship, aircraft or hovercraft. These establishments are governed by the special rules mentioned earlier in this chapter.

Duties of employees

As already mentioned, if your organisation is a large one, it is likely that many employees will be involved in making selection and other personnel decisions, and interviewing job applicants and promotion candidates. The following three rules are clearly set out in Sections 32 and 33 of the RRA and Sections 41 and 42 of the SDA:

1. Anything done by a person in the course of that person's employment is treated as having also been done by the employer.
2. You as employer have a defence against a discrimination complaint if you can prove that you took all reasonably practicable steps to prevent the discrimination.
3. Whether or not you as employer make out the above defence, the offending employee is also personally liable. The quaint expression used in the legislation is that the employee is treated as 'aiding' your discrimination and has a defence only if he or she did not do so 'knowingly'.

The course of the employment

You have a defence to a complaint against you as employer if you can show that the person who did the act complained of was not acting in the course of his or her employment.

It is not enough, however, to show that you had not authorised the act complained of or even that you had expressly forbidden it; you have to show that the person was in effect no longer acting as your employee when the act complained of was done.

It is hard to imagine any circumstances in which managers and other employees could be said not to be acting in the course of their employment when going about your business in terms of recruiting, interviewing, supervising and making other personnel decisions.

In practice, the defence is likely to be put forward only in cases of racial or sexual harassment (a subject dealt with in Chapter 9); it is only very rarely that the defence can be expected to succeed even in those cases.

Partners and directors

Is a company responsible for the actions of a non-executive director, or a partnership for the actions of a partner? They are not employees.

Although not employees, partners are the agents of their partners and a director is the agent of the company. The rules regarding persons who act as agents, with express or implied authority, are similar to those regarding employees.

Reasonably practicable steps

The main defence which is in practice sometimes put forward by employers is that all reasonably practicable steps were taken to prevent either the specific act of discrimination complained of or acts of that kind.

This defence can be made out only by proving that:

(a) nothing could in practice have been done to prevent the discrimination; or
(b) all reasonably practicable steps were taken.

This defence is also considered in more detail in Chapter 9, in the context of racial and sexual harassment. It is difficult to imagine the defence being made out in other cases, for example where a manager discriminates in shortlisting, interviewing or selecting job applicants, unless you have at least taken the following steps:

(a) explained the relevant legislation to the manager;
(b) given the manager training on relevant matters, such as interviewing techniques;
(c) made it clear that discrimination will be treated as a disciplinary offence;
(d) complied with any other guidance contained in the codes of practice.

It must also be remembered that comparatively junior employees may be involved in the recruitment process and that you are responsible for their acts as well. They include, for example, the receptionists and gate keepers who may be the first port of call for some job applicants.

Liability of the employee

In practice, employees are rarely made personally liable for acts of discrimination on their part, except in cases of racial and sexual harassment. However, it does occasionally happen that a manager is held personally responsible for discriminating in relation, for example, to promotion or dismissal, or some disciplinary measure.

The prospect of managers and other employees being made to pay compensation for acts of discrimination on their part is likely to become an increasingly real one as more and more employers carry out effective equal opportunity policies. More employers will then be able to defend complaints by showing that they have taken all reasonably practicable steps to prevent the discrimination complained of. By making out that defence, they leave the offending employee directly in the firing line.

Practical advice

The most important advice to be given is that employers should adopt and carry out effective equal opportunity policies and comply with the recommendations in the codes of practice. By doing so, you may be able to avoid liability for unauthorised acts of discrimination by your employees. Detailed advice on specific matters has been given already in Chapters 2, 3 and 4 and is also given in later chapters of this book.

As part of the programme for instructing and training your employees you should make it clear to them that racial and sex discrimination on their part may lead not only to disciplinary action but also to industrial tribunal complaints against them and liability to pay compensation.

You should also remember, and explain to managers and other employees, that your obligations under the discrimination laws extend to many individuals who are not employees in the conventional sense of the word; as explained earlier in this chapter, many self-employed workers, partners and contract workers also have rights under the discrimination laws.

Summary

1. Employers of all kinds and sizes are subject to the discrimination laws.
2. They owe duties to partners, contract workers and technically self-employed workers as well as to conventional employees.

3. Workers at all establishments in Great Britain are covered, with special rules for ships, aircraft, hovercraft and other cases where work is done partly overseas.
4. The only general exception, under the RRA only, is for domestic employment, and even that exception is not unqualified.
5. Discrimination by an employee, in the course of his or her employment, or by a director or partner, generally gives rise to dual liability.
6. Employers can escape liability for discrimination by an employee in the course of that employee's employment only if all reasonably practicable steps have been taken to prevent such discrimination.

6
Discrimination in Filling Vacancies, Promotion and Training

This chapter deals with perhaps the most important subject in this book. A fundamental object of the RRA and the SDA is to eliminate racial, sex and marriage discrimination in relation to job vacancies and career development.

The main (but not the only) problems to be tackled by the law are:
(a) racial discrimination which prevents black employees being recruited at all by a particular company, organisation or unit;
(b) sex, marriage or racial discrimination in relation to particular kinds of work, eg against women as labourers and men as secretaries;
(c) direct discrimination or more subtle barriers to prevent women and black employees from rising within an organisation or gaining places on management and other training courses.

The law

All these matters and others are dealt with comprehensively. The relevant provisions of the RRA are Section 4(1) and the first part of Section 4(2)(b); the corresponding provisions of the SDA are Section 6(1) and the first part of Section 6(2)(a). These provisions are to be found in Appendix 1; they are almost identical.

The law covers racial, sex and marriage discrimination in the following respects in relation to employment at establishments in Great Britain:
(a) refusing a job application, or deliberately omitting to offer the job;
(b) the arrangements made for determining who should be offered a job;
(c) the way in which employees are afforded access to opportunities for promotion, transfer or training;
(d) the terms on which a job is offered.

The RRA and the SDA prohibit direct discrimination, indirect discrimination and victimisation in relation to any of these matters, each of which will now be considered in turn.

Refusal or deliberate omission

The following are examples of unlawful refusals of employment:

(a) A man who, from his accent, appears to be of West Indian origin, telephones about a vacancy which has been advertised. Because he is thought to be black, he is falsely told by one of your managers that the vacancy has been filled. There has been direct racial discrimination in refusing him the employment.

(b) When interviewing a woman for a secretarial post, you ask why she left her last job. She states that she left because of sexual harassment by her boss and that she successfully took her case to an industrial tribunal. You are aware that some of your own managers have a tendency to 'try it on' with female employees and you tell yourself that it would not be fair to the applicant to bring her into that kind of environment. Accordingly, a day or two later, you send her a letter in which you turn down her job application and falsely state that one of the other applicants was better qualified. You have discriminated against the applicant in refusing to offer her employment, because your victimisation of her is discrimination as defined by the SDA.

(c) A woman and several men are interviewed for a technical sales post. The woman is the best qualified candidate, but you send her a rejection letter and appoint one of the men because you believe that the customers would respond better to a man. You have directly discriminated against her in refusing her the post.

Discrimination in *omitting* to offer employment is also unlawful. For example, you engage a firm of 'headhunters' to find a new finance director for your company. They come up with the name of a woman who is the outstanding candidate. You decide not to offer the post to her, because you cannot see a woman in the role of finance director. You have acted unlawfully by directly discriminating in omitting to offer her the post.

Hypothetical comparisons

In many cases of direct discrimination it is possible to make a comparison between, for example, the treatment of a woman complaining of discrimination and the treatment of a man who has been appointed in spite of being less suitable for the job. However, it will be recalled from Chapter 2 that direct discrimination can occur even without such a comparison. For example:

(a) The only qualified candidate for a technical post is black. The manager dealing with the appointment is racially prejudiced and therefore decides to make no appointment and to re-advertise the post. No actual white candidate has been treated more favourably; but a qualified white candidate would have been.

(b) A woman applies for a managerial post. She is the outstanding candidate. When she tells you that she is about to get married, you become concerned that she may have children and leave in a short time. You decide therefore that the job should go to one of the other applicants, an older woman with a grown up family. Would you have rejected an outstanding male candidate because he was about to marry? If not, you have directly discriminated in refusing to offer the post to the best candidate, because you have treated her less favourably than a man would have been treated in similar circumstances; it is immaterial that another woman was in fact appointed.

The point is also illustrated by the case of *Owen and Briggs v James*, which was mentioned in Chapter 2. It is unlawful to discriminate in refusing or omitting to offer a post to a person, even though, for example, the sex or colour of the complainant was not the only reason for the failure to appoint him or her. So long as it was an important reason, it is immaterial that there was some other reason for which he or she could have been rejected.

Recruitment and selection arrangements

Discrimination in the arrangements for filling a vacancy can be unlawful, even where there is no direct contact between you and the complainant. For example:

(a) A vacancy for a post as a barperson has been placed with your local job centre. You receive a telephone call from the job centre. A man with considerable experience of bar work is interested in the job and would like to attend for an interview. You state that you are not prepared to see him. Your customers prefer to be served by a woman and you already have more men than women working behind the bar. You therefore ask the job centre to send a woman along instead. You have directly discriminated against the man who was interested in the job, even though you have never spoken or written to him.

(b) You have advertised a post as a driver/salesperson. An Irish candidate asks for a form and reads on it that candidates must have held a clean UK driving licence for at least three years. The candidate cannot comply with this requirement, because he has only recently come to England from Eire. There has been indirect racial discrimination against him in the arrangements for filling the vacancy.

Failure to shortlist

A common complaint is that of failure to shortlist the complainant and invite him or her for interview. It is not necessary for the complainant to prove that he or she would probably have been appointed even if there had been no discrimination and an interview had been offered. Consider the following example.

You have a vacancy for a senior laboratory technician. You are looking for academic qualifications and experience. You receive many written applications and you prepare a shortlist of three men and three women. A woman is left off the shortlist, even though she has better qualifications and more relevant experience than two of the men who have been shortlisted. If she had been shortlisted, she would have had little or no chance of being appointed, because the third man, who is in fact offered the job, is streets ahead of her and all the other candidates. You have nevertheless unlawfully discriminated against the complainant by depriving her of the opportunity of competing for the job at the interview. The fact that she would almost certainly have been unsuccessful is relevant only to the amount of the compensation.

Offensive or discriminatory questions
What is the position where a candidate does reach the interview stage but then faces questions which are offensive and which would not be put to a candidate of the opposite sex or a different racial group? This was the issue in the case of *Saunders v Richmond-upon-Thames Borough Council*. In this case, Vivien Saunders, the well-known golfer, applied for the job of professional at a municipal golf course. She was one of several candidates to be interviewed, but her application did not proceed any further because of a mistaken belief by the committee that she was not available for a second interview. Her claim failed because it was this mistaken belief, and not her sex, which prevented the success of her job application. However, she also complained that questions which were put to her were themselves unlawful, because the committee would not have put these questions to a man. The questions included: 'Do you think men respond as well to a woman golf professional as to a man?' and '...don't you think this type of job is rather unglamorous?'

In this particular case, it was held by the EAT that it was not unlawful to ask such questions, even though a man would not have been asked the same questions. The judge said that the importance of such questions is not that they are unlawful in themselves but that in many cases they will be strong evidence that bias and prejudice are the reason for refusing a job application.

Discouraging questions and remarks
This decision does not mean, however, that offensive questions can *never* in themselves amount to unlawful discrimination in the arrangements for filling a vacancy. In the case of *Simon v Brimham Associates*, Mr Simon replied to an advertisement for a job in central London and was interviewed by the chief executive of a firm of employment consultants. He was told that the job would involve working for Arab employers and he was asked his religion. He refused to answer and the interviewer explained that 'if, for instance, you were of the Jewish faith, it might preclude your selection for the job.' Mr Simon, unknown to the interviewer, was Jewish and withdrew his application.

Mr Simon had not pursued his application to the point of being turned down for the job, but he complained that the discouraging comment was itself discriminatory. His complaint failed. The same comment would have been made to any other job applicant who had been offended by the question about religion. It was also held to be relevant that the comment was made in ignorance of the fact that Mr Simon was himself Jewish; accordingly, it was open to the industrial tribunal to find that the comment was not made on racial grounds.

The important aspect of the case, however, lies in the following comments made in the Court of Appeal by Lord Justice Balcombe:

> For my part, as a proposition of law, I am prepared to accept that, in appropriate circumstances, words or acts of discouragement can amount to treatment of the person discouraged less favourable than that given to other persons.

These words mean that there could, for example, be direct racial discrimination if ethnic minority candidates, but not white candidates, are asked questions such as:

Will you need time off to 'go home'?
Will you be able to work on all your religious feast days?
Can you read and write?

A job applicant who happens to have a brown skin but who was born in England, has received a first class education and has no strong religious views could well be discouraged and put off his stride by questions such as these. If the questions were not also put to white applicants then they could amount to direct racial discrimination against him.

Similarly, questions such as the following could amount to direct sex discrimination if addressed only to female job applicants:

Do you have any plans to start a family?
What arrangements will you make for looking after your children when you have to work late?
Will you need time off when the children are sick?
Why did you bother having children if you farm them out like this?
Would your husband object to you working long hours?
Might you have to move if your husband changes jobs?

If a woman is upset and discouraged by questions such as these and if the same questions are not put to male applicants, then she has been less favourably treated on the ground of her sex in the arrangements for filling the job vacancy.

A double risk
There is therefore a double risk for employers and interviewers who ask questions of this kind. First, the questions themselves may amount to direct discrimination, if not asked of all the applicants. Second, the attitudes revealed by the questions may result in a finding that any subsequent decision not to appoint the applicant was discriminatory. If, for example, Vivien Saunders had been invited for the second interview but then turned down for the job, the questions

put to her would have been evidence that she was turned down because of her sex. Similarly, if Mr Simon had revealed that he was Jewish but pressed his job application to its conclusion, the comment made to him would have been evidence of direct discrimination if in the event he had proved to be unacceptable to the Arab employers.

Discriminatory tests
There is also direct discrimination in the arrangements for filling a vacancy if women or ethnic minority candidates are made to jump through hoops which other candidates are not. For example:

(a) You are interviewing applicants for a clerical job. The applicants born overseas are required to take a written test; those born in the UK are not. By imposing this extra requirement on them you are treating the former candidates less favourably on grounds of national origin.

(b) A woman who applies for a labouring job is required to demonstrate her ability to lift heavy weights. Men who apply for similar jobs, whatever their size and physique, are never required to take a test of this kind. You have therefore treated the woman less favourably on the ground of her sex.

In both the above examples, therefore, there has been direct discrimination in the arrangements for filling the job vacancy.

Promotion, transfers and training

Whenever you have a specific job vacancy which could be of interest to existing employees, there must be no racial, sex or marriage discrimination against any employee, either in the arrangements which you make for filling the vacancy or by refusing or omitting to appoint the employee. In other words, when filling job vacancies you have the same obligations towards your existing employees as you have towards job applicants from outside. For example:

(a) When a supervisor leaves, you decide to promote one of the existing shop floor workers. The most experienced and suitable candidate is black, but you decide not to appoint her because the great majority of the workers are white and you are concerned that some of them could resent the appointment on racial grounds. You have unlawfully discriminated in not affording the employee access to this opportunity for promotion.

(b) A man applies for a transfer to a vacant post at a branch in another area because his wife is being transferred to that area by her employers. You turn down his application, even though it is the company's policy to allow any female employee to transfer when her husband's job gives rise to a move. You have unlawfully discriminated against the employee in not affording him access to the opportunity for a transfer.

Reasons for discrimination
There are two very common reasons for discrimination in relation to

promotion. The first is that many employers tend to underestimate the qualities of women and ethnic minority employees. For example, a company employs unqualified clerks of both sexes. The men are nearly all promoted and become managers. The women remain clerks until they leave, even when they are as intelligent, hard-working and long-serving as the men who are promoted. Male clerks are invited to apply for managerial vacancies; the vacancies are not even mentioned to the women. Each time this happens, there is direct sex discrimination in the arrangements for filling the vacancy.

The second problem is an even more difficult one. Promotion to many senior posts depends on an assessment of personal qualities, such as leadership ability, which are difficult to assess objectively. As mentioned in Chapter 2, women and ethnic minority candidates are at risk of an adverse subjective assessment whatever they do. On the one hand, if they stand up for themselves, they can be accused of being awkward and argumentative; if, on the other hand, they try to fit in as members of the team, then they can be condemned for lack of authority and individuality and other leadership qualities.

Grading and appraisals

Discrimination in affording 'access to opportunities for promotion' need not involve a specific vacancy, because these words are very broad. For example:

(a) Employees in your organisation are promoted to higher grades if they meet certain criteria, even where no change of job is involved. Moving to a higher grade brings a pay increment and a better chance of promotion when there is a vacancy. However, the higher grades are not open to part-time workers. This rule, unless it can be objectively justified, amounts to indirect discrimination against the women to whom it is applied. The reason, as explained in Chapter 3, is that many women, because of their family responsibilities, cannot comply with the requirement of full-time working.

(b) In your company a written appraisal of the work of each employee is carried out each year by his or her manager. These appraisals form part of the material on which future decisions about promotions are made. A black employee complains that his manager has appraised him unfavourably and done so on racial grounds, understating or ignoring his achievements and exaggerating any difficulties. If the complaint is made out, the act of discrimination in carrying out the appraisal is unlawful, since the unsatisfactory appraisal is restricting the complainant's access to opportunities for future promotion.

Training

The avoidance of discrimination in giving access to opportunities for training is particularly important. In many organisations, training is either essential or an important advantage for employees seeking promotion to management or technical jobs. Discrimination against women and ethnic minority employees in providing access to training can block or hold up their career development very seriously. The discrimination is unlawful, whether the training is provided by you or by some third party. For example:

(a) Your company takes on two management trainees, one white and one black. The white trainee is given the opportunity to work in several departments and to do a variety of interesting work. The black trainee is restricted to one department, doing routine work, because you fear that some of the other managers would be hostile to her on racial grounds. This is direct racial discrimination by you against the black trainee in the way in which she is afforded access to opportunities for training.

(b) You are selecting employees to go on a weekend residential management course which is being run by an outside organisation. You exclude a woman who would otherwise have been selected because you assume that she would not be able to make arrangements for her young children to be looked after. No such assumption is made in the case of male employees who have young children. The exclusion of the woman from the course is direct sex discrimination against her.

The last example illustrates again the difference between direct and indirect discrimination. A strict requirement to attend residential courses, in order to receive training, could amount to indirect sex discrimination against women who, because of their family responsibilities, cannot comply with it. You will be able to justify the requirement only if you have explored all the reasonable alternatives and drawn a blank. However, to *assume* that a woman could not comply with the requirement, while making no such assumption about male employees in similar circumstances, is *direct* discrimination, not indirect.

It will be seen in Chapter 8 that the law permits a limited measure of positive discrimination, usually in favour of women or ethnic minority employees, in giving access to opportunities for training.

Terms of job offer

Cases in this remaining category are comparatively rare. There would be unlawful racial discrimination in the following example.

You interview a suitable black candidate for a job vacancy. You believe that because he is black he is at a disadvantage in seeking employment. You exploit his position by offering him the job at less than the advertised wage. Your offer on these terms, whether or not he accepts it, amounts to direct racial discrimination.

The position is more complicated when a woman wishes to complain about the amount of the pay offered to her or any other financial term of the proposed contract. The offer to her is unlawful only if, on accepting the offer, she would then have a good claim under the Equal Pay Act. For example, a woman applies for a job as a clerk and you offer the job to her. You have existing male clerks who are doing work which is similar or of equal value to the work set out in the woman's proposed job description. However, the rate of pay which you offer her is less than that paid to the men and you cannot point to any reason, other than the difference in sex, for this differential. The offer amounts to unlawful sex discrimination, whether or not it is accepted.

Identifying and proving discrimination

There are several ways in which over the years complainants have been able to identify and prove discrimination against them. It is important for employers and managers to be aware of these methods, for the following reasons:

(a) If you receive a complaint of discrimination, you should use similar methods for your internal investigation. If a complaint appears to be well founded, there is no point at all in fighting a losing tribunal case, with the attendant cost and publicity. It is far better to offer redress immediately and take disciplinary action against the offender.
(b) Similar methods can also be used to carry out spot checks and other monitoring exercises to ensure that the law is being complied with. It is better to take pre-emptive action to eliminate discrimination than to wait for a complaint to be made.
(c) Interviewers who are aware of the ways in which the wrong signals can be given to interviewees will be better equipped to avoid giving a false impression of discrimination.

The following are ways in which direct discrimination can be (and has been) proved:

1. Openly admitted discrimination.
2. Questions or comments indicating a discriminatory attitude.
3. A hostile or superficial approach towards the job applicant.
4. Giving a false reason for the decision taken.
5. The appointment of a less suitable candidate than the complainant.
6. Statistical evidence.

Open discrimination

When the SDA and the RRA came into force in the mid-1970s, it was still quite common for female job applicants to be told that a man was required for the job and for male applicants to be told that a woman was required. There were also still cases of racial prejudices being quite openly displayed by employers and managers.

Overt discrimination is now less common, but there are still cases where the discrimination is quite open. In some cases the discrimination is admitted to a third party; in others the employer or manager openly discriminates because he believes that he is acting lawfully. For example:

(a) A job centre officer telephones the manager of a factory to tell him that there is a woman interested in an advertised vacancy for a job in the warehouse. The manager states that he is not prepared to see the applicant, because the job involves lifting heavy weights and a man is required. The refusal to see the applicant is blatant direct sex discrimination. The job centre officer would be an important witness in any proceedings brought by the woman herself or by the EOC.

(b) You turn down a job application from a national of an east European country (who has the necessary work permit). You tell him that in a time of high unemployment you prefer to give priority to British workers. You are not aware that the RRA covers discrimination on grounds of nationality, whatever the colour of the applicant.

(c) You tell a woman who applies for a job in your factory that all your present employees are men and that you do not have separate toilets for women. You believe, wrongly, that the absence of suitable toilet facilities gives you a lawful excuse for not employing her.

The case of *James v Eastleigh Borough Council*, which was explained in Chapter 2, is also a case where there was no dispute as to the facts, because the council believed that they were acting lawfully.

Questions and comments

Several examples have been given earlier in this chapter of questions and comments which, if put to a woman or a black applicant, could reveal a discriminatory attitude. Questions put to male applicants for certain jobs can be equally revealing. For example, you are a female manager interviewing a man who has applied for a job as your secretary. You ask him a number of questions which you would not put to a female applicant:

> Is not this a very unusual job for a man?
> How would you feel about working for a woman?
> Would it humiliate you to have to make tea for her?
> Could you put up with teasing from the other typists, who are all women?

Questions such as these reveal a discriminatory attitude. If the man is turned down for the job then the questions are themselves evidence that the decision was made at least in part on the ground of his sex.

Employers and managers who ask questions such as these, particularly if they are accompanied by colleagues at the interview, may well take the view that there is no real risk involved in asking the questions. They can always deny having done so and the interviewee will have no supporting evidence. This is an unduly complacent view. There have been very many cases where the unsupported evidence of a complainant has been believed and where the evidence of a whole panel of interviewers has been rejected.

Interview notes

Comments which are written down by interviewers can also be used as evidence. It will be seen in Chapter 15 that there are legal rules and procedures for the disclosure of relevant documents, including interview notes. Derogatory comments written by interviewers for their private amusement or that of their colleagues can be used as evidence of a discriminatory attitude.

Hostile or superficial approach

If as an interviewer you are rude and inconsiderate, the explanation may simply be that you are unpleasant to everyone. If you ask irrelevant questions, the reason may well be that you have had no training or experience in preparing for and conducting an interview.

Such matters may, however, be treated as evidence of a discriminatory attitude. If, for example, you only ask questions which have nothing to do with the post for which you are interviewing, the inference may be drawn that you are merely going through the motions, because you have already made up your mind not to appoint the applicant, either because of his or her sex or marital status, or on some racial ground.

False reason for decision

If you justify your selection or promotion decision by giving a reason which is demonstrably untrue, then the inference may be drawn that you have something to hide and that there was in fact a discriminatory motive for your decision. For example:

(a) There is a notice outside your factory advertising vacancies for machinists. A black woman who enquires about these posts is told that the vacancies have been filled. A white friend who calls ten minutes later is offered an interview.

(b) Your defence to a claim of sex discrimination is that the successful candidate had a specific qualification which the complainant lacked. When, as part of the preparation for the hearing, you are obliged to disclose all relevant documents, including job applications, it turns out that the successful candidate did not have this qualification.

(c) The reason which you give for having turned down a black candidate for a sales post is that he had difficulty in making himself understood. He complains of racial discrimination and when the industrial tribunal hear his evidence they find him clear and articulate.

All the above examples are based on actual cases in which the industrial tribunal was prepared to draw an inference that discrimination had occurred.

Less suitable candidate appointed

In many cases where direct discrimination is complained of, nothing is said to the complainant or any third party to indicate that discrimination is taking place. The complainant is interviewed, treated courteously and asked all the relevant questions and then sent a polite rejection letter in which no reason is given. How can racial or sex discrimination be proved in circumstances such as these?

The answer is that there are procedures to ensure that all relevant information and documents are available to the complainant and to the industrial tribunal. The complainant can use a questionnaire procedure, which is explained in more detail in Chapter 15, to obtain relevant information; there is also a rule, as already mentioned, that if proceedings are brought, you must disclose the relevant documents in your possession. If the complainant has been interviewed but not appointed, the industrial tribunal will be able to compare the complainant's qualifications, experience and general suitability with those of the successful candidate; if the complainant has not been shortlisted, then the complainant's application can be compared with those of the shortlisted candidates.

Suppose that these documents and the other evidence show that a black or female complainant has been left off the shortlist and that a less qualified white or male applicant has been included. There could then be a finding of direct discrimination, unless you can give some satisfactory explanation for the different treatment.

A similar approach can be adopted where the complainant has been interviewed but not appointed. If the successful candidate is of a different sex or racial group to the complainant and has made an inferior application for the job, then you will need to be able to explain the difference in treatment. It may well be easier to give a satisfactory explanation in this case, because weight will have been given to the interview performances of the complainant and the successful candidate. However, the relevant documents which must be disclosed will include any notes taken during or after the interviews.

These principles, relating to the objective comparison between the complainant and the successful or shortlisted candidates, were clearly established by the Court of Appeal in the case of *Noone v North West Thames Regional Health Authority*. In this case, the complainant, who was born in Sri Lanka, applied for a post as a consultant microbiologist. She was interviewed for the post but was not appointed. She had superior qualifications, experience and publications to the successful candidate. Her complaint of direct racial discrimination was upheld. It was ruled by the Court of Appeal that the industrial tribunal were entitled to draw an inference of discrimination because her application was stronger than that of the successful candidate and the employer was unable to give a satisfactory explanation for having rejected her application.

Statistical evidence

As an employer, you are not required to meet any racial quota or employ equal numbers of men and women in any particular job. If, for example, you employ large numbers of black workers and women, but have no black or female managers, it does not automatically follow that there has been direct racial or sex discrimination. The reason may simply be that there have been very few applications and that the black and female employees who have applied for promotion have not been the strongest candidates.

This does not mean, however, that evidence of a pattern of unsuccessful applications for jobs or promotions is irrelevant. The evidence can give rise to an inference of discrimination unless you can give a satisfactory explanation, such as that mentioned above.

This principle was established by the decision of the Court of Appeal in *West Midlands Passenger Transport Executive v Singh*. In this case, Mr Singh complained of racial discrimination in relation to the rejection of his application for promotion from inspector to senior inspector. He asked for the production of details of the ethnic origins of successful and unsuccessful candidates for comparable posts over a two-year period. The employers resisted this request, but it was held by the Court of Appeal that the details requested should be supplied.

Lord Justice Balcombe said:

> Statistical evidence may establish a discernible pattern in the treatment of a particular group: if that pattern demonstrates a regular failure of members of the group to obtain promotion to particular jobs and of under-representation in such jobs, it may give rise to an inference of discrimination against the group.

He went on to say:

> If a practice is being operated against a group then, in the absence of a satisfactory explanation in a particular case, it is reasonable to infer that the complainant, as a member of the group, has himself been treated less favourably on grounds of race. Indeed, evidence of discriminatory treatment against the group in relation to promotion may be more persuasive of discrimination in the particular case than previous treatment of the applicant, which may be indicative of personal factors peculiar to the applicant and not necessarily racially motivated.

The above judgement has been quoted at some length, since it is of great importance. Employers risk successful complaints of direct discrimination if they fail to take the following steps:

(a) keep records of job applications and promotions, showing the sex, marital status and ethnic origin of the successful and unsuccessful candidates;
(b) examine those records and investigate the reasons for any apparent pattern of unsuccessful applications or under-representation.

Victimisation

The methods by which victimisation can be proved are very similar to those which are used in cases of direct discrimination. In particular, it is very common, when an employee is dismissed for having made or supported a complaint, for the employer to give a demonstrably false reason for the dismissal, such as incompetence or redundancy.

Indirect discrimination

In most cases of indirect discrimination, the requirement or condition complained of is expressly stated, for example in an advertisement or job application.

If you or one of your managers applies the requirement or condition without actually mentioning it and subsequently denies having done so, a complainant can use the procedures under the legislation for obtaining information and documents. For example:

(a) You advertise a senior scientific or medical post for which degrees and relevant experience are required. The applications submitted include several from ethnic minority candidates, of whom some have obtained their degrees and experience in the UK and some overseas. You shortlist one person from the former group but not one from the latter group, even though two of them have better qualifications and more relevant experience than any of the shortlisted candidates. On these facts, there could be a finding that you have applied to the candidates a requirement that to be shortlisted they must have obtained their degrees and experience in the UK.

(b) You advertise a post with a 'preferred' upper age limit of 35. A woman of 40 who applies but is not shortlisted complains of indirect sex discrimination. Like Mrs Price, in the case referred to near the end of chapter 3, she was unavailable for work during her late twenties and early thirties because she was bringing up her children. Examination of the applications shows that all the candidates over 35 have been excluded from the shortlist, even though several of them had put in stronger applications than those of most of the shortlisted candidates. This is strong evidence that the upper age limit was a strict requirement, not a mere preference, and that you have therefore acted unlawfully unless you can justify the age limit.

Practical advice

Some of the practical advice given in earlier chapters is particularly relevant to decisions relating to recruitment, promotion and training. Anyone involved in such decisions must be on their guard against the effects of generalised assumptions and prejudices (Chapter 2);

requirements and conditions must be kept under constant review, to avoid indirect discrimination (Chapter 3).

Other practical advice will be given in later chapters. The *Singh*, case mentioned on page 91, demonstrates the importance of monitoring, particularly in a large organisation, so as to identify branches, departments or units where there are patterns of recruitment which need explanation. This whole question of monitoring is considered in more detail in Chapter 18.

Chapters 17 and 18 also deal with the subject of instruction and training. In a large organisation, a large number of people could be involved in recruitment, promotion and training decisions. Instructions must be given even to people who are only marginally involved, such as gate staff and receptionists. More detailed training is required for staff responsible for shortlisting, interviewing and selecting candidates, and other personnel decisions.

The matters which will now be considered are:

1. Recruitment and promotion arrangements.
2. Interviewing.

Recruitment and promotion arrangements

The following are some of the key rules, whether you are recruiting from outside or dealing with internal candidates for a promotion or transfer or training:

(a) Adopt objective criteria.
(b) Exclude irrelevant factors.
(c) Treat individuals with efficiency and consideration.
(d) Where practicable, involve more than one person in all decisions.

Objective criteria

The rules for efficient recruitment and selection are well established and well understood by personnel staff and by many other managers. For example:

(a) Before a job is even advertised, a job description should be prepared.
(b) Essential requirements (such as a driving licence where applicable) should be stated in any advertisement or application form. Workers should not be encouraged to waste their time in applying for jobs for which they are not qualified.
(c) A specification of the qualities required for the job should then be prepared, with the various factors either placed in order of priority or given points. This document should then be used for purposes of shortlisting and selection.

The CRE code, in paragraph 1.14 (b), refers to the importance of giving clear guidance to staff responsible for shortlisting, interviewing and selecting. They should be told what the selection criteria are and also the need for the consistent application of these criteria.

Excluding irrelevant factors

If you have an equal opportunity policy, you will need information about matters such as the colour, ethnic origin, sex and marital status of all candidates. You may also need further details about the successful candidate for your personnel records. Where practicable, this information should be obtained on a separate or detachable form and the reason for asking for it should be clearly explained. Otherwise there are risks of the selection process being affected by such factors or the wrong impression being given to candidates.

The EOC code makes the fundamental point, in paragraph 23(b), that applications from men and women should be processed in exactly the same way and that there should not be separate lists of male and female or married and single applicants. Similarly, you should not keep separate lists of white and black applicants.

Efficient and considerate treatment

You may well give a false impression of discrimination if you are casual and inconsiderate in your treatment of candidates. If you cancel interviews at the last minute, keep candidates waiting for hours and fail to write to the unsuccessful candidates, they may well, rightly or wrongly, gain the impression that the applications are not being taken seriously.

Involving more than one person

It is now increasingly the practice for more than one person to be involved in shortlisting, interviewing and selecting candidates. While there is a risk of a panel decision being tainted by the prejudice of one member of the panel, experience has shown that decisions are more likely to be made objectively if they are discussed by a panel (usually of two or three members), rather than made by one person.

This practice is in accordance with guidance in the CRE code. The code states (in paragraph 1.14 (c)) that, wherever possible, shortlisting and interviewing should not be done by one person alone but should at least be checked at a more senior level.

It is particularly useful if a member of the personnel department can be involved in all decisions of this kind and be present at all interviews. This helps to achieve consistency in decision making.

Similarly, where promotion decisions are based on performance appraisals, these should where practicable be checked by a more senior manager. The subject of the appraisal should in any event be given the right to see and challenge what is said about him or her.

Interviewing

Most of the above rules also apply to interviewers. When interviewing a candidate for a job or promotion you should:

(a) Read carefully the application form and any other relevant document, such as performance appraisals and references. It does not inspire confidence in the interviewee if you start off

DISCRIMINATION IN FILLING VACANCIES 95

with a series of questions which have been answered in the application form.
(b) Plan the interview beforehand and decide what you need to tell the candidate about the job and what you need to find out about the candidate.
(c) Try to put the candidate at ease and treat him or her with courtesy at all times.
(d) Ask questions which relate to the requirements of the job. This point is made in the EOC code (paragraph 23(c)), which goes on to make a further point. It may sometimes be necessary to assess whether personal circumstances will affect the performance of the job, for example where the job involves unsocial hours or extensive travel. The matter should be discussed objectively and positively (with *all* the candidates), without detailed questions based on assumptions about marital status, children and domestic obligations.
(e) Avoid asking questions about marriage plans or family intentions (this point is also made in the EOC code, paragraph 23(c)). You should also avoid asking any other questions which could indicate prejudice or discriminatory assumptions (like some of the examples mentioned earlier in this chapter).
(f) Avoid asking irrelevant questions and try to be positive in your general approach.
(g) Make notes, recording your impression of the candidates, and keep them afterwards. Ideally, you should use some form of point scoring system, since otherwise it can be difficult to make objective comparisons between interviewees, particularly where the first and last interviews are separated by several hours or even by two or three days. The EOC code (in paragraph 23(b)) makes the point that records of interviews should be kept, where practicable, showing why applicants were or were not appointed.

Summary

1. The law covers discrimination not only against job applicants but also against existing employees in relation to promotion, grading, training, appraisals and transfers.
2. The law covers discrimination in recruitment and other arrangements as well as in actual selection decisions. A person who is not shortlisted or who is put off by a discriminatory requirement could have a valid claim even if not the strongest candidate for the post.
3. Questions and comments by interviewers can be evidence of discriminatory attitudes and can also amount to discrimination in themselves.
4. There are comprehensive procedures for disclosure of information and documents, to enable objective comparison of the

complainant with successful or shortlisted candidates. A complaint could be upheld if there is no satisfactory explanation for any apparent discrimination revealed by such comparison.
5. It is essential that clear guidance and training be given to interviewers and others. Objective and consistent criteria should be used and questions which indicate discriminatory assumptions and attitudes should not be asked.

7
Genuine Occupational Qualifications and Other Exceptions

When the current discrimination laws were passed in the mid-1970s, most of the exceptions, under which some discrimination was permitted, were based on one of the following principles:
1. Avoiding interference in relationships where the law would be ineffective or widely seen to be intrusive.
2. Permitting employers to discriminate where the discrimination is necessitated by or reflects discrimination by the state itself.
3. Exempting the handful of jobs where a person's sex or some racial factor can genuinely affect that person's suitability for the job.

Exceptions which no longer apply

Many of the exceptions based on 1. and 2. have now disappeared. There have been the following changes to the SDA:
(a) There is no longer an exception for domestic employment (although there still is under the RRA, as mentioned in Chapter 5). Instead there is the more limited exception mentioned later in this chapter.
(b) There is no longer an exception for businesses with fewer than six employees.
(c) Exceptions which are based on the 'protective laws' have largely disappeared, along with most of the protective laws themselves. These were laws which, for example, prohibited the employment of women on the night shift in many manual jobs.
(d) Because of the effect of EC law, employers may no longer discriminate in the age at which men and women are made to retire.
(e) While the state itself still has different pension ages for men and women, the right of employers to discriminate in this way has been successfully challenged, as mentioned in Chapter 13, under EC law.

This chapter is concerned mainly with the third category of exceptions, those occasional cases where a person's sex or racial group can be a genuine qualification for a particular job. There are, however, still some exceptions based on or reflecting statutory or official discrimination and also a few other general exceptions; these will be dealt with first.

There are two general points which should be clearly understood:

1. In practice, if you are a private sector employer, there are hardly ever likely to be any circumstances in which you could rely on any of the exceptions mentioned in this chapter.
2. Most of the exceptions apply so as to permit some discrimination in appointing a person to a particular job or training a person for that job; they do not generally permit other acts of discrimination against existing employees, such as dismissing an employee because the job should be done by a person of the opposite sex or of a different racial group.

Statutory and official discrimination

There are the following three matters to be considered:

1. The general provisions under which discrimination may be authorised by statute.
2. The rules under which discrimination may be authorised on grounds of national security.
3. The specific cases of employment in the civil service and the armed forces.

Statutory discrimination—the SDA
There are a few jobs (eg working with certain chemicals) which a pregnant or breastfeeding woman (or, exceptionally, any woman) cannot do without risk to her health.

The current law is contained in section 51 of the SDA (which was amended by the Employment Act 1989). The principle is that you may in certain circumstances refuse to employ a woman on some particular work, but that you must not dismiss her if some suitable alternative work is available. If she is pregnant when dismissed, she has the same statutory right to return to work as she would have had if she had continued to work until the eleventh week before the expected week of confinement.

Before dismissing the employee (or transferring her to other work) you must ask yourself the following questions:

(a) Is there a statutory requirement not to employ the woman on this work?
(b) Is the purpose (or one purpose) of that requirement to protect women as regards pregnancy, maternity or other circumstances giving rise to risks specifically affecting women?

(c) Is the requirement contained in (or in regulations made under) an Act which was passed before the SDA (or a re-enactment of such an Act)?

If the answer to all these questions is yes, then the dismissal will be lawful, so long as there is no suitable alternative work. If the answer to any of them is no, you must then ask the following further questions:

(d) Does the work in question involve risks which specifically affect women in general or pregnant women or mothers?
(e) Is it necessary, for her own protection, for me to stop the woman from doing the work in question?
(f) If I fail to do so, shall I be in breach of my statutory duty to have regard to the health, safety and welfare of my employees?

If the answer to these three questions is yes, then again it will be lawful for you to dismiss the woman, so long as there is no suitable alternative work.

Similar principles apply where a woman applies for a job involving work of the kind in question or where an existing employee applies for a transfer to such work.

There is a new Bill, the Trade Union Reform and Employment Rights Bill, which will be referred to in more detail in Chapter 11. One purpose of this Bill is to bring UK law into line with a recent EC Directive, the Pregnant Workers Directive. The law will be changed in cases where you are unable to employ a woman on some particular work because she is pregnant, has recently given birth or is breast-feeding and there is no suitable alternative work available. In these circumstances you will be obliged to suspend the employee on full pay, not dismiss her.

The Directive provides for a new first step to be taken before the employee is transferred to alternative work or suspended. If the risk to the employee can be removed by a temporary adjustment to her working conditions and/or working hours, then that is the step which must be taken, unless, viewed objectively, it is not technically possible or there is some other reasonable objection.

Statutory discrimination—the RRA

The exceptions contained in Section 41 of the RRA are much broader. An act of racial discrimination is lawful if it is done:

- in pursuance of any Act or Order in Council;
- in pursuance of any statutory rules or regulations;
- in order to comply with any condition or requirement imposed by a minister by virtue of any Act.

It does not matter whether the Act or regulations, etc, were passed before or after the RRA.

This exception has, however, been given a narrow interpretation by the courts. The *Hampson* case has already been mentioned in

Chapter 3. This was the case where a teacher from Hong Kong was required by the Department of Education and Science to take an extra qualification in order to teach in the UK. One of the defences put forward by the department was that their requirement was authorised by statutory regulations. This defence was rejected by the House of Lords. The department would have had a defence only if the regulations had *required* them to act in the way they did; it was not sufficient that the regulations purported to *authorise* them to act in this way.

Immigration control
Section 41 also permits direct discrimination on the ground of nationality and indirect discrimination in relation to residential requirements or conditions, if the act of discrimination is done:

- in pursuance of arrangements made or approved by a minister; or
- to comply with a condition imposed by a minister.

The implications of this exception, for you as an employer, are that the law does not require you to offer employment to a person who:

- needs a work permit and does not have one; or
- would be prevented by the conditions on his work permit from doing the job in question.

It would be direct discrimination in the arrangements for recruitment if you were to single out black job applicants and those who look or sound foreign in order to ask them to produce work permits or evidence that no work permit is required. You should, however, investigate the position where a new employee, of whatever colour or origin, is unable to produce a national insurance card.

National security

Both the SDA (Section 52) and the RRA (Section 42) contain provisions under which discrimination is lawful if it is for the purpose of safeguarding national security. A certificate to that effect by a minister is conclusive under the RRA (Section 69(2)), but not under the SDA.

It is possible to understand the sense of this provision in the context of racial discrimination. For example, your company makes highly secret equipment under a contract with the Ministry of Defence. The Secretary of State certifies that it would be in the interests of national security for you not to employ at the particular establishment any national of certain countries which are potential enemies or a person born in one of those countries. It would be lawful for you to refuse to employ a person at the establishment if he or she has the relevant nationality or national origin. The certificate from the Secretary of State would be a complete defence to any proceedings.

It is, however, bizarre to find the similar exception in the SDA. It is difficult to envisage circumstances in which a person could be a security risk by reason of being a man, being a woman or being married.

The civil service and armed forces

Under the SDA, discrimination is forbidden both in the treatment of civil servants and in appointments to the civil service. The RRA, on the other hand, provides that rules made by the Minister for the Civil Service may lawfully restrict employment in the service of the Crown (or by some public bodies) on grounds of nationality, descent or residence. However, even in these areas direct discrimination against an applicant on the ground of colour is unlawful.

The armed forces

The RRA provides that racial discrimination is lawful in recruitment to the armed forces, if it is in accordance with the appropriate regulations. It is only on grounds of nationality or national origins that the regulations permit any discrimination. If a recruit is turned away on any other racial ground (for instance, because of his or her colour), he or she may present a complaint to an industrial tribunal. Once a person has become a serving member of the armed forces, any kind of racial discrimination against him or her is forbidden, but he or she cannot make a complaint to an industrial tribunal. Instead, the complaint must be made and dealt with in accordance with the provisions for the redress of grievances contained in the Army Act or in the corresponding Acts for the Air Force and the Navy.

The SDA and the Equal Pay Act exclude claims by members of the armed forces. That is not the end of the story, however. It has been conceded by the Ministry of Defence (in the Divisional Court cases of *Lane* and *Leale*), that a former provision (in the Queen's Regulations) for the automatic discharge of all pregnant women was contrary to the EC Equal Treatment Directive. This meant that any woman who had been discharged under these Regulations was given the right to apply to an industrial tribunal for compensation, relying on the Directive. Furthermore, it now seems to be open to any member of the armed forces to take a sex discrimination or equal pay claim of whatever kind to an industrial tribunal, relying on an EC Directive or on Article 119 of the EC Treaty.

EC law

The above case illustrates an important general principle. Parliament can create exceptions to the requirements of domestic legislation, including the RRA and the SDA; however, no domestic legislation can exempt employers (including the Crown) from any directly enforceable obligations under EC law.

Other general exceptions

There are three general provisions under which discrimination in the employment field (as well as other fields) is occasionally permitted. These relate to:

1. Charitable benefits.
2. Sport.
3. Communal accommodation (the SDA only).

Charitable benefits

A charitable organisation or trust may lawfully exist to provide benefits:

- only for men; or
- only for women; or
- only for members of a particular racial group (defined otherwise than by reference to colour).

Any reference to *colour* in the definition of the beneficiaries must be ignored. For instance, a charitable trust for the benefit of *black* West Indians would take effect as a trust for the benefit of *all* West Indians of whatever colour.

These general exceptions for charitable benefits are contained in Section 34 of the RRA and Section 43 of the SDA. The following would be an example of lawful discrimination pursuant to these provisions.

You are the director of a sheltered workshop set up under a charitable trust to provide employment for disabled women born in Scotland. You may lawfully refuse places in the workshop both to a man (wherever born) and to a woman born outside Scotland. If a black woman who was born in Scotland applied for employment in the workshop you would be acting unlawfully if you rejected her application on the ground that she was black, even if the charitable instrument provided for employment to be offered only to white Scotswomen.

It should be noted that the exception only applies where the employment to be offered is a benefit provided in accordance with the charitable trust. If, in the above example, a man born in England applied to you for a job as a fund-raiser, you would be contravening both the RRA and the SDA if you turned down his application on the grounds of his national origin and his sex. If appointed he would be an ordinary paid employee, not a beneficiary, of the charity.

Sport

The general principle is that sports clubs and organisations are not permitted to discriminate against employees or applicants for work, whether the employment is as a player, a referee or other official, or an administrator. However, both the SDA and the RRA contain exceptions to this general rule.

GENUINE OCCUPATIONAL QUALIFICATIONS

Sport—the SDA

The exception in the SDA (Section 44) relates to sports, games and other activities of a competitive nature, where the 'physical strength, stamina or physique' of the average woman puts her at a disadvantage to the average man. Events involving such activities may be lawfully confined to competitors of one sex. It is lawful, for example, for a football club to refuse to employ women or girls on the playing staff. Sport is very much a special case. There is no other provision in the SDA permitting discrimination on the basis of a comparison of the 'physical strength, stamina or physique' of the average woman with that of the average man. The exception does not cover administrators, referees or other officials.

Sport — the RRA

Under the RRA, certain acts of direct or indirect discrimination, both in and outside the employment field, are lawful in either of two circumstances. The acts which are permitted in these circumstances are:

(a) direct discrimination on the ground of nationality or place of birth;
(b) any indirect discrimination which results from the application of a residential requirement.

Such acts are permitted both in the selection of persons to represent a country or area and under rules stating who is eligible to take part in a competition. For instance, Yorkshire County Cricket Club were not breaking the law in the days when they refused to employ cricketers born outside the county.

Communal accommodation

The SDA contains a provision (in Section 46) under which sex discrimination in the provision and management of dormitory or other shared sleeping accommodation may sometimes be lawful. This exception, like the other general exceptions mentioned above, applies both in the employment field and in other areas, such as the provisions relating to the supply of services to the general public. The following would be an example of the working of the exception.

You employ labourers on a long-term contract in a distant part of the country. It is necessary for them to live in the area of the site during the week and they then generally travel home at the weekend. You have provided a large caravan in which several of the labourers can sleep at any one time. You recruit a woman to work on the site, having previously employed only men. You would not necessarily be breaking the law if you refused to offer the woman the right to share the use of the caravan.

There are, however, two important requirements before the exception can apply, as follows:

(a) You must alter or extend the accommodation or provide additional accommodation if it would be reasonable to do so, having

regard to the frequency of the demand or need for use of the accommodation by both sexes. In the above example you should consider whether an additional, smaller, caravan should be provided for use by the female employee.
(b) You must make such arrangements as are reasonably practicable to compensate for the detriment caused by the discrimination. In the above example, an appropriate step would probably be for you to pay a lodging allowance to the woman.

There is, of course, no exception as regards communal accommodation in the RRA.

Genuine occupational qualifications

The law recognises that there are exceptional circumstances in which a person's sex or racial group can be relevant and indeed crucial in determining his or her suitability for a particular job. Accordingly, the SDA and (to a much smaller extent) the RRA define circumstances in which it can be a genuine occupational qualification (or GOQ) for a job that the person appointed should:

- be a man; or
- be a woman; or
- belong to a particular racial group.

General principles

The detailed wording of the GOQ exceptions is set out in Section 7 of the SDA (as amended by the SDA 1986) and Section 5 of the RRA. These two sections are to be found in Appendix 1. Section 7 of the SDA refers throughout to cases where 'being a man' is a GOQ for a job; cases where being a woman is a GOQ are also covered; throughout the section, 'woman' must also be read for 'man' and 'man' for 'woman'.

Where the GOQ exception applies to a job, you may discriminate not only in recruitment to the job but also in promoting or transferring employees to the job, or in training them for it. Where you can lawfully discriminate against a job applicant who lacks the necessary qualification, you may also discriminate on that ground against a person wishing to become a partner. You may also refuse the services of a contract worker who lacks the necessary qualification.

The GOQ exception is very limited. It is important to bear in mind that no occupation should be classified as being one to which the exception always applies. The GOQ exception can apply where only part of the work requires a person of a particular sex or racial group, but it is always necessary for you to consider whether it would be reasonable for you to use existing employees to carry out the relevant work.

Whenever you rely on the GOQ provisions, the industrial tribunal will look carefully at the circumstances of the particular case in the light of the statutory provisions. In practice, the defence rarely succeeds.

The Specific Cases

The SDA lists various GOQ exceptions under a number of headings. Those under the first two headings are matched by similar exceptions in the RRA, but these are the only GOQ exceptions in that Act.

Authenticity and physiology
The RRA (but not the SDA) permits discrimination for reasons of authenticity in filling jobs which involve working in a place where food or drink is served to the public. The obvious examples are jobs which involve serving in an Indian or Chinese restaurant.

The RRA also permits discrimination for reasons of authenticity:

- when casting parts in plays or other entertainments;
- when employing an artist's or photographic model.

However, it is not always necessary on grounds of authenticity to cast parts in a play or other performance on the basis of the character's racial group. Many white actors have played the role of Othello; the lead in the Scottish play can be played without an authentic Scots accent.

The SDA contains a similar exception which applies to many jobs in entertainment and modelling. The questions to be considered are:

(a) If the job involves working in a dramatic performance or other entertainment, does the essential nature of it call for a man (or woman) for reasons of authenticity?
(b) Alternatively, whatever kind of job it is, does the essential nature of it call for a man (or woman) for reasons of physiology (excluding physical strength or stamina)?
(c) In either case, would the essential nature of the job be materially different if carried out by a woman (or a man)?

The word 'physiology', in (b) above, is a strange one to be used. It presumably covers cases where a person is required to model clothes. It should be noted that the fact that a job requires physical strength or stamina can never bring the GOQ exception into play.

Personal services
There is only one other ground on which membership of a particular racial group can qualify a person for a job. Where a job includes providing members of a particular racial group with personal services promoting their welfare, the job may be reserved for a person of that same racial group if, but only if, these personal services can most effectively be provided by such a person. The Home Office guide to the RRA suggests that 'there may be circumstances in which, for example, some members of a particular racial group might respond

best to help offered by a social worker who belongs to the same racial group.'

The case of *Tottenham Green Under Fives' Centre v Marshall*, which came before the EAT in 1989 and again in 1991, illustrated the working of this exception.

The centre ran a nursery for children aged between two and five, of whom 84 per cent were of Afro-Caribbean origin. One of the five nursery workers was also of Afro-Caribbean origin and, when she left, the advertisement for her replacement stated that the post was for an 'Afro-Caribbean worker.' One of the reasons was that the duties included reading books in Afro-Caribbean dialect and talking to the children in that dialect. A white man applied for the job and complained that he had been refused an interview on racial grounds.

An industrial tribunal took the view that the GOQ exception did not apply, but the EAT ruled that the wrong approach had been adopted by the tribunal and sent the case back for re-hearing. The tribunal again decided that the exception did not apply, but for different reasons this time; once again the EAT said that these reasons were not valid and sent the case back. The decisions of the EAT established the following principles:

(a) The centre did not have to prove that any of the personal services to be provided to the children *could only* be provided by a worker of Afro-Caribbean origin; only that personal services could *most effectively* be provided by a person of that racial group.

(b) The work of reading and talking in dialect was a genuine duty and not one invented to claim the benefit of the GOQ exception; that being the case, it was not open to the industrial tribunal to disregard that duty as being less important than the other duties of the post.

In contrast, in the case of *London Borough of Lambeth v CRE* in 1990, the council required an assistant head and a group manager for the housing benefits department. Over half of the tenants were of Afro-Caribbean or Asian ethnic origin. The advertisement for the posts stated that they were confined to Afro-Caribbean and Asian applicants.

It was held by the Court of Appeal in the above case that the GOQ exception did not apply. There must generally be direct contact between the holder of the job and the person to whom personal services are to be given; in this case the posts were management jobs involving minimal contact with the public. It was not sufficient that managers of Afro-Caribbean or Asian origin would possibly be better placed to train housing benefit officers to empathise with claimants. The court also rejected an argument that the discrimination was permissible on the ground that employees of Afro-Caribbean and Asian origin were under-represented in the council's workforce. The law does not permit positive discrimination in selection, however well intentioned.

There is a similar exception, for cases where personal services are to be provided, in the SDA. The 1974 white paper *Equality for Women* gives the example of a team of probation officers, where it may be 'necessary to maintain a team including members of each sex.'

In the following two respects, the exception in the SDA is broader than that in the RRA:

(a) Sex discrimination may be lawful where personal services are provided to promote not the welfare but the education of the recipients.
(b) The discrimination need not be in favour of a person of the same sex as the recipients of the services. For instance, where a school of ballroom dancing offers individual tuition to the pupils, it would probably be lawful for the proprietors to discriminate in recruiting teachers, so that the female pupils can be taught by a man and the male pupils by a woman; the tuition is a personal service which can be most effectively provided by a person of the opposite sex.

Decency and privacy—physical contact
In the SDA, there are two GOQ exceptions relating to decency and privacy.

There are two conditions before the GOQ exception can apply in the first of these cases:

■ the job is likely to involve physical contact with men (or women);
■ they might reasonably object to the job being carried out by a woman (or man).

It is probably lawful for a health farm or any other legitimate establishment where patients are massaged so to arrange its recruitment policy that men are massaged by masseurs and women by masseuses. However, similar discrimination would not be lawful in any ordinary hospital (as opposed possibly to a special single-sex hospital). It would be unreasonable for a patient to object to the well-established tradition that doctors and nurses treat patients of both sexes indiscriminately.

The benefit of the exception is sometimes claimed when assistants are taken on to work in a clothing store, where the job involves physical contact with customers. However, you should always bear in mind the important general principle, which applies to all the GOQs, that the exception cannot apply where there are already enough employees to perform those duties for which the sex of the employee is a legitimate criterion. This principle has been illustrated by the two cases mentioned below.

In *Wylie v Dee & Co (Menswear) Limited* in 1978, a lady who had considerable experience in men's tailoring was turned down for a job as a sales assistant at a men's clothing store, because the job involved carrying out inside leg measurements for men's trousers. Her complaint of sex discrimination succeeded. The tribunal considered that the need to take an inside leg measurement did not arise on very many occasions, and had regard to the fact that there were already seven male assistants employed at the store.

In *Etam plc v Rowan*, some ten years later, a man was turned down for a post as a sales assistant at a shop selling women's and girl's clothing. The employers argued that being a woman was a GOQ because a major part of the job was working in the fitting rooms and measuring customers when they were in a state of undress. This defence was rejected; there were normally 16 women employees in the shop; a man could have adequately carried out the bulk of the work involved in the job and there were sufficient women available to meet the likely requirements in terms of measuring customers in the fitting rooms.

Decency and privacy—toilet facilities, etc
The other decency and privacy case is that where work is likely to be done in circumstances where men (or women) might reasonably object to the presence of a woman (or man) because they are:

■ in a state of undress; or

■ using sanitary facilities.

The obvious examples would appear to be such jobs as lavatory and changing room attendant.

In the case of *Sisley v Britannia Security Systems Limited*, in 1983, the EAT doubted (probably incorrectly) whether the exception did in fact cover cases such as these. They thought that the exception would only apply where it was the holder of the post, not fellow employees or customers, who would be in a state of undress or using the sanitary facilities. The case illustrated how the exception may occasionally apply in that context.

Women were employed, on shifts of up to 12 hours, at a security control station. They had lengthy rest periods, during which they stripped to their underwear to avoid crumpling their uniforms. It was ruled that the GOQ exception applied so as to permit the employers to refuse a job application from a man. The rest periods were a necessary aspect of the work and, accordingly, employees could be regarded as doing their work while they were in a state of undress during the rest periods.

The exception would not, however, permit discrimination on the ground that you do not have toilets or showers for both sexes. The use of these facilities is an interruption to the work which your employees are employed to do, not part of it. Where you have facilities for only one sex, then these must be adapted or extended to provide for both sexes.

Domestic employment
Before the SDA 1986, there was a complete exception for discrimination in relation to employment for the purposes of a private household (except in cases of victimisation and cases where contract workers

were involved). This is still the position under the RRA. Under the SDA there is now a much more limited exception, under which the following conditions must be met:

(a) The job involves working or living *in* a private home.
(b) It *needs* to be held by a man (or woman).
(c) The job is likely to give rise to physical or social contact with a person living in the home or knowledge of the intimate details of such a person's life.
(d) Objection might reasonably be taken to allowing a woman (or man) that degree of contact or that knowledge.

It is unlikely that the exception could ever now cover jobs such as that of a gardener or cleaner. The exception could possibly apply where, for example, an elderly woman requires a paid companion to live with her in her home.

Living accommodation required
There are cases where your employees may have to live in accommodation which you provide because there is no practicable alternative. Employees on a ship, an oil rig or a remote construction site cannot generally commute to work from their homes each day. The GOQ exception may apply in such cases if the premises are not equipped with:

- separate sleeping accommodation for both sexes; or
- sanitary facilities which can be used by both sexes in privacy.

There is, however, an important proviso. You cannot claim the benefit of the exception if it would have been reasonable for you to cater for both sexes by:

- extending or modifying the premises in order to include the separate sleeping accommodation or sanitary facilities; or
- providing additional premises.

Single-sex establishments
The next GOQ exception covers cases where the job involves working in certain single-sex establishments. The following questions must all have been answered yes before the exception can apply:

(a) Will the person appointed be working in a hospital, prison or other establishment for persons requiring special care, supervision or attention?
(b) Are those persons all of the same sex (disregarding any whose presence is exceptional)?
(c) Is it reasonable, having regard to the essential character of the establishment (or the part where the work is to be done), that the job should only be held by a person of that same sex?

This exception does not cover *all* single-sex establishments; there are some (such as hospitals) where objection could not generally be taken to the presence of qualified employees of both sexes. Furthermore, it is unlikely that the exception would ever cover *all jobs* in *any* establishment; the essential character of the establishment is not generally affected by the sex of, for example, a gardener.

Overseas duties
Many employees at establishments in Great Britain have to do some work outside the country, for example when selling goods to overseas customers or escorting or driving parties of tourists. A GOQ exception can apply to such jobs where the job is likely to involve some work in a country where, because of the laws or customs of the country, the duties could not effectively be performed by a woman (or man).

This is the only ground on which an employer is ever permitted to pander to the prejudices of others, whether customers or other employees. There is no corresponding provision in the RRA.

For example, a Jewish man and a woman both apply to you for a job as a sales manager. It will be necessary every few months for the successful applicant to visit the company's most important customers, who are based in an Arab Muslim country. You refuse to employ the woman, on the ground that being a man is a GOQ for the job. Because the country is a fundamentalist Muslim country, its customs are such that selling could not effectively be carried out by a woman; customers would refuse to discuss business with her. Your GOQ defence to a complaint by the woman would probably succeed. You also, however, refuse to employ the male applicant, because he is Jewish and the country is an Arab country. You would have no defence to a complaint by him under the RRA.

Married couples
A person's sex can also be a GOQ where a job is one of two to be held by a married couple. If you are, for instance, a brewery manager looking for a married couple to manage a public house, you are not bound to offer the jobs to the two most suitable individuals if they are not married to each other, even if they are an unmarried couple or two men or two women who are prepared to live and work together. You may legitimately seek not the two most suitable individuals but the most suitable married couple.

Practical advice

1. The EOC code (in paragraph 15) makes the following points:
    (a) There are very few instances in which the GOQ exception applies.
    (b) The exception cannot be used to justify discrimination against women on the ground that a job requires strength or stamina.
    (c) A GOQ exception cannot be used to justify dismissing any employee.

2. You must not assume that any job can automatically be classed as one to which the GOQ exception applies. The legal annex to the EOC code makes the point that a GOQ 'is not an automatic exception for general categories of jobs. In every case it will be necessary for an employer to show that the criteria detailed in the SDA apply to the job or part of the job in question.'
3. If the GOQ exception has previously been used in order to fill a particular kind of post, do not assume automatically that the exception will apply next time that a similar post (or even the identical post) has to be filled. The relevant circumstances may have changed. The EOC code expressly recommends (in paragraph 17) that any such job should be re-examined whenever the post falls vacant to see whether the GOQ exception still applies.
4. All the above points apply equally to the few GOQ exceptions under the RRA.
5. The remaining point applies to the more general exceptions mentioned earlier in this chapter rather than to the GOQ exceptions. Remember that finding an exception in the RRA or the SDA is not the end of the story. Discrimination which is permitted by domestic legislation may nevertheless be unlawful under EC law. This point is particularly important for public sector employers, since they are particularly vulnerable to proceedings based on an EC Directive.

Summary

1. There are very few cases in which discrimination is permitted. The circumstances of any particular case need to be carefully examined.
2. The RRA has general provisions permitting discrimination which is *required* by some other law. There are also special rules regarding entry to the civil service and armed forces.
3. There is a more limited exception in the SDA, where it would be unlawful for employers to employ (or continue to employ) a person because of special risks affecting women in general, or pregnant women or mothers in particular.
4. The SDA does not apply to the armed forces; but EC Directives do.
5. Both Acts have general exceptions for:

    (a) some discrimination in the employment of playing staff in certain sports;
    (b) discrimination in relation to charitable benefits;
    (c) national security.

6. There are a few cases in which being a man, being a woman or belonging to a particular racial group can be a GOQ, so as to permit discrimination in appointments to or training for the post.

8
Positive Action

The law makes absolutely no distinction between reverse discrimination, in relation to shortlisting and job offers, and other acts of discrimination. You cannot lawfully penalise white or male job applicants or promotion candidates in order to achieve a reasonable quota of black or female workers, or to atone for past discrimination against these groups. The law does not permit discrimination in job selection as a method of meeting quotas or targets and does not recognise a benevolent motive for unlawful discrimination. These principles were illustrated by the case of *London Borough of Lambeth v CRE* which was mentioned in Chapter 7.

On the other hand, the effects of past discrimination by employers or discriminatory attitudes in society generally may linger on, continuing to blight the lives of some employees for decades to come. For example:

(a) A particular factory or other establishment, or a whole occupation, may be so dominated by, for example, white workers and men that black workers and women are deterred from applying for jobs.

(b) Individuals who have been denied vocational training or lack formal educational qualifications may be condemned to working at a level far below that justified by their natural abilities.

The law accordingly permits limited exceptions to the general rule that positive or reverse discrimination is unlawful. In the words of the 1975 white paper *Racial Discrimination*:

> The Government considers that it would be wrong to adhere so blindly to the principle of formal legal equality as to ignore the handicaps preventing many black and brown workers from obtaining equal opportunities.

A similar approach was followed in relation to the SDA.

The legal exceptions

The law recognises five ways in which employers may lawfully discriminate in order to help employees and potential employees overcome disadvantages and enjoy genuine equality of opportunity. It is important to note that these provisions may in certain circumstances be relied on in order to discriminate in favour of men rather than women or even in favour of white workers rather than black workers. The five exceptions are:

1. Inviting job applications.
2. Training for certain existing employees.
3. Participating in training initiatives for non-employees.
4. Measures to meet the special needs of ethnic minorities.
5. Special treatment for pregnant employees.

Inviting job applications

Under Section 48(1) of the SDA (which is set out in Appendix 1), you may discriminate by encouraging only women (or only men) to take advantage of opportunities for some particular work. The only condition is that at some time during the previous 12 months there must have been no or comparatively few women (or men) doing that work at the establishment in question.

The following examples illustrate how the exception works in practice:

(a) Your company's goods are sold by sales representatives who visit customers and potential customers and who are supported by sales staff in the office. All the sales representatives are men; the sales staff in the office, who have less interesting and lower paid work, are nearly all women. You could lawfully discriminate by encouraging one or more of the women to apply for the next vacancy for a post as a sales representative.

(b) You have a large office in which all the filing clerks and office juniors are female. This is because the school leavers who apply for vacancies are always female. You may lawfully ask your local job centre and the careers officer at the local school to bring the next vacancy specifically to the attention of male school leavers who are interested in doing office work.

But for the exception, the steps taken in both the above examples would have been unlawful. In (a), the discrimination would have been in the way you afforded access to opportunities for promotion or transfer; in (b), you would have been discriminating in the arrangements for determining who should be offered employment.

In both cases, however, there must still be no discrimination at the point of selection. If a man applied for the sales job in (a) or a woman applied for the clerical work in (b), then those applications must be dealt with on their merits.

Encouragement under the RRA

There are similar provisions under the RRA (in Section 38(1) and (2), which is also set out in Appendix 1). Under these provisions, you may encourage black workers or workers of some other racial group to apply for some particular work at your factory or other establishment. Before you can take advantage of these provisions you must be satisfied that one of the following conditions was complied with at some time during the previous 12 months:

1. There were no members of the racial group doing that work at the establishment in question; or
2. Of the employees doing that particular work, the proportion belonging to the racial group in question was smaller than that which would have reflected the racial composition of your total labour force at the establishment or the population of the area from which you normally recruit employees for the establishment.

The expression commonly used, where the statistical conditions are met, is that members of the racial group are 'under-represented' in relation to the particular work. This expression is, however, very much a shorthand expression and should not be understood as meaning that the law recognises any policy of racial quotas; indeed any policy of discriminating in selection to achieve a racial quota (or equal numbers of men and women) is unlawful.

The following examples illustrate the working of these provisions:

(a) You have a large store in a town with a high ethnic minority population. All the assistants in the store are white, because there have been only white applicants for the jobs. You may lawfully discriminate in relation to the next vacancy by advertising the vacancy predominantly in the local minority language newspapers.
(b) A large proportion of the jobs in your factory are held by workers of Asian origin, but they are nearly all unskilled jobs. All the apprentices are white. As above, you may advertise the next apprenticeship in Asian language newspapers; or produce vacancy notices in those languages, to be displayed at the factory gate or sent to the local job centre; or ask careers officers to bring the apprenticeship to the notice of school leavers of Asian origin.

As in the case of the SDA, there must be no discrimination at the point of selection. If a white worker becomes aware of a vacancy and applies for it, then that white worker must be appointed if he or she is the most suitable candidate (subject in some circumstances to the 'special needs' exception mentioned later in this chapter).

There are many cases where the exceptions under the RRA could overlap with those under the SDA. If, in example (b), all your apprentices are not only white but also male, you could tell local careers officers that you would particularly like to interview female school leavers (of whatever racial group), as well as school leavers of Asian origin.

Training

There is one respect in which the law *does* permit direct or indirect discrimination in *selecting* an existing employee for preferential treatment.

Under Section 48(1) of the SDA and Section 38(1) and (2) of the RRA (both to be found in Appendix 1) you may discriminate in affording employees access to training facilities to help fit them for some particular work.

Under the RRA, the conditions are similar to those already mentioned in relation to encouraging job applications. You must be satisfied that the work in question is work which (either now or at some time in the last 12 months) is being done in your factory (or other establishment):

(a) by no employees of the same racial group as the proposed trainee; or
(b) by comparatively few employees of that racial group in relation to the racial composition of your total workforce in the establishment or that of the population of your recruitment area.

The conditions under the SDA are more straightforward. You simply need to satisfy yourself that the work in question is (now or at some time in the last 12 months) being done in your establishment either by no women or by comparatively few women (or men if the trainee is a man).

The following examples illustrate the working of these provisions:

(a) Your factory has a high proportion of black workers, but they are nearly all shop floor workers. There is not a black or brown face to be seen in the accounts office or sales office and all the drivers are white as well. The law permits you to discriminate in favour of one or more of your black employees in selection for a computer course (to help fit them for work in the accounts department); a sales course; or a driving course.
(b) Your factory employs a large number of women as well as men, but all the managers are men. You may discriminate in favour of one of your female employees if there is a vacancy on a management development course.

The above exceptions apply whether you are providing the training yourself or helping your employee to take advantage of training provided by a third party. The ways in which you could help include:

- day release;
- giving the employee paid or unpaid leave to attend a training course;
- paying the whole or part of the course fees and other expenses.

An employee who has received training may then be the strongest candidate when a suitable vacancy arises. However, at that stage the employee must compete on merit with any other candidates for the post; any discrimination in selection for the post would be unlawful.

Skills to be used overseas
The RRA (in Section 6) contains special provision for workers who are ordinarily resident outside Great Britain. You may lawfully

discriminate in allocating jobs to such workers in order to provide training in skills which you believe the employee intends to exercise wholly outside Great Britain.

For example, your company has a subsidiary company in an African country. Each year you take two management trainees and two apprentices from that country, so that they can then use their skills for the benefit of your company in their own country. The racial discrimination in their favour is lawful.

Other training initiatives

It could be partly for selfish reasons that you take advantage of the above provisions. It can make sound business sense to find new sources of untapped ability and to help employees to realise their full career potential.

You may also, however, wish to provide training and encouragement for individuals who do not work for you and who are not seeking employment with you. Many employers recognise a moral obligation to contribute time or resources for the benefit of their own industry, profession or locality, or that of the community generally.

Both the RRA (in Section 37) and the SDA (in Section 47) contain provisions under which you may lawfully discriminate in providing training or encouragement for individuals who are *not* your employees and who are *not* job applicants. You may provide this training and encouragement either on your own initiative; or through an employers' or trade or professional association to which you belong; or in conjunction with a local authority or private or public sector training body.

The exception under the SDA applies if:

- no women or comparatively few women in Great Britain are doing the relevant work; or
- you are encouraging or training women for work in some particular area and there are no women or comparatively few women doing the work in that area.

The exception may, subject to the same conditions, be relied upon in order to permit discrimination in favour of men. For example:

(a) You own a large garage. You are aware that in Great Britain there are few women working as mechanics and few men working as secretaries. You offer work experience to pupils from a local school, but on the understanding that the boys will work with the secretaries in the office and the girls will work with the mechanics in the workshop.

(b) Your engineering company provides a scholarship for women taking engineering degrees; the sex discrimination is lawful because comparatively few of the people working as engineers in Great Britain are women.

The conditions for the exception under the RRA are similar. Suppose, for example, that you wish to offer training or encouragement to black workers in relation to some particular work. You need to look at the figures as at a date within the last 12 months. There are then the following possibilities:

1. Only a small percentage of the people doing that work in Great Britain are black, compared with the percentage of the total population of Great Britain who are black.
2. You wish to train or encourage black workers to do the work in some particular area; in that area, only, say 2 per cent of those doing the work are black, but, say, 10 per cent of the local population are black.

The following examples illustrate the working of these provisions:

(a) Your factory is in an area where there are many people of Asian origin but a comparatively small number of Asian teachers and youth leaders. You pay for advertisements in national minority newspapers encouraging Asians to apply for jobs as teachers and youth leaders in the area.
(b) Your profession has a very low percentage of black members compared to the percentage of the population of Great Britain who are black. You sponsor black school leavers on degree and professional education courses in order to help increase the percentage of those entering the profession.

Special needs—domestic and family responsibilities
There is a further training initiative which you may take for the benefit of persons who are *not* your employees, even though it may involve direct or indirect sex discrimination.

Many women (and some men) spend years during which they would otherwise be pursuing full-time careers in bringing up children or looking after sick or elderly relatives. During those years, they have a complete break from their careers or are able to work only intermittently or part time. A person wishing to return to full-time work, after discharging domestic or family responsibilities for some years, may be in special need of vocational training. You may lawfully provide such training, either on your own account or in conjunction with your local authority, or a local college or some other body. For example:

(a) You provide, using your own premises and your own staff, refresher courses on secretarial work and computer technology for women wishing to return to work. Your direct discrimination, in providing the course for women returners only, is lawful; there must, however, be no discrimination in dealing with job applications from those women or from any other person.
(b) The local schools from which you recruit many employees are short of maths and science teachers. You join with your local authority in paying for refresher courses for men and women who wish to return to teaching those subjects after a break of some years. Restricting the courses to returners probably means that there will be more women than men on the courses.

Because of the exception in the SDA, a man who had not had a break from the profession but wished to take advantage of the extra training could not complain of indirect discrimination and require you to justify the restriction.

Employees and non-employees

Apart from the special case of skills to be exercised overseas, details have been given in this chapter of three sets of exceptions which permit discrimination in relation to training, as follows:

1. Under both the RRA and the SDA, you can discriminate in providing career development and other training for your own employees, so long as certain statistical conditions are met. The conditions in the RRA involve looking at the numbers employed in your own establishment and sometimes also at the population of the recruitment area for the establishment.
2. Under both Acts you can discriminate in providing, or participating in the provision of, training strictly for persons who are *not* employed by you. Again, there are statistical conditions, which involve looking at the numbers doing the work in question either in Great Britain as a whole or in some particular area.
3. The SDA also contains special provisions for discrimination in providing training for those returning to work after an absence from full-time work for domestic or family responsibilities; again, it is only persons who are *not* employed by you who can benefit from this exception and you must not then discriminate in offering them employment.

Special needs of ethnic minorities

There is a very broad provision in the RRA which authorises discrimination in favour of both employees and non-employees. Under Section 35 of the RRA, you may lawfully discriminate in affording persons of a particular racial group access to facilities or services to meet the special needs of persons of that group in regard to their education, training, welfare or any ancillary benefits. For example:

(a) Your factory employs a large number of workers of Asian origin. Some of them came to Great Britain as adults and have difficulty in understanding and speaking English. You provide language courses for them and also arrange for safety notices and the company newsletter to be translated into Asian languages. Employees from other ethnic groups would have no valid complaint on the ground that they would like to have the newsletter translated also into, for example, Welsh and Polish.

(b) Your company has a good many driving jobs and several employees also qualify for company cars. You employ a number of refugees from eastern Europe, hardly any of whom have driving licences. This is partly because of language difficulties and partly because they came to Great Britain with no money and could not afford tuition. You may lawfully discriminate in favour of these employees by providing driving tuition in their own language, as well as the language tuition which they will need to understand the Highway Code.

It is possible that you may also in certain circumstances be able to rely on this 'special needs' provision to discriminate in favour of members of a particular racial group by offering them apprenticeships and similar employment. The main purpose of an apprenticeship and similar employment is to provide training; so long as the members of the racial group in question have special needs in regard to such training, then the discrimination will be lawful.

However, the 'special needs' provision emphatically does not give licence for discrimination of a more general nature. If, for example, members of a particular racial group have been particularly hard hit by unemployment and you wish to discriminate in their favour in dealing with job applications, you cannot expect to convince an industrial tribunal that employment itself is a facility or service of which members of the group have a special need in relation to their welfare. Employment itself cannot properly be regarded as a facility or service and if Parliament had intended to authorise discrimination in job selection it would have done so expressly.

Pregnancy

Some employers, when they learn that an employee is pregnant, congratulate and dismiss the employee in virtually the same breath. This question of discrimination against pregnant employees is considered in Chapter 11.

Other employers, however, wish to treat pregnant employees more generously than the law requires; partly because this seems a fair and reasonable thing to do; partly because employees who are generously treated are more likely to be loyal and hard working in the future.

The law permits discrimination *in favour of* pregnant employees. The SDA (in Section 2) follows up the definition of discrimination by excluding from it special treatment afforded to women in connection with pregnancy or childbirth.

You may therefore, for example:

(a) pay full wages, rather than statutory maternity pay;
(b) extend the period of maternity leave;
(c) give these benefits to employees who do not have long enough service to qualify for them by right;
(d) make a lump sum payment towards maternity expenses;
(e) provide a refresher course for an employee returning to work after maternity leave, particularly where she works in a field of rapid technical change.

Male employees cannot complain of sex discrimination on the ground that they can never qualify for these benefits by becoming pregnant or on the ground that they are not given similarly generous treatment if they have time off, for example for sickness or study.

It is, of course, open to you as an employer to allow male employees to take paternity leave, although this is not (yet) a legal requirement.

Local authorities

Local authorities have a particularly important part to play in relation to education and training for employment. Many local authorities, for example:

- are major employers in their own right;
- are also education authorities;
- also provide a wide range of adult education courses;
- also have the function of promoting local industry and commerce.

Local authorities are, therefore, particularly well placed to provide training on their own account and also to support and co-ordinate the training activities of local employers and colleges.

The RRA (in Section 71) imposes on every local authority the duty to carry out their functions with due regard to the need:

- to eliminate unlawful racial discrimination; and
- to promote equality of opportunity, and good relations, between persons of different racial groups.

Non-discriminatory steps

This chapter has explained how you may in certain circumstances, through discriminatory encouragement and training, help to increase the numbers of (usually) women or ethnic minority workers doing particular kinds of work.

Quite apart from the specific exceptions contained in the legislation, there are many other steps which you may take in order to help employees and job applicants overcome disadvantages which tend to affect mainly, for example, women and ethnic minority workers. Some of these possible further steps are considered in the next section of this chapter.

There is, however, one important legal principle which you must at all times bear in mind. It is entirely laudable and sensible that you should take steps to remove unnecessary obstacles to the career development of particular groups of workers, such as women and ethnic minority workers. Indeed, many such steps are obligatory, in order to avoid unlawful indirect discrimination. However, unless you are relying on one of the express statutory exceptions mentioned earlier in this chapter, you must ensure that all the actions which you take and all the facilities which you offer are free from unlawful discrimination. For example:

(a) If you offer female employees the opportunity to work part time with no loss of seniority or career prospects, then (except where

you are giving special treatment to pregnant employees) you must offer similar opportunities to male employees who may themselves have family responsibilities or medical conditions which make full-time working difficult or impossible.
(b) Assistance with child care (whether financial assistance or an offer of a place in a nursery or creche) should not be restricted to female employees; there are single parent families where the parent is a man and other families where the man has the main or shared responsibility for children.

Practical advice

If you propose to discriminate in the way in which you provide encouragement or training for particular work, make sure that you do so lawfully, in accordance with the conditions described earlier in this chapter. If you are a manager committed to equal opportunities you may face the temptation to discriminate in selection for jobs, in order to redress the disadvantages faced by many women and ethnic minority workers in trying to break through to more senior posts. However, reverse discrimination in job selection:

- is unlawful;
- may cause resentment on the part of male and white workers who are rejected for jobs for which they are the most suitable candidates;
- could damage the credibility of the equal opportunity policy in the eyes of the main decision makers in your company or other organisation and cause them to withdraw their backing even for the positive actions which you can take lawfully.

Discriminatory encouragement and training

Subject to this important proviso, the law permits a great deal of discrimination in training and encouragement for particular work, as mentioned earlier in this chapter. The CRE code (in paragraph 1.3(c)) suggests that, where appropriate and where permissible under the RRA, you should aim as part of your equal opportunity policy to give employees of under-represented racial groups training and encouragement, to help them achieve equal opportunity within your organisation.

The code recommends (in paragraph 1.45) several steps to be taken to help combat under-representation of particular racial groups in particular work. If, for example, your factory has many employees but no managers of Asian origin (the code does not use this specific example), you should consider the following measures:

(a) Advertise posts for trainee managers in Asian language newspapers as well as other newspapers.

(b) Use employment agencies and careers offices in areas with a high population of Asian origin.
(c) Run recruitment and training schemes for school leavers designed to reach Asian school leavers.
(d) Encourage existing employees of Asian origin to apply for promotion or transfer opportunities.
(e) Give management or supervisory or skills training to employees of Asian origin who show potential—including language training where necessary.

The CRE code itself (in paragraph 1.44) makes the fundamental point, however, that discrimination at the point of selection for work is not permitted under the positive action provisions contained in the RRA.

The EOC code also refers to the kinds of positive action which are permitted. The examples given (in paragraph 42) include:

(a) Training your own employees for work which is traditionally the preserve of the other sex, for example training women for skilled manual or technical work.
(b) Giving positive encouragement to women to apply for management posts and providing special courses where necessary.

Language and communications

The CRE code (in paragraph 1.26) draws attention to language training as being particularly important. It states that difficulties in communication can endanger equal opportunity in the workforce; good communications can also improve efficiency, promotion prospects and health and safety, and create a better understanding.

Certain measures are suggested (in paragraph 1.27) in order to improve the working conditions of ethnic minority workers. These include:

(a) Provision of interpretation and translation facilities (for example to help employees pursue grievances and also understand the terms of their employment).
(b) Training for managers and supervisors in the background and culture of racial minority groups.
(c) The use of alternative or additional methods of communication, for example translating safety notices and giving instruction combined with industrial language training.

Where ethnic minority employees have difficulties in understanding or communication in English, language training is a very important method of helping them to work more safely and effectively, and also to improve their promotion prospects. The code recommends (in paragraph 1.27) training in English language and communication skills.

Non-discriminatory steps

As mentioned earlier in this chapter, there are many steps which you can take to promote equality of opportunity without any discrimination being involved; indeed, there are some which you must take in order to avoid indirect discrimination.

Some of the non-discriminatory measures which you could consider taking as part of a positive action programme fall broadly into the following four categories:

- language and other training;
- flexible selection arrangements;
- help with maternity and childcare;
- flexible working and training practices.

Language and other training

Language training to meet the special needs of some ethnic minority employees has already been mentioned, but they are not alone in needing such training. There are workers of all racial groups and all colours who, for one reason or another, have language and communication difficulties. It is unsatisfactory if any employee, of whatever ethnic group or colour, has innate abilities which cannot be fully used because of language difficulties. It is therefore good employment practice to provide, so far as resources permit, language and communication training for all employees who need it or could benefit from it.

Flexible selection arrangements

If you find that the formal requirements for some posts represent a barrier to, for example, women rather than men or black workers rather than white workers, the steps which you could consider taking are as follows:

(a) Retain the requirement, whatever the consequences, because it serves an important purpose and there appears to be no reasonable alternative to it.
(b) Simply abandon the requirement, if it cannot be justified.
(c) Make a special exception for women and for black workers—but that would be unlawful direct discrimination.
(d) Provide special training for women and black workers already employed by you in other jobs—such positive action could, subject to conditions, be permissible, as explained already in this chapter.
(e) Modify the requirement to the extent of providing alternative avenues for job applicants and promotion candidates of both sexes and all racial groups.

The following are examples of the approach suggested in (e) above:

(i) You require a minimum level of intelligence for certain work and you require job applicants to demonstrate that intelligence by having obtained a minimum number of GCSE passes. You find that many ethnic minority job applicants cannot meet this educational requirement, even though they have the innate intelligence required. The answer is not to make a special case of them but to allow all job applicants, of whatever racial group or colour, to take a non-discriminatory intelligence test as an alternative to the formal educational qualifications.

(ii) You require candidates for a senior managerial post to have substantial and recent experience of running a business. A woman returning to work after bringing up her family will be unable to meet this requirement, but may well have substantial and recent experience of running a voluntary organisation and managing its staff and helpers. If you were to broaden your requirements to take account of the management experience of women (and men) in managing charitable and other voluntary organisations, this would be a non-discriminatory way of promoting equality of opportunity.

There are circumstances where this kind of flexible approach should also be exercised in relation to internal promotions, transfers and training. The EOC code recommends (in paragraph 25(d)) that, when general ability and personal qualities are the main requirement for promotion, care should be taken to consider favourably candidates of both sexes with differing career patterns and general experience.

Maternity and childcare
The EOC code (in paragraph 43) gives several examples of action to help provide continuity of employment to working parents, many of whom will have valuable experience or skills. The steps which you can take in order to avoid losing employees (or having them distracted from their work) because of their childcare commitments include:

(a) Establishing nursery facilities on the premises, if feasible, or combining with other employers in the area to provide such facilities.
(b) Where residential training is necessary, inform the employees well in advance to enable them to make childcare and other personal arrangements.
(c) If you have your own residential training centre, consider whether childcare facilities might be provided.
(d) Ensure that personal leave arrangements are adequate and available to both sexes.

All the above facilities should be provided in a non-discriminatory way to employees of both sexes who need the facilities. The code points out that men as well as women need to undertake domestic responsibilities on occasion.

It is also lawful, as already mentioned, to improve the statutory maternity leave provisions, either by reducing the qualifying service period, extending the leave period or giving access to part-time arrangements on return to work.

Paternity leave is another option to be considered.

Flexible working and training practices
Many women, some men and some ethnic minority workers of both sexes are unable to undertake a conventional career pattern of full-time working, for one or more of the following reasons:

(a) Many women, and some men, are unable to work full time or have breaks in their working life because of domestic and family commitments, including bringing up young children and looking after other relatives.
(b) Workers of both sexes are unable to work full time or without breaks in their careers, for medical reasons.
(c) Some ethnic minority workers are able to work full time but need flexible hours of work because of the need to observe prayer times and religious holidays, a point made in the CRE code (paragraph 1.24(a)).

The EOC code suggests (in paragraph 43(a)) that measures which you could consider include allowing certain jobs to be carried out on a part-time or flexi-time basis. Other facilities which you could consider offering to employees of both sexes and all racial groups include:

- job sharing;
- working from home, where the job lends itself to an arrangement of this kind;
- career breaks, with arrangements for continuing access to training and information and a guarantee of favourable consideration when a return to full-time work becomes practicable.

It is important not to see these facilities in terms only of special arrangements for women. Job sharing, for example, could be undertaken between a working mother and a man who wishes to reduce his hours as he approaches retirement or who needs time off each week for hospital treatment.

Summary

1. Positive discrimination in selection for any job is unlawful. The only exception is in regard to apprenticeships and other jobs where training is the dominant purpose of the employment, if:
    (a) the employee is not ordinarily resident in Great Britain and intends to exercise his or her new skills outside Great Britain;
    (b) the employment can be regarded as a facility or service to meet the special needs of persons of a particular racial group in regard to their education or training.
2. There are provisions under which you can discriminate in favour of employees (with separate provisions for non-employees) in

giving encouragement or training for particular work. The condition is that the persons receiving the encouragement or training must (according to one of several possible criteria) be 'under-represented' in relation to the particular work.
3. The 'special needs' provision mentioned above also authorises certain acts of racial discrimination in providing facilities or services to existing employees in relation to their education, training, welfare or ancillary benefits.
4. The law permits special treatment afforded to women in connection with pregnancy or childbirth.
5. There are also many steps which can be taken in a non-discriminatory way in order to promote equality of opportunity.

9
Sexual and Racial Harassment

Sexual and racial harassment take many forms, verbal and physical. Examples include:

(a) The persecution of ethnic minority employees, ranging from patronising and demeaning remarks through open aggression and racial insults to physical violence.
(b) The subjection of employees (usually but not always women) to suggestive and obscene remarks, unwelcome sexual advances or indecent assaults.
(c) Promises or hints of career advancement in return for sexual favours, and threats or hints of stagnation or demotion if sexual favours are refused.

There is an EC code of practice *Protecting the Dignity of Women and Men at Work*, which is mentioned in more detail later in this chapter and which was adopted in October 1991. The code states, on the basis of research, that for millions of women in the European Community sexual harassment is an unpleasant and unavoidable part of their working lives. The code defines sexual harassment as 'unwanted conduct of a sexual nature, or other conduct based on sex affecting the dignity of women and men at work'. The code goes on to say that sexual harassment pollutes the working environment and can have a devastating effect upon the health, confidence, morale and performance of those affected by it.

From an employer's point of view, both sexual and racial harassment have the following unacceptable consequences:

(a) The victims of racial and sexual harassment are not allowed to get on with the work for which they are paid and may even be driven out of their jobs.
(b) Managers who harass their subordinates are abusing their positions and the trust placed in them.
(c) Other employees who indulge in sexual or racial harassment are misusing their working time to behave in a way which is at best immature and at worst vicious.
(d) A poisonous working atmosphere is created when harassment is seen to go unchecked.

The legal approach to harassment

The word 'harassment' does not appear at all either in the SDA or the RRA. However, both the SDA (in Section 6(2)(b)) and the RRA (in Section 4(2)(c)) forbid employers to discriminate by subjecting an employee to a 'detriment'. The word 'detriment' means no more than a real disadvantage. Sexual and racial harassment are among the most serious of the detriments to which employees can be subjected; other examples of detrimental treatment are considered in Chapter 10.

Matters to be proved

If a complaint of sexual or racial harassment against you is to succeed, there are four matters which the complainant will need to prove. You will have a defence to the complaint if any one of the following matters is not proved:

1. The complainant must show that he or she has been *treated* in the way complained of.
2. It must also be shown that the treatment amounts to a *detriment*.
3. There is no unlawful discrimination unless there is a *sexual or racial element* to the treatment complained of.
4. The treatment complained of must also be in the *employment context*.

Treatment

The starting point in any complaint of sexual or racial discrimination is to determine whether the matters complained of actually took place. In most cases the individual accused of harassment denies the allegations and usually there is no clear independent evidence on either side. An employer investigating the allegations and subsequently an industrial tribunal hearing the complaint has to decide where the truth lies, on the basis of the respective credibility of the complainant and the alleged harasser. As an employer, however, you should not delude yourself into thinking that a complaint is unlikely to succeed without any independent witnesses; many complaints are upheld on the unsupported evidence of the complainant.

There is also a legal sense in which it has to be shown that the complainant has been *treated* in the way complained of. The harasser must have done something which was in some way *aimed* at the complainant. In the case of *De Souza v The Automobile Association*, an employee overheard a conversation in which a racially derogatory word was used to describe her, but the person making the remark did not intend her to overhear it or become aware of it and had no reason to believe that she would become aware of it. Accordingly, her complaint of racial discrimination was unsuccessful.

Similarly, a female employee who goes into a working atmosphere in which swearing and bad language are to be found is not being subjected to any kind of treatment, and has no complaint, if the swearing and bad language continue unabated. It is different, however, if the bad language is directed at her or intensified in an attempt to make her feel uncomfortable. Most women who take jobs on a male-dominated shop floor or building site expect and are prepared for a certain amount of swearing and bad language; when such women complain of sexual harassment, the complaints usually relate to very much more serious matters.

Detriment

A detriment can take the form of one serious incident, as in the *Darby* case mentioned below, or a series of incidents which have a cumulative effect.

An employee is subjected to a detriment if made to feel:

- fear, degradation or humiliation, even on one occasion;
- helpless anger caused by being made to listen to offensive remarks and being afraid to do anything about it;
- worry or uncertainty about the risk of career prospects being blighted by a refusal to respond to sexual advances.

A detriment does not always involve a physical assault; words can suffice. It is usually inoffensive for one employee to ask another for a date; many marriages have resulted from office romances. However, repeated propositions and suggestions, once they are known to be unwelcome, can amount to a detriment.

One very sensitive issue is the extent to which the complainant's own words and conduct are relevant. In *Snowball v Gardner Merchant Limited*, a 1987 case, a catering manager complained about repeated suggestions of a sexual nature which she said had been made by her district manager. It was alleged that she had talked freely to her fellow employees at work about sexual matters. The allegations on both sides were denied. The question was whether evidence of her own sexual attitudes and of what she was supposed to have said at work was at all relevant to the case.

It was ruled by the EAT that the industrial tribunal was entitled to hear the evidence about these matters. The evidence could be relevant to the question of whether any detriment had occurred and also, for compensation purposes, the question of the degree of detriment.

The above case was one where the complaint related to unwelcome suggestions, not a physical assault, and where the counter-allegations related to remarks made at work. Evidence about the complainant's sexual attitudes is far less likely to be relevant and admissible if it relates to things which have been done or said outside work, or if the complaint relates to a physical assault of a sexual nature. It is not permissible to respond to a complaint of sexual harassment with a generalised attack on the complainant's character; however liberated the complainant's behaviour and attitudes outside work may be, this does not give a licence for all and sundry to commit indecent assaults in the work place.

These principles were illustrated by the case of *Wileman v Minilec Engineering Limited*, in 1988. An employee complained of salacious remarks and unwanted physical contact by a director of the company. The employers wished to introduce evidence that the complainant had posed for a national newspaper in a flimsy costume. This 'evidence' was ruled by the EAT to be irrelevant and inadmissible. It could not affect in any way the question of physical harassment and its value in relation to the salacious remarks by the director was almost minimal.

As a general rule, therefore, evidence about the complainant's own words or behaviour is likely to be relevant or admissible only if the complainant has said or done things at work which can be said to fall into a similar category to the matters now complained of.

Sexual or racial element
In most harassment cases, there is a fairly obvious discriminatory motive for the treatment complained of. Sometimes the harassment is furtive, with no witnesses; on other occasions it takes place quite openly. For example:

(a) A shy, young woman in her first job works with an older and senior male colleague. He takes advantage of the situation by making suggestive remarks to her and brushing against her at every opportunity, calculating that she will be too embarrassed to complain. He would not treat a male colleague in this way.

(b) A woman obtains a job on a previously all-male shop floor. One or two irresponsible and immature men react to the unfamiliar presence of a woman by making repeated comments about her appearance, within her hearing, and leaving pornographic magazines on her work-bench.

Sometimes racial harassment takes place in circumstances similar to those in (b) above. Workers who are not normally obsessed by racial hatred can react in an unthinkingly insulting and offensive way to the arrival of the first black worker in a previously all-white establishment, unit or department.

On occasion a discriminatory motive leads to the sexual harassment of male employees. This can happen, for example:

- when a man, especially a young man, is given a job in a department or a factory floor among a previously all-female work-force;
- if a man is subjected to repeated or physical homosexual advances by a male colleague;
- if a man is expected to respond to sexual overtures from his female boss as the price of a favourable annual appraisal.

There is also, however, unlawful harassment when a person's sex or colour determines the *methods* used to give vent to personal hostility. This principle was established in the case of *Strathclyde Regional Council v Porcelli* in 1986.

For many months, a female science laboratory technician was subjected to a campaign by two male colleagues to try to persuade her to leave the school. The methods used included suggestive remarks and comments on the complainant's physical appearance in comparison with that of a nude female depicted in a newspaper. Eventually the campaign succeeded and the complainant left her job.

In this case, the complaint was rejected by the industrial tribunal on the grounds that the motive for the hostile campaign was personal dislike, not a sexual motive, and that a disliked male colleague would also have received hostile treatment. However, the EAT and the Court of Session (the Scottish equivalent of the Court of Appeal) took a different view. Although the hostility was personal in origin, the methods used were not those which would have been used against a male colleague. Accordingly, there had been direct sex discrimination against the complainant.

In the Court of Session, Lord Emslie commented that:

> Sexual harassment is a particularly degrading and unacceptable form of treatment which it must be taken to have been the intention of Parliament to restrain.

The employment context

There are two separate questions to be considered in order to determine whether an act of sexual or racial harassment is covered by the employment provisions in the SDA or the RRA. These questions are:

1. Was the complainant subjected to the harassment in his or her capacity as an employee?
2. Was the act of discrimination committed by the employer personally or by a person for whose actions the employer can be held accountable?

Where the harasser is a director or a partner, there is usually no difficulty in establishing the liability of the company or firm.

Where the harasser is a fellow employee of the victim, the question to be determined is whether the act complained of was done by the harasser in the course of his employment. The law draws a distinction between, on the one hand, doing what you are employed to do, but in a wrongful and perverted way; and on the other hand, doing something which is entirely outside the scope of your employment. In the following example, there would be no breach of the SDA.

A man and woman employed by you also have a social relationship and go to a party together. He has too much to drink and indecently assaults her. She has not suffered any discrimination in her capacity as an employee; he was not acting in the course of his employment when he committed the assault.

In practice, a breach of the SDA will usually be involved where sexual harassment takes place at work in circumstances where the complainant and the harasser are working in the same room or are required by their work to communicate with each other. In *Bracebridge Engineering Limited v Darby*, an employee of a small company had finished her shift and was about to wash her hands. She was grabbed by her chargehand and the works manager, and taken to the latter's office, where she was threatened with a written warning for leaving early and was indecently assaulted. The EAT upheld a finding by the industrial tribunal that the complainant had suffered a detriment in the context of her employment and that the harassers had been acting in the course of their employment; they had been engaged in exercising a disciplinary and supervisory function, albeit in a wholly improper way.

It is clear from the above case that an act can be in the course of the harasser's employment even if it was one which the employer would have forbidden if he had known about it. Indeed, an act can be in the course of employment even if expressly forbidden.

An act of sexual harassment can be unlawful even if it takes place away from the work place; for example, at a sales conference which the harasser and the complainant are required to attend.

Your responsibility as employer

Where sexual or racial harassment takes place in the course of the harasser's employment, both you as employer and the individual harasser can be held legally accountable. The victim of the harassment can bring proceedings against both of you, and you can both be ordered to pay compensation. As explained in Chapter 5, the legal fiction adopted is that the offending employee's act is treated as your act but that he is regarded as having 'aided' you to do it.

There is, however, a possible defence open to you. If you can show that you have taken all reasonably practicable steps to prevent the act complained of, or acts of that kind, then you as employer have a defence. If this defence is made out, the offending employee remains liable—an important distinction between this defence and the defence that what happened was outside the course of the employment. Where the latter defence is made out the harasser is also let off the hook, however inequitable this result may be.

There are two ways in which you can seek to demonstrate that you have taken all reasonably practicable steps to prevent unlawful acts by your employees, as follows:

- that there was nothing you could have done to prevent the act complained of; or
- that there are things which you could have done, but you have done them all.

The former approach was successful in the *Balgobin* case mentioned below, but that case was decided in 1987. It is most unlikely that a similar defence would succeed now, particularly since the EC code published in 1991 specifies a number of measures which employers can and should take. These measures are mentioned later in this chapter, under the heading of 'Practical advice'.

The EC code is not referred to in the SDA, since it saw the light of day long after the Act. A decision of the European Court in a case named *Grimaldi* is, however, authority for the proposition that

Recommendations like the EC code do have legal effect and must be taken into consideration by national courts and tribunals.

Failure to deal effectively with complaints
The question considered so far is whether you can be held responsible for misconduct by your employee. Can you yourself, as employer, be held to have acted unlawfully if you fail to take a complaint of harassment seriously enough or if you compel the complainant to continue working side by side with the alleged harasser?

The latter question arose in the case of *Balgobin and Francis v London Borough of Tower Hamlets*. In that case, two women working as cleaners in the canteen area of a hostel were sexually harassed by a male cook. The employers were unaware of what was happening and indeed neither of the cleaners knew about the harassment of the other. After they complained, an investigation was inconclusive and they had to continue working in the same area as the cook. It was held by the industrial tribunal that by having to work with the harasser the women were subjected to intolerable conditions; but there had been no sex discrimination by the employers in this respect.

This decision by the tribunal was upheld by the EAT. It was not because they were women but because the investigation had been inconclusive that the two cleaners had been required to continue working with the harasser. There would have been discrimination against them only if it had been found that the employers would have acted differently if the cleaners had been men complaining of homosexual advances against them.

Nevertheless, it is not good practice to require a complainant to continue to work side by side with an alleged harasser, if this can possibly be avoided. This question is considered later in this chapter.

Unacceptable defences

There are still employers who take an insufficiently serious view of complaints of harassment, particularly sexual harassment. The following are some of the defences and 'mitigating factors' still put forward:

(a) She never complained — she may have been too embarrassed or afraid of losing her job.
(b) She's still here—many victims of harassment do continue working in intolerable conditions because they need the money.
(c) No one else saw anything—many harassers wait until there are no witnesses before striking.
(d) I never even touched her—suggestive and obscene remarks made repeatedly can amount to serious harassment, even if there is no physical contact whatsoever.
(e) It only happened once—one serious incident can be sufficient, as in the *Darby* case.
(f) I didn't even fancy her—a sexual motive is not essential, as in the *Porcelli* case.

(g) It was only a bit of fun—not from where the victim was standing.
(h) She's that kind of girl—whatever her attitudes and life style, she does not lose the right to say no.
(i) Everybody's doing it—harassers who hunt in packs become even more intimidating.
(j) It's traditional—some traditions should be stamped out.

Practical advice

There are two separate questions to be considered:

1. What steps should you take to prevent sexual and racial harassment?
2. How should you deal with a complaint of harassment?

Preventing harassment

The CRE and EOC codes contain little in the way of detailed advice. The latter, for example, simply says (in paragraph 32(e)) that all reasonably practical steps should be taken to ensure that a standard of conduct or behaviour is observed which prevents members of either sex from being harassed.

The Employment Department have however issued guides on sexual harassment in the workplace. The titles of these guides and the address from which they can be obtained are given in the section on *Further Reading* at the end of the book. The *Further Reading* also includes a guide published in 1992 by the Institute of Personnel Management, *Statement on harassment at work*.

There is also more detailed advice in the EC code and you should have regard to this advice, which contains the following elements:

(a) Adopt a clear policy statement and publicise it.
(b) Give instructions and training to managers and supervisors.
(c) Impose a positive duty on *all* employees.
(d) Have a clearly defined complaints and support system for victims of harassment and make employees aware of it.
(e) Make sexual harassment a disciplinary offence.

Policy statement
The statement should expressly state 'that all employees have a right to be treated with dignity, that sexual harassment at work will not be permitted or condoned, and that employees have a right to complain about it should it occur' (EC code).

The statement should make clear what behaviour at work is unacceptable and also explain that such behaviour may be unlawful.

Steps should then be taken to communicate the policy effectively to all employees. If possible give them all a copy, as well as displaying it on the notice boards and referring to it in any newsletters you produce.

In general, the policy itself and the way in which you communicate it should 'highlight management's commitment to eliminating sexual harassment thus enhancing a climate in which it will not occur' (EC code).

Managers and supervisors
The policy statement should impose a positive duty on managers and supervisors to implement the policy and take corrective action to ensure compliance with it.

As part of the policy you should give managers and supervisors clear instructions and training. You must ensure that they know what steps to take if a complaint is made.

The training could include matters such as:

(a) Recognition of signs of possible harassment, for example where a woman changes her working pattern in what could be an attempt to avoid working with a particular male colleague or where a woman shows clear signs of distress.
(b) Awareness of situations where harassment is most likely to occur, for example where an employee is given a job in an environment where all the existing employees are of the other sex.

Specialist training should be given to managers who are made responsible for dealing with complaints.

Managers should also have a role to play in communicating the policy to their staff and promoting it.

Positive duty
The policy statement should make it clear that all employees have a positive duty to comply with the policy and to ensure that their colleagues are treated with respect and dignity.

You should make it clear to all employees, not only managers and supervisors, that they are expected to intervene and report the matter if they see harassment taking place. They must not simply stand by.

Complaints and support system
Your policy statement should clearly explain to employees what they should do to obtain assistance and to whom they should complain. Many victims of harassment are too afraid or embarrassed to complain; your policy statement should give an undertaking that allegations of sexual harassment will be dealt with seriously, expeditiously and confidentially. The policy statement should also assure employees that they will be protected against victimisation or retaliation for bringing a complaint.

In the first instance, there should be a system for trying to resolve problems informally. You should appoint one or more persons (depending on the size of your organisation) to give advice and assistance and to try to resolve matters informally and confidentially. You should make sure that all your employees are aware of the name of the person appointed.

There must then be a formal complaints procedure to be used where informal procedures are unsatisfactory or where the offence is too serious. Your formal procedure, of which employees should be made aware, should (the EC code suggests):

(a) specify the person to whom a complaint should be made;
(b) provide an alternative, for example where the person specified is the employee's line manager and that person is himself the alleged harasser;
(c) if possible, make provision for employees to complain in the first instance to someone of their own sex, if they wish.

You should monitor and review any complaints of sexual harassment to ensure that your procedures are working effectively.

Disciplinary offence
Your disciplinary rules should be amended (under the EC code):

(a) to make clear what is regarded as inappropriate behaviour at work;
(b) to state the range of possible penalties;
(c) to make it clear that it will also be a disciplinary offence to victimise or retaliate against an employee for bringing a complaint of sexual harassment in good faith.

Your policy statement on sexual harassment, as well as your disciplinary rules, should make it clear that disciplinary action will be taken against employees found guilty of sexual harassment, victimisation or retaliation.

Dealing with complaints

The EOC code (in paragraph 31(c)) recommends that particular care is taken to deal effectively with all complaints of harassment. It should not be assumed that they are made by those who are over-sensitive.

There are the following questions to be considered:

1. How should complaints be investigated?
2. What if any disciplinary action should be taken?
3. How should future problems be avoided?
4. What instructions and training should be given to managers and supervisors about these matters?

Investigating complaints
The EC code contains detailed guidance and recommends the following steps:

(a) The investigation should be handled with sensitivity and with due respect for the rights of both the complainant and the alleged harasser. The implications of this advice are that you should not pre-judge the matter or give the impression that you have done so. A complaint of sexual harassment is a very serious matter and the alleged harasser is entitled to a fair hearing.

(b) The investigation should be seen to be independent and objective.
(c) Those carrying out the investigation should not be connected with the allegation in any way.
(d) The matter should be resolved as quickly as is consistent with a thorough investigation. Grievances should be handled promptly and a time limit for completing the investigation should be set. This advice is particularly important, because a protracted investigation can cause considerable worry and uncertainty both for the parties themselves and for witnesses and other colleagues who are aware of the complaint.
(e) Both the complainant and the alleged harasser should have the right to be accompanied and/or represented, eg by a trade union representative.
(f) The alleged harasser must be given full details of the complaint and the opportunity to respond.
(g) Strict confidentiality should be maintained throughout the investigation (although in practice this can be very difficult to achieve). In particular, the importance of confidentiality should be emphasised to all witnesses who are interviewed.
(h) A complainant should not be required to recount the facts repeatedly except where this is unavoidable.
(i) The investigation should focus on the facts of the complaint.
(j) A complete record should be kept of all meetings and investigations.

The fact that an industrial tribunal complaint has been made or threatened should not prevent you from carrying out a full investigation. If the complaint is false, your investigation will help you to gather the evidence to resist the complaint; if it is well founded, it is in your interests to establish the truth and to concede or settle the complaint at the earliest possible time.

One question which the EC code does not deal with is that of keeping the complainant and the alleged harasser apart while the investigation is being carried out. In a large organisation, it may be possible for the two employees to continue working without meeting. There may, however, be no alternative to offering them both paid leave until the investigation is concluded. It should be made clear that the purpose of any such arrangement is to spare them personal embarrassment while the investigation is being carried out.

Disciplinary action
Where a complaint is upheld as a result of an investigation, disciplinary action against the harasser should follow. In a bad case, dismissal may be the appropriate penalty.

You should also consider disciplinary action against any other employee who has connived at the harassment and in particular any manager or supervisor who has stood by, knowing of the complaint but taking no action.

If an investigation establishes that a complaint has been made falsely and maliciously, as an act of spite or revenge against the alleged harasser, then disciplinary action against the complainant would be appropriate. It is a very serious matter to make a false allegation which puts at risk a fellow employee's career.

You should, however, take such action only if you are quite sure that the complaint was false and malicious. If the complaint was made in good faith, then action against the complainant would amount to unlawful victimisation. If you discipline an employee for making a complaint which is subsequently upheld by a tribunal, you will put yourself in a very bad light and also face the prospect of having to pay compensation both for the sexual harassment and for the victimisation.

The CRE code recommends (in paragraph 1.23) that in applying disciplinary procedures to any employee consideration should be given to the possible effect on the employee's behaviour of racial abuse or other racial provocation. If a black employee retaliates when subjected to racial harassment, you should take the harassment into account as a mitigating factor.

Avoiding future problems
Whatever the outcome of your investigation into a complaint of sexual harassment, you should ensure where possible that the complainant and the alleged harasser do not have to work together in the future.

The EC code recommends that where a complaint is upheld, consideration should be given, wherever practicable, to allowing the complainant to choose whether he or she wishes to remain in his or her present post, or to be transferred. No element of penalty should be seen to attach to a complainant whose complaint is upheld.

If a complaint of harassment against a senior manager is upheld, there may be strong commercial or practical reasons for not transferring the manager. In the last resort, however, if neither the complainant nor the manager wishes to be transferred, then it is the latter who should be compelled to move, however difficult this decision may be.

The EC code goes on to deal with the case where a complaint is not upheld, for example because the evidence is regarded as inconclusive. The code suggests that consideration be given to transferring or re-scheduling the work of one of the employees concerned, rather than requiring them to continue to work together against the wishes of either party.

The code also suggests that where a complaint is upheld you should monitor the situation to ensure that the harassment has stopped.

Managers and supervisors
The EC code recommends that the instructions and training given to managers and supervisors should cover the following matters:

(a) Managers should be responsive and supportive to any member of staff who complains about sexual harassment.

(b) They should also provide full and clear advice on the procedure to be adopted.
(c) They should maintain confidentiality.
(d) They should ensure that there is no further harassment and that there is no victimisation after a complaint has been resolved.

Racial harassment

The EC code deals only with sexual harassment. However, you should also have a clearly defined and publicised policy for preventing racial harassment and dealing with complaints. The main elements of the policy and procedures should be the same as those for dealing with sexual harassment. For example, you should:

(a) Make it clear that racial harassment will be dealt with as a serious disciplinary offence.
(b) Make employees aware of the formal and informal complaints procedures and the name of the person to complain to.
(c) Give instructions and training to managers and supervisors.
(d) Investigate any complaints quickly, thoroughly and objectively.
(e) Take disciplinary action where a complaint is upheld.
(f) Take effective action to prevent any repetition or victimisation.

Summary

1. You may be held responsible, as an employer, for racial or sexual harassment if:
   (a) an employee has been treated unfavourably;
   (b) because of his or her sex or colour, etc, or in a way which is affected by his or her sex or colour, etc;
   (c) by being subjected to a detriment; and
   (d) in his or her capacity as an employee by you personally or by a fellow employee acting in the course of his or her employment.
2. You have a defence if you can prove that you took all reasonably practicable steps to prevent the discrimination complained of or acts of that kind; if the defence is made out then the offending employee remains liable.
3. You are unlikely to be able to establish this defence unless you have followed the recommendations contained in the EC code; similar steps should also be taken to prevent racial harassment.

10
Benefits, Detriment and Dismissal

Chapter 6 dealt with the vital subject of equal opportunity for job applicants and for existing employees who wish to further their careers with you; Chapter 9 dealt with the very different subject of employees who are subjected to sexual or racial harassment.

There are also many other management and personnel decisions which involve good news or bad news for your employees. Discrimination in making any of these decisions is likely to involve a breach of the UK or EC laws on discrimination and equal pay.

These laws cover discrimination in the following four areas:

1. Terms of employment.
2. Access to benefits, facilities or services.
3. Detrimental treatment.
4. Dismissal

Terms of employment

The RRA (in Section 4(2)(a)) forbids discrimination in the terms of employment. There must be no direct or indirect discrimination or victimisation in fixing or negotiating the rate of pay or any other term of the contract.

For example, all the white workers in your factory have fixed hours of work. For all the black workers, however, you use a contract under which they can be required to work a variable shift pattern. Your theory is that high rates of unemployment among black workers will cause them to accept whatever contract terms you decide. This direct discrimination on your part is unlawful.

The law on discrimination in contract terms as between men and women is rather more complicated. Most such complaints are dealt with under the Equal Pay Act. As will be seen in Chapter 13, complainants under that Act bring proceedings to obtain the same rate of pay or same contract terms as a person, usually a fellow employee, of the opposite sex, who is known as the comparator. Most cases involve a comparison of the two jobs to determine whether they are broadly similar or of equal value. There is, however, a defence, where it can be shown that the difference in pay or other contract terms is caused by some material factor other than the difference of sex.

The relationship between the SDA and the EPA is not an easy one. There is also the complication that gaps in domestic legislation can sometimes be filled by EC law. The rules are as follows:

(a) If one of your employees wishes to complain about a contract term for payment of money (whether basic pay, expenses, bonus, commission or any other payment) the claim cannot be brought under the SDA. This exclusion is contained in Section 6(6) of the SDA.

(b) Such a claim can be brought under the EPA, if a comparator can be identified; it can also be brought under Article 119 of the EC Treaty, if the woman's immediate predecessor in the employment was of the opposite sex and had a higher rate of pay or better contract terms.

(c) If the complaint relates to some other contract term, not one for the payment of money, then it cannot be brought under the SDA if there is a valid claim under the EPA, or would be but for a material factor defence (Section 8(5) of the SDA).

(d) A complaint can be brought under the SDA (or perhaps under EC law) if the contract term is not one for the payment of money and if a claim under the EPA would fail for lack of a suitable comparator.

The following examples illustrate the position:

(a) In your small company the management team consists of yourself and a female manager; you have never employed a male manager. She complains that she is being paid less than a man would be; however, she has no claim under the EPA because there is no comparator. She does not have a claim under the SDA either, because her complaint relates to a contract term for the payment of money.

(b) Your company has a female office manager and a male sales manager, doing work of equal value. He is entitled, under his contract, to a company car; she is not. There is a material factor which explains this difference in contract terms. He is required to travel to do his work; she is not. You would have a material factor defence to a claim by the woman under the EPA and she would not be entitled to present a complaint under the SDA.

(c) None of your employees has the right to a company car. A woman whom you appoint as a manager was the second choice for the job; she subsequently meets the man who was the first choice but who turned the job down. He tells her that you offered him the contractual right to a company car as part of the employment package. The woman can bring a complaint under the SDA and such a complaint will succeed unless you can show that there was some reason other than the difference of sex for the difference in contract terms enjoyed.

Benefits, facilities or services

The RRA (in Section 4(2)(b)) prohibits discrimination in access to benefits, facilities or services. There is a similar provision in the SDA (Section 6(2)(a)), subject to the proviso mentioned above, where benefits are regulated by the contract of employment.

Where benefits or facilities such as company cars, access to overtime and payment of relocation expenses are discretionary, not contractual, any complaint of sex discrimination in relation to such benefits will be brought against you under the SDA, not the EPA.

Sometimes complaints relate to matters which have little or no significance in financial terms but which can nevertheless cause ill feeling and give rise to a considerable sense of injustice. For example:

(a) You arrange a golf competition for your customers. The men in the sales department are all invited to play; women of the same seniority and doing the same work are not invited. You do not even bother to ask them if they play golf. This is a case of blatant sex discrimination.

(b) You give all your female employees a day off for Christmas shopping. Men are not allowed this facility, even those who are single parents. Again, this is a clear case of direct sex discrimination.

An important facility to employees is access to a *grievance procedure*. There must be no racial or sex discrimination in access to the procedure or the way in which it operates. For example:

(a) One of your managers is patient and considerate when white employees bring complaints to him under the grievance procedure, but is rude and impatient whenever a black employee presents a grievance.

(b) Complaints of sexual harassment by female employees under your grievance procedure are taken very seriously, but you are scornful and dismissive when a young male employee complains of sexual harassment by his female boss.

In both the above examples there is direct discrimination in relation to the grievance procedure.

A further important facility enjoyed by many employees is that of access to *collective bargaining*. This facility must also be made available without discrimination. For example:

(a) Your factory is non-unionised, but you negotiate pay, contract terms and working conditions with a staff committee containing a representative from all but one of the departments and manufacturing units. The exception is a unit in which all the employees are of Asian origin. Unless you can give some other credible explanation, the circumstances give rise to an inference of direct racial discrimination.

(b) Your plant employs approximately equal numbers of men and women, both doing a variety of different jobs. Some jobs are done mainly by men, others mainly by women. You and the union operate a practice under which the plant bargaining committee contains five representatives of the men employed in five separate departments, but only one representative of all the women employed in those departments. This is direct discrimination in relation to access to collective bargaining.

In example (b) above, any complaint under the SDA would be quite distinct from any claims brought by women under the EPA in respect of the pay and other contract terms resulting from the collective bargaining process. While any financial losses would be the subject of the EPA claims, compensation for injured feelings could be claimed in the SDA proceedings.

Detrimental treatment

Both the RRA (in Section 4(2)(c)) and the SDA (in Section 6(2)(b)) prohibit discrimination in dismissing an employee or subjecting the employee 'to any other detriment'.

The word 'detriment' means simply a disadvantage. In the 1979 case of *Jeremiah v Ministry of Defence*, male examiners at an ordnance factory were required, if they volunteered for overtime, to work in a part of the factory where the conditions were dusty and dirty. They had to wear protective clothing and to take a shower after work. They received a small extra payment to compensate them for having to work in these conditions. The female examiners were never required to work in this part of the factory; they did not wish to take showers, because their hair would be affected.

Both the EAT and the Court of Appeal upheld a decision by an industrial tribunal that this sex discrimination was unlawful, even though the male examiners had suffered no financial loss. It was immaterial that the employers believed that they had sound administrative reasons for the discrimination. Furthermore, an employer cannot obtain a licence to discriminate by paying extra money to compensate for the detriment.

This case related to the allocation of work and such cases can be viewed in either of two ways. The complainant has either been denied the benefit of doing pleasant and satisfying work or subjected to the detriment of having to do dirty and unpleasant work.

Trivial complaints

How serious must a detriment be before it can lead to a complaint? This was one of the questions answered by the Court of Appeal in the 1978 case of *Peake v Automotive Products Limited*. Mr Peake complained of a rule by his employers under which women were allowed to leave the factory at 4.25pm, while men had to wait until 4.30pm. The purpose of the rule was to protect the women from being injured in the rush through the gates.

The Court of Appeal held that this rule did not amount to unlawful sex discrimination. The SDA is designed to redress the genuine grievances caused by sex discrimination and not, in the words of Lord Justice Shaw, 'to provide a basis for capricious and empty complaints of differentiation between the sexes.'

Courts and Tribunals are generally very reluctant to adopt this approach. In the later case of *Gill and Another v El Vino Company Limited*, in a well-known wine bar, two women were refused service at the bar. They were told that if they sat down at a table their drinks would be brought to them. This was in accordance with a house rule at the wine bar. It was held by the Court of Appeal that there had been a breach of the SDA.

Whilst the above case was not an employment case, the principle of it is equally applicable in employment cases.

Racial segregation

The approach adopted in the *Peake* case would never be appropriate when dealing with a complaint under the RRA. The definition of direct racial discrimination includes racial segregation, which can be a very real detriment, involving serious injury to feelings, even where no financial loss is incurred.

For example, your company employs both white and black workers. There have recently been several fights at the factory gates. To avoid racial conflict, you insist that all the black workers must leave work five minutes early. The rule amounts to direct racial discrimination and, indeed, it is likely to be the black workers, who leave early, who suffer the greater injury to their feelings.

The different treatment of white and black workers gave rise to a successful complaint in the 1983 case of *B L Cars Limited v Brown*. The company wished to keep out a black employee who had been charged with theft. It was suggested that he might try to re-enter under a false name. The chief security officer issued a written instruction to check the identity of black workers and to subject them to special investigation before they could go into their place of work. Complaints were made by 28 employees of the company and its contractors. It was ruled by the EAT that the issue of the instruction (even before it had been implemented) could mean that the company was subjecting its black employees to a detriment.

Rules on dress

In the 1977 case of *Schmidt v Austicks Bookshops Limited*, an employee in a book shop objected to the company's rules on dress. Women employees were required, when serving the public, to wear skirts and overalls; they were not allowed to wear trousers. An employee complained that these rules amounted to discrimination against women. It was held by the EAT that her complaint had been rightly dismissed.

Mr Justice Phillips said, of the requirement to wear overalls, that 'something is only to be said to constitute a detriment when there is something serious or important about it.' This was the *de minimis* approach adopted by the Court of Appeal in the *Peake* case.

So far as the requirement to wear a skirt was concerned, both sexes were treated alike in that they were both subjected to restrictions on the choice of clothing to be worn at work. The fact that the restrictions were different was immaterial.

The above case should be viewed with some caution, in view of changing standards since 1977. A different approach has already been adopted by Industrial Tribunals and by the Northern Ireland Court of Appeal (in the case of *McConomy v Croft Inns Limited*) in cases involving men with, respectively, long hair and earrings.

Chivalry and administrative convenience

A second reason for the decision in the *Peake* case was that the arrangement for the women to leave early was a sensible administrative arrangement motivated by chivalry and was therefore lawful. A similar approach was, however, rejected in the *Jeremiah* case. Discrimination in subjecting employees to a detriment is unlawful, however strong the administrative arguments for the discrimination and however pure the chivalry which gave rise to the discrimination.

For example you have a young male assistant and a young female assistant in your shop. You always send him to the bank with the takings, even though there is not much to choose between them in size, because you do not like the idea of her being bashed on the head in the event of the takings being stolen. Your sex discrimination in this case is unlawful. It would, of course, be legitimate for you to send them both to the bank each time or to reduce the danger by laying on a taxi.

Disciplinary action

There must be no racial or sex discrimination in the way in which employees are disciplined, for example by suspending a man and giving a woman a warning for similar offences in similar circumstances.

Dismissal

The question of pregnancy-related dismissals is considered in Chapter 11. The other most common ways in which a dismissal could give rise to a complaint of discrimination are:

1. Discrimination in dismissal for misconduct.
2. Different ages of compulsory retirement for men and women.
3. Discrimination in selection for redundancy.
4. Discrimination in relation to lump sum payments on dismissal.
5. Constructive dismissal resulting from sexual or racial harassment or other acts of discrimination.

A discriminatory dismissal is often also an unfair dismissal under the employment protection legislation. However, there are important differences between the rights which your employees have under the two sets of legislation. For example:

(a) In general, an employee must have two years' service before acquiring the right not to be unfairly dismissed; you must not *discriminate* by dismissing an employee even on that employee's first day at work.
(b) There are restrictions on unfair dismissal rights relating to hours of work and employees over retirement age; all employees have rights under the discrimination laws, whatever their age and hours of work.
(c) The compensation for a discriminatory dismissal is in some respects less than that for unfair dismissal; there is no basic award based on the accrued redundancy rights.
(d) In another respect, extra compensation can be payable for a discriminatory dismissal; this is because compensation for injured feelings can be awarded in discrimination cases but not in ordinary unfair dismissal cases.

Misconduct dismissals

There must be no discrimination in the way in which you investigate and penalise disciplinary offences. A female employee or black employee must be treated neither more nor less harshly than a male or white employee would be treated in similar circumstances and with a similar disciplinary record.

It is, on the other hand, entirely legitimate for you to have regard to mitigating circumstances, for example where a black worker who has committed a serious offence has been provoked by racial abuse.

Different retirement ages

Initially, both the SDA and the EPA contained a very broad exception for discrimination in relation to retirement. It was lawful for employers to have compulsory retirement ages of, say, 65 for men and 60 for women.

This discrimination was challenged under EC law in the case of *Marshall v Southampton and South-West Hampshire Area Health Authority*. In this case, Mrs Marshall, a senior dietician, was compelled to retire at 62, even though a man in her position would have been entitled to continue working until the age of 65.

This discrimination was permitted under the original provisions of the SDA, but because Mrs Marshall was employed in the public sector she was able to bring a complaint under the EC Equal Treatment Directive. As a result of her successful complaint, the UK law was changed by the SDA 1986. It is now unlawful for any employer to have different compulsory retirement ages for men and women doing comparable jobs.

Selection for redundancy

It would be a clear case of direct sex discrimination if you were to have regard to the sex or race of any employee when deciding which employees should be made redundant. There was a time when some employers used to select married women for redundancy, rather than men or unmarried women, on the ground that a married woman was less likely to be the family breadwinner; selection on these grounds would now be direct sex discrimination and also direct marriage discrimination.

Care should also be taken, in fixing or negotiating the criteria for redundancy selection, not to adopt any which are indirectly discriminatory. In the 1982 case of *Clarke v Eley (IMI) Kynoch Limited*, the employers were faced with declaring a number of redundancies. They adopted a policy of first of all dismissing all the part-time workers. Two women who worked part time and had many years' service were dismissed; full-time male employees with very short service were retained.

A complaint of indirect sex discrimination was successful. The reasoning was as follows:

(a) The employers had applied to the women a requirement that to avoid selection in the first batch of redundancies they must be full-time workers.

(b) The proportion of the women in the factory who could comply with the requirement was considerably smaller than the proportion of the men who could comply—many of the women, but hardly any of the men, worked part time;

(c) The requirement could not be justified in the particular circumstances.

(d) The requirement was to the detriment of the complainants—they were dismissed because they could not comply with it.

Redundancy and other payments

Under the SDA and the EPA, you could freely discriminate in relation to the payments which you made to men and women when they left your employment.

Such discrimination is, however, contrary to EC law. The case of *Barber v Guardian Royal Exchange Assurance Group*, with its implications for pension schemes, is referred to in Chapter 13. However, it was also ruled in this case that lump sum payments on dismissal or retirement amount to pay for the purposes of Article 119 of the EC Treaty. Under this Article, men and women are entitled to equal pay for equal work. Accordingly, redundancy payments, severance payments and other lump sum payments must be calculated in the same way for both men and women. It is immaterial whether the payments are made under the statutory redundancy scheme, or whether there is a contractual right to them, or whether they are discretionary.

You should also note that there must be no discrimination in relation to non-financial benefits after retirement. In *Garland v British Rail Engineering Limited*, male rail employees were entitled, after their retirement, to concessionary travel for themselves and their dependants; female employees were entitled to the concessionary travel only for themselves. It was ruled by the European Court that the concession amounted to pay for the purposes of Article 119 and that accordingly the discrimination was contrary to EC law. The House of Lords then went on to decide that it was not clear whether the exceptions in the SDA applied to the case or not; accordingly, the SDA should be interpreted in accordance with EC law; Mrs Garland succeeded under the SDA as well.

Constructive dismissal

Sometimes an employee who walks out can be said to have been dismissed. This happens where there has been a serious breach by the employer of an express or implied term of the contract and in consequence the employee is justified in treating himself or herself as dismissed.

One implied contractual term is that of mutual trust, confidence and support. This implied term was held to have been broken in the *Darby* case, which was a serious case of sexual harassment mentioned in Chapter 9. The breach of the implied term took place because the employers failed to take the allegation of sexual harassment seriously. The employee had been greatly upset and suffered shock and trauma as a result of the incident, and was justified in treating herself as constructively dismissed. This dismissal was unfair.

A constructive dismissal could be both unfair and discriminatory, if it results from a serious act of discrimination by an employer personally, or possibly by a manager. This is because the discrimination itself would be a breach of the implied term of mutual trust, confidence and support.

Practical advice

The EOC and CRE codes give advice relating to benefits, disciplinary matters (including dismissal) and redundancy.

Benefits

The CRE code (in paragraph 1.20) recommends the following steps to avoid both direct and indirect discrimination:

(a) All staff concerned with terms of employment and the provision of benefits, facilities and services to employees should be instructed in the need not to discriminate.
(b) The criteria governing eligibility should be examined to ensure that they are not unlawfully discriminatory.

The code goes on to advise (in paragraph 1.21) on dealing with requests for extended leave. It points out that employees may request extended leave from time to time in order to visit relations in their countries of origin or relations who have emigrated to other countries. If you have policies which allow annual leave entitlement to be accumulated, or extra unpaid leave to be taken, you should take care to apply these policies consistently and without unlawful discrimination.

There would, for example, be unlawful racial discrimination in the following circumstances. You allow a worker of Asian origin to accumulate leave in order to visit relatives in India. A white employee, doing the same job and with a similar length of service and employment record, asks to be allowed to accumulate leave to visit relatives who have emigrated to Australia. You refuse this request.

The EOC code (in paragraph 28) recommends that all terms of employment, benefits, facilities and services are reviewed to ensure that there is no unlawful discrimination on grounds of sex or marriage. It gives examples of benefits and facilities which should be available to both male and female employees, if the circumstances are the same or not materially different. The examples given are part-time work, domestic leave, company cars and benefits for dependants.

The EOC code also makes the point (in paragraph 29) that treating part-time workers less favourably than full-time workers can amount to unlawful indirect discrimination, if it is without justification. This possibility arises in an establishment where the part-timers are solely or mainly women. If the part-time workers do not enjoy pro-rata pay or benefits with full-time workers, the arrangements should be reviewed to ensure that they are properly justified.

Grievance procedure

The CRE code (paragraph 1.22) recommends that grievances from members of particular racial groups should not be ignored or treated lightly on the assumption that those complaining are over-sensitive about discrimination. Furthermore, no individual should be victimised because he or she has complained or given evidence about a complaint.

The EOC code makes a similar point (in paragraph 31). Employees should be advised to use the internal grievance procedure where appropriate, without prejudice to the individual's right to complain to an industrial tribunal. Particular care should be taken to deal effectively with all complaints of discrimination, victimisation or harassment. It should not be assumed that they are made by those who are over-sensitive.

Disciplinary matters

The CRE code recommends (in paragraph 1.23) that in applying disciplinary procedures you should give consideration to the possible effect on an employee's behaviour of:

- racial abuse or other racial provocation;
- communication and comprehension difficulties;
- differences in cultural background or behaviour.

The EOC code (in paragraph 31(a)) recommends that particular care is taken to avoid victimisation. An employee who has taken action in good faith under the SDA or the EPA must not be disciplined or dismissed because of this.

The EOC code also recommends (in paragraph 32(a)) that care is taken that members of one sex are not disciplined or dismissed for performance or behaviour which would be overlooked or condoned in the other sex.

Redundancy and short-time working

The CRE code (in paragraph 1.17) recommends the following steps to avoid discrimination in relation to redundancy:

(a) Staff responsible for selecting employees for dismissal, including redundancy, should be instructed not to discriminate on racial grounds.
(b) Selection criteria for redundancies should be examined to ensure that they are not indirectly discriminatory.

The EOC code also deals (in paragraph 32(b)) with indirect discrimination in selection for redundancy. Procedures affecting a group of employees predominantly of one sex should be reviewed, to remove any effects which could be disproportionate and unjustifiable. An example of indirect discrimination in redundancy selection was the *Clarke* case mentioned earlier in this chapter. This was the case where the part-timers were selected first, irrespective of length of service.

The code also deals (in paragraph 32(c)) with conditions of access to voluntary redundancy benefits. These should be made available on equal terms to male and female employees if the circumstances are the same or not materially different.

Sometimes a fall in the volume of business can be dealt with by way of short-time working. The EOC code points out (in paragraph 32(d)) that where there is short-time working or downgrading, the arrangements should not unlawfully discriminate on the ground of sex.

Summary

1. Both the RRA and the SDA forbid discrimination (direct, indirect or by way of victimisation) in:
    (a) access to benefits, facilities or services;

(b) detrimental treatment;
(c) dismissal (including redundancy).
2. The RRA also forbids discrimination in relation to the terms of employment. Any complaint of unequal treatment between men and women in relation to terms of employment is normally brought under the EPA and *must* be brought under that Act (or EC law), not the SDA, if it relates to a contract term for the payment of money.
3. The SDA and the EPA both contain exceptions covering redundancy and severance payments, but the gap has been filled by EC law.
4. Employees can complain under the SDA or the RRA about dismissal or any other treatment irrespective of age, length of service or hours of work.

11
Pregnancy Related Discrimination

It is a sad fact that many employers and managers react with panic or hostility to the news that an employee has become pregnant. The following cases are typical:

(a) The employee is dismissed, on the (nearly always false) assumption that she will disrupt the business by taking time off every other day or that she will be unfit for any physical work.

(b) She is dismissed shortly before she has two years' service, so that she will not acquire her statutory right to return to work and her employer will not need to find a temporary replacement for her.

(c) If her job involves sales or reception work, she is transferred to a job where she will be out of sight, or even dismissed altogether, on the strange assumption that customers will be put off if they are served by a pregnant employee.

(d) She is assumed to be ineligible for any promotion or training, even if her maternity leave is not due to start for several months and she intends to return to work very quickly after the baby has been born.

If she loses her job, or is already unemployed when she becomes pregnant, her pregnancy gives her a greatly reduced prospect of obtaining a new job.

The law and pregnancy

If you dismiss an employee because she is pregnant, she has a cast iron claim for unfair dismissal if dismissed after more than two years' continuous service. The dismissal is automatically unfair. The only exceptions (which are to be modified by the new Bill, mentioned later in this chapter) are where:

(a) she cannot do her work adequately because of her pregnancy; or
(b) her continued employment would be unlawful (for example where she is doing work which presents particular dangers for pregnant women or the unborn baby).

Many pregnant employees who are dismissed, however, do not have the necessary two years' service to bring a complaint of unfair dismissal. They either have a right to complain of sex discrimination or they have no right of action at all (until the new Bill becomes law). If the dismissal is contrary to the SDA or EC law, then they can bring tribunal proceedings, even if they have been employed for only a matter of days.

Furthermore, even where an employee does have the necessary service to complain of unfair dismissal, the right to complain under the SDA as well is a useful additional right. An industrial tribunal can award compensation for injured feelings in cases of direct discrimination; there is no compensation for injured feelings in ordinary unfair dismissal cases.

The comparable man approach

The question first came before the EAT in 1980, in the case of *Turley v Allders Department Stores Limited*. In that case it was ruled that dismissal of a woman on the ground of pregnancy could not amount to direct sex discrimination. The reason for the decision was that since a man could not become pregnant it was impossible to compare like with like as required by section 5(3) of the SDA.

A different approach was adopted by the EAT five years later, in the case of *Hayes v Malleable Working Men's Club and Institute*. The approach adopted in that case and subsequent cases has been as follows:

1. Men do not of course become pregnant.
2. However when a pregnant woman is dismissed the reason is not generally the fact of her pregnancy, but some real or imagined consequences of the pregnancy, for example that:
   (a) she will be taking some months off work (her maternity leave) and then wishing to return to work;
   (b) she could become unfit, for several months of her employment, to lift heavy weights or do other strenuous physical jobs; or
   (c) her appearance will be affected by her pregnancy.
3. Although men do not become pregnant, they do have medical or other conditions which can give rise to similar consequences from the employer's point of view. For example:
   (a) One of your male employees may need several months off work in order to have a major operation and convalesce from it.
   (b) There are several medical conditions (such as a broken leg, a hernia or a back complaint) which can impair a male employee's ability to lift weights or do other heavy work.
   (c) There are also medical complaints and personal characteristics (such as skin complaints or gluttony) which can affect a male employee's physical appearance.

4. The first step then is to identify the particular aspect of the employee's pregnancy which caused you to dismiss her—for example the fact that she would need several months off work.
5. The next step is to consider how you have treated male employees in comparable circumstances. If a male employee has needed several months off work for an operation or some other medical reason, have you dismissed him or have you allowed him to return?
6. If there has been no case of a male employee needing a long absence from work, the more difficult question then to be considered is how you *would* treat a male employee in these circumstances.
7. The complaint of direct sex discrimination will succeed if it can be shown that you have dismissed a pregnant employee and that you would not have dismissed a male employee in comparable circumstances.

There have been many successful complaints of discrimination in relation to pregnancy related dismissals, using this comparable man approach. Commonly, in such cases, the employer argues that the dismissal was for some quite different reason, such as the incompetence or misconduct of the employee. If this reason is shown to be false, then the inference can be drawn that the employer has something to hide and that sex discrimination was the true reason for the dismissal.

The automatic discrimination approach

There were two main difficulties about the comparable man approach:

(a) In many cases there was no evidence to show how an *actual* male employee had been treated in relevant circumstances, and it can be very difficult to establish how a *hypothetical* man would have been treated.
(b) It seems rather unjust that an employer who has acted unfairly, by dismissing a pregnant employee with less than two years' service, can escape all liability by showing that he would have behaved equally badly towards a man who needed time off.

At the time of writing, a new Bill, the Trade Union Reform and Employment Rights Bill (TURER), is before Parliament. This Bill has been introduced partly to bring UK law into line with the EC Directive on Pregnant Workers 1991, which must be implemented by 19th October 1994. One of the key provisions of the Bill is to remove the two year qualifying period in unfair dismissal cases, where pregnancy is the reason for the dismissal.

In the meantime, the other method which has been adopted of extending the rights of women dismissed on account of pregnancy is to treat all such dismissals as automatically discriminatory. The European Court moved towards this approach in two cases in 1991, known as *Dekker* and *Hertz*. These cases related to the EC Equal Treatment Directive. The point was then argued in the British case of *Webb v EMO Air Cargo (UK) Limited*. In this case, a company had 16 employees, including four members of an import department. In 1987, an import operations clerk became pregnant. She proposed to start her maternity leave at the end of the year. Mrs Webb was recruited at the beginning of July; she would need six months' training from the import operations clerk and would then act as the latter's temporary replacement when she went on maternity leave. However the possibility that she would be available for this purpose throughout the relevant period disappeared a few weeks later, when Mrs Webb found that she was pregnant and informed her employers. She was dismissed.

Mrs Webb's case was taken to the House of Lords, which in its decision (in November 1992) appears to have adopted the automatic discrimination approach, but with one modification. Lord Keith said:

> There can be no doubt that in general to dismiss a woman because she is pregnant or to refuse to employ a woman of child-bearing age because she may become pregnant is unlawful direct discrimination. Child-bearing and the capacity for child-bearing are characteristics of the female sex. So to apply these characteristics as the criterion for dismissal or refusal to employ is to apply a gender-based criterion.

Applying a gender-based criterion was direct discrimination, by reason of the decision of the House of Lords in *James v Eastleigh Borough Council* (Chapter 2).

However, the House of Lords took the view that Mrs Webb's dismissal was not in breach of the SDA, viewed in isolation. Her dismissal was not caused by the mere fact of her pregnancy and its ordinary consequences, but by her expected non-availability during the period when her services were particularly required.

This was not the end of the story, however. The House of Lords referred to the European Court of Justice (the ECJ) the question of whether Mrs Webb's dismissal was in breach of the Equal Treatment Directive. If the ECJ rules that there was a breach of the Directive, the House of Lords will then have to consider whether the SDA can be construed in such a way as to accord with the Directive. There are accordingly the following possibilities in future cases brought by employees on similar facts to those of Mrs Webb's case:

(a) Breach of both the SDA and the Directive.
(b) No breach of either the SDA or the Directive.
(c) Breach of the Directive but not the SDA—in that case claims can be brought against public sector employers, based on the Directive, but not against private sector employers.

The new Bill, when it becomes law, will reduce the importance of *Webb* by removing the two year qualifying period for unfair dismissal in pregnancy cases. However the House of Lords decision in *Webb* will still be relevant in, for example, cases where a woman has her job application turned down or is refused promotion because she is pregnant. The general principle seems to be that there is a breach of the SDA in these circumstances, because a gender-based criterion has been applied to her.

The Section 51 defence

At present, under section 51 of the SDA, the dismissal of a pregnant employee, even where it is to be treated as discriminatory, can be permitted, under section 51 of the SDA, if it is on health and safety grounds relating to her pregnancy. As mentioned in Chapter 7, when the new Bill (TURER) becomes law, dismissal will no longer be permitted. You must either offer her suitable alternative work or, if there is no such work available, suspend her on pay.

Other legal issues

There are other circumstances in which a complaint of discrimination could arise either before pregnancy, during maternity leave or on the exercise of the right to return to work.

Before pregnancy

There are cases where employers make decisions which are influenced by the possibility of a female employee becoming pregnant in the future. If a person appointed or promoted to a job will require substantial training they appoint a man rather than a more suitable woman because if the latter becomes pregnant and leaves, the cost of the training will have been wasted.

These are clear cases of direct sex discrimination. A man would not be rejected for a job or promotion on the ground that he may one day become a father.

Moreover, as explained in Chapter 6, if job applicants are asked when interviewed if they intend to start a family, such questions can raise an inference of a discriminatory attitude; they could even in themselves amount to unlawful discrimination if only women are asked the questions and if any of the women are upset by this line of questioning.

Maternity leave

Could a woman who leaves work to have a baby have a claim under the SDA or Equal Pay Act or EC law in any of the following cases?

(a) Her absence is not treated as pensionable service.
(b) The period of her absence is disregarded for the purpose of calculating her seniority.
(c) She is not allowed to retain benefits in kind, such as use of a company car.

There has been no authoritative ruling on these points, but it is likely that under current law the employee will have a claim if she has been denied rights which would have been enjoyed by a comparable male employee who is absent on sick or study leave.

When the new Bill (TURER) becomes law, there will be a maternity leave period of 14 weeks during which the employee will be entitled to the terms and conditions of employment (excluding pay but presumably including benefits in kind) which she would have enjoyed if she had still been at work. However there could be a significant gap between the end of this 14 week period and the date by which the woman exercises her right to return to work. The existing law (which as mentioned has not yet been fully clarified) will apply once the 14 week period has ended.

A further question which has still to be determined under the current law is whether employers who give enhanced pay and other benefits to employees on sick leave must also give enhanced pay and benefits to women on maternity leave. In general, there is probably a liability under both the Equal Pay Act (or sometimes the SDA in the case of non-financial or discretionary benefits) and under Article 119 of the EC Treaty.

In one respect, the new Bill (TURER), when it becomes law, will curtail rights currently enjoyed by pregnant employees. Under the current law, a woman may choose not to start her maternity leave until a very short time before the baby is born and if she is off sick for a few days in the meantime then the SSP provisions will apply. Under the new Bill, if she is absent from work during the 11 weeks before the expected week of childbirth, and her absence is wholly or partly because of her pregnancy, then her maternity leave will commence whether she likes it or not. This particular provision is not one which needs to be in the Bill to comply with the Pregnancy Directive and the Bill may of course be amended before it becomes law.

The return to work

The general rule is that a woman who is not allowed to exercise her right to return to her work is treated as dismissed. The only exceptions are:

(a) where it is no longer practicable to take her back in her old job, but a suitable alternative is offered;
(b) where you have fewer than six employees and it is not practicable either to take her back in her old job or to offer any suitable alternative job.

Even where there is an automatic dismissal, the dismissal is not automatically unfair. If, for example, a redundancy situation arises during an employee's maternity leave, you will be entitled to consider selecting her for redundancy, so long as you act reasonably. The dismissal would almost certainly be unfair if you selected her for redundancy because she was on maternity leave or if there was no adequate consultation with her before you made your decision.

A dismissal in these circumstances could also be discriminatory, if it could be shown that a male employee of similar seniority and with a similar employment record would not have been dismissed in comparable circumstances, i.e. whilst on sick leave or on any other leave. You should also bear in mind that if an employee is selected for redundancy because she is pregnant then the dismissal is automatically unfair.

Practical advice

As a minimum, when you find that an employee or job applicant is pregnant, you should react reasonably and objectively. If you panic and act hysterically, for example by dismissing a pregnant employee who is fully capable of doing her work, this dismissal:

(a) could lead to a successful complaint of direct sex discrimination;
(b) will almost certainly lead to a successful complaint of unfair dismissal, if the woman has the necessary two years' qualifying service, (and irrespective of length of service, when the new Bill becomes law);
(c) will show you in a bad light, as someone who cannot make management decisions on a rational basis;
(d) will do nothing for staff morale, particularly if you expect other employees to give evidence on your behalf at the industrial tribunal.

There is a great deal to be said for a positive approach. If you demonstrate to a pregnant employee that she is a valued employee and treat her generously and considerately, then you will not only be complying with the law but also encouraging her to show loyalty to you for the rest of her career and also enhancing staff morale generally.

The EOC code (in paragraph 43(e)), refers to the possibility of enhancing the statutory maternity leave provisions, for example by:

- reducing the qualifying service period;
- extending the leave period;
- giving access to part-time arrangements on return.

Promotion and training

You should not overlook pregnant employees when making decisions relating to promotion and training. Such treatment could be unlawful and is in any event short-sighted.

Redundancy

If a redundancy situation arises, either while an employee is pregnant or during her maternity leave, you should deal with the matter exactly as you would if she were still at work and not pregnant. Whether she is at work or at home, you must not overlook the need for proper consultation with her before you make any decision to dismiss her on the ground of redundancy.

Summary

1. The dismissal (or selection for redundancy) of a woman because she is pregnant will usually involve a breach of both the SDA and the EC Equal Treatment and Pregnancy Directives. The exceptions (if any) to this principle will be determined by the rulings of the ECJ and the House of Lords in *Webb*.
2. Dismissing a woman (or selecting her for redundancy) because she is pregnant is also unfair dismissal, so long as she has two years' service. When the new Bill (TURER) becomes law, the dismissal will be unfair whatever the length of service.
3. There will also generally be a breach of the SDA and of the Equal Treatment Directive if a woman has her job application rejected or is overlooked for promotion or training (or is otherwise unfavourably treated) because she is pregnant.
4. Women on maternity leave (including the period after their right to SMP expires) could have rights under the Equal Pay Act (or sometimes the SDA) and under Article 119 of the EC Treaty if they are denied enhanced benefits enjoyed by men on sick or study leave. Such benefits include:
    (a) pay which is more than the statutory requirement;
    (b) the accrual of benefits (eg in relation to pension and seniority) during the period of absence;
    (c) the retention of benefits in kind, such as use of a company car.
5. There will be an express statutory right in respect of some of the above matters when the new Bill (TURER) becomes law (and also rights under the Pregnancy Directive in the case of public sector employees), but only for the maternity leave period of 14 weeks specified in the Bill. If the woman exercises her right to return to work after this period of 14 weeks has expired, the existing law will continue to apply between the end of the 14 weeks and the date when she returns.

12
Unlawful Advertising and Pressure to Discriminate

Most complaints under the SDA or the RRA arise because of unlawful discrimination against an individual. There are, however, certain actions which are declared to be unlawful, even where no individual suffers discrimination as a result of them. Proceedings in respect of such actions can be taken against you by the EOC or the CRE (as the case may be) in order to obtain a finding that you have acted unlawfully. No penalty of any kind can be imposed, but further infringements (or the threat of them) could lead to an application for an injunction, as explained in Chapter 16.

The law concerns itself with three kinds of 'victimless' offences:

1. Discriminatory practices.
2. Advertisements which indicate an intention to discriminate.
3. Instructions or pressure to discriminate unlawfully.

This chapter deals mainly with (2) and (3) above; proceedings are rarely, if ever, brought in respect of a discriminatory practice.

Discriminatory practices

A discriminatory practice is defined by the SDA (Section 37) and the RRA (Section 28). It includes unlawful acts of indirect discrimination. These could lead to proceedings against you by an individual who is detrimentally affected or by the relevant commission. The definition also includes acts of indirect discrimination which would be unlawful if an individual victim could be identified. For example:

(a) All the workers in your factory are white and vacancies are always filled through personal recommendations by existing employees. Black workers who would be interested in working for you never even hear about the vacancies. Unless you could show your recruitment policy to be justifiable (which is unlikely), you are operating a discriminatory practice and the CRE could take proceedings against you.
(b) Whenever you have a secretarial vacancy, you recruit through

the head of an all girls' school. You do not advertise the vacancies in any way. Accordingly, only girls hear about the jobs and apply for work with you. You are operating a discriminatory practice and the EOC could take proceedings.

Advertisements

The SDA and the RRA deal differently with advertisements.

The SDA

Under the SDA (Section 38), it is unlawful to publish or place an advertisement which indicates your intention to discriminate *unlawfully*. Even if you do not intend to discriminate unlawfully, publishing the advertisement or causing its publication is unlawful if the advertisement might reasonably be understood to indicate such an intention.

The Act also refers to job descriptions which have a sexual connotation, such as 'waiter', 'salesgirl', 'postman' and 'stewardess'. The use of terms such as these is automatically taken to indicate an intention to discriminate, unless the advertisement contains an indication to the contrary. You can give the contrary indication in one of two ways:

(a) by also using the description which applies to the other sex, such as 'waitress' and 'salesman'; or
(b) by expressly stating that the job is open to both sexes.

It is safer to use terms which have no sexual connotation, such as 'salesperson', wherever you can think of such a term which describes the job accurately and is not unduly clumsy.

The SDA expressly provides that publishing the advertisement is not against the law if the intended discrimination would be lawful, for example when you are advertising for someone to work wholly or mainly at an establishment overseas.

The RRA

The RRA does not contain any general defence of this kind. The Act (in Section 29) prohibits the publication or causing the publication of an advertisement indicating an intention to discriminate, even if the discrimination would be lawful. As with the SDA, the law is also broken if the advertisement could reasonably be understood to indicate such an intention.

This means that, for example, while you can generally discriminate when recruiting a person to work in a private household, you cannot lawfully state this intention in any advertisement. The reason for this distinction between the two Acts was stated in the white paper, *Racial Discrimination*, as follows: 'The public display of racial prejudices and preferences is inherently offensive and likely to encourage the spread of discriminatory attitudes and practices.'

Publication of the intention to discriminate is lawful, however, if the discrimination itself would be lawful under:

(a) one of the GOQ provisions mentioned in Chapter 7;
(b) the exceptions relating to sport and statutory discrimination mentioned in Chapter 7; or
(c) the exceptions for positive action mentioned in Chapter 8.

If you are advertising a job outside Great Britain, you may lawfully refer to a nationality or residential requirement. However, you may not lawfully indicate an intention to discriminate directly by reference to colour, race or ethnic or national origins.

Placing an advertisement

If you place an advertisement which is published unlawfully in a newspaper, you cannot escape liability on the ground that you did not actually 'publish' the advertisement; the publication was by the editor or proprietor of the newspaper. Both the SDA and the RRA cover causing the publication of an advertisement so as to catch the person who places it.

Furthermore, you will be committing a criminal offence if you knowingly or recklessly make a false or misleading statement in order to have your advertisement published. The offence would be committed, for example, if you told the staff at the newspaper office that the job was covered by a GOQ exception and if you knew the statement to be false.

Meaning of advertisement

The provisions in the SDA and the RRA about advertisements do not apply only to newspaper advertisements. The SDA (in Section 82) and the RRA (Section 78) both define 'advertisement' in the widest possible terms. The definition includes every form of advertisement or notice, whether to the public or not. It would include, for example:

- a television or radio advertisement;
- a notice at the factory gate;
- a notice on the factory or office noticeboard;
- a notice in an internal staff magazine, newsletter or circular.

Complaints by individuals

Only the EOC or the CRE (as the case may be) can take proceedings on the ground that an advertisement has been published unlawfully. No individual can take proceedings against you on the ground that he or she was upset or offended by the advertisement; his or her remedy is to complain to the appropriate commission and ask them to take action.

The terms of a discriminatory advertisement may, however, be relied on as evidence by an individual complaining of unlawful discrimination in the arrangements which you make for filling a vacancy or (where the complaint is made by an existing employee) in the way in which you provide access to opportunities for promotion, transfer or training. It is arguable that such a person could complain of unlawful discrimination even if he or she does not actually apply for the post. You could, however, have a defence on the ground that there is not enough of a link between you and a person who has simply read the advertisement and done nothing more; you have not *treated* that person unfavourably because you have never had any dealings with him or her.

Pressure to discriminate

Both the SDA (Sections 39 and 40) and the RRA (Sections 30 and 31) make it unlawful:

(a) to give instructions to discriminate unlawfully; or
(b) to put pressure on a person to discriminate unlawfully.

The instructions to discriminate are unlawful if they are given to a person over whom you have authority (such as an employee) or a person who is accustomed to act in accordance with your wishes. Your conduct is still unlawful if you avoid giving a direct instruction but try indirectly to *cause* the subordinate or other person to discriminate unlawfully.

Under the SDA, you are acting unlawfully if you use a benefit (or the offer of one) or a detriment (or the threat of one) to *induce* a person to act unlawfully. It is immaterial whether the pressure is applied directly or indirectly. Under the RRA, directly or indirectly inducing or attempting to induce a person to discriminate unlawfully is forbidden whether or not accompanied by threats or promises.

The following are examples of the working of the above provisions:

(a) You are accustomed to using your local job centre for filling vacancies. You telephone the job centre to place a vacancy for a job in the kitchens of your restaurant; you tell the job centre not to send along any women who wish to apply, since the job involves heavy lifting.

(b) You are using a private employment agency for the first time, to fill a vacancy in your office. They telephone to tell you that a black woman is interested in the post. You say that your existing staff are all white and that they might object to working with a black person; you ask the agency to tell the job applicant that the post has already been filled.

Both job centres and private employment agencies are under a duty not to discriminate in the way in which they provide their services. In (a) above, you are instructing the job centre to discriminate unlawfully. Because you have placed previous vacancies with them, the job centre is accustomed to act in accordance with your wishes. Giving the instruction to discriminate is an unlawful act on your part; it is immaterial that the job centre has refused to comply and that no individual applicant has yet been affected by the instruction. The unlawful instruction could lead to a complaint against you by the EOC, although you may be able to avoid proceedings by giving satisfactory assurances to comply with the law in the future.

In (b), you have unlawfully attempted to induce the private employment agency to discriminate unlawfully. Because the case involves racial rather than sex discrimination, the attempted inducement is unlawful even if not accompanied by a threat (such as an express or implied threat to take your business elsewhere). Furthermore, since in this case there is an individual job applicant who has been refused an interview, there could also be a complaint against you (either by the CRE or by the applicant personally) that you have unlawfully discriminated in the arrangements for filling the job vacancy.

Victimisation

It is clear that you will be acting unlawfully if you instruct an employee or (if you yourself are an employee) a subordinate to discriminate unlawfully. Would there then be a further breach of the law if the employee or subordinate refuses to obey the instruction and is dismissed or disciplined as a result?

For example, you instruct a personnel manager to prepare a short list of applicants for a post as your personal assistant. You state that you are not prepared to see any men who apply, but a man is included on the shortlist. The personnel manager tells you that it would have been unlawful for him to comply with your instruction; you dismiss him.

In the above example, the personnel manager would be able to bring a complaint against you under the SDA, because of the broad definition of victimisation. In refusing to do something because it was forbidden by the SDA, he was acting 'under or by reference to' the Act.

If the instruction had related to racial discrimination, there would have been a further possibility because of the very broad definition of 'racial grounds' which is contained in the RRA. In the case of *Zarczynska v Levy*, in 1979, a part-time barmaid at a public house was dismissed because she refused to obey an instruction that she must not serve black customers. It was said by the EAT that the barmaid had received less favourable treatment on racial grounds than the treatment which would have been received by a barmaid prepared to apply the embargo.

Pressure on you to discriminate

It has already been explained, in Chapter 2, that it is no defence to a complaint of discrimination for you to say that you were discriminating in response to instructions or pressure. If, however, you are at the receiving end of pressure to discriminate unlawfully, then it is open to you to report the circumstances to the EOC or CRE (as the case may be) and ask them to consider taking proceedings. For example:

(a) You give a woman a job on a previously all-male shop floor. Some of the existing employees threaten to go on strike unless you transfer her to other duties.
(b) A customer objects on racial grounds to a black sales representative and threatens to take his business elsewhere if you persist in sending this representative to see him.

The employees in (a) and the customer in (b) have acted unlawfully; proceedings could be taken against the employees by the EOC and against the customer by the CRE.

Practical advice

Both the EOC code (paragraphs 19 (b), (c) and (d), and paragraph 20) and the CRE code (paragraphs 1.10 and 1.11) warn against the kind of discriminatory practice mentioned at the beginning of this chapter.

Advertising

The CRE code (paragraph 1.5) reminds employers that it is unlawful to publish an advertisement indicating an intention to discriminate, whether the discrimination would be direct or indirect. The code gives (in paragraph 1.6(b)) the following examples:

(a) You should avoid specifying requirements such as length of residence or experience in the UK.
(b) If a particular qualification is required, you should make it clear that this does not mean only UK qualifications; a fully comparable qualification obtained overseas will be equally acceptable.

A positive approach is to be recommended. Advertisements are a very good method of putting over to job applicants and employees the message that you are an equal opportunity employer. The CRE code recommends (in paragraph 1.7) that when sending literature to job applicants you should demonstrate your commitment to equality of opportunity by including a statement that you are an equal opportunity employer. It is sensible to adopt a similar approach in relation to advertisements of all kinds.

The EOC code recommends (in paragraph 19(a)) that job advertising should be carried out in such a way as to encourage applications from suitable candidates of both sexes. This is not just a matter of the wording of the advertisements. You should also, for example:

(a) place advertisements in publications likely to reach both sexes;
(b) review all advertising material and accompanying literature to

ensure that it avoids presenting men and women in stereotyped roles.

The EOC code makes the point (in paragraph 42(c)) that if you use the positive action provisions mentioned in Chapter 8, your advertisements should make it clear that selection will be on merit without reference to sex. You should also make it clear that selection will be on merit when you use the corresponding provisions under the RRA.

If you have a large organisation, in which several people are involved in placing advertisements, you should have a written statement of the legal requirements and of your own policy. Ensure that they are all familiar with it. The consent of a senior manager should be required before the benefit of the GOQ or any other exception is claimed.

Remember that the definition of advertisements extends far beyond newspaper advertisements. You should ensure that the necessary standards are maintained in all other relevant documents, such as notices and newsletters.

Instructions and pressure to discriminate

The CRE code (in paragraph 1.28) gives the following examples of unlawful instructions and pressure respectively:

(a) An instruction from a personnel or line manager to junior staff to restrict the numbers of employees from a particular racial group in any particular work.
(b) An attempt by a shop steward or group of workers to induce an employer not to recruit members of particular racial groups, for example by threatening industrial action.

The code makes the following recommendations (in paragraph 1.30):

(a) Give guidance to all employees, particularly those in positions of authority or influence, on the relevant provisions of the law;
(b) Instruct decision makers not to give way to pressure to discriminate;
(c) Treat giving instructions or bringing pressure to discriminate as a disciplinary offence.

This last advice is particularly important. If anyone tries to make you discriminate unlawfully, you should not even consider giving in to the pressure. Instead, you should strike back by whatever means are appropriate. If the unlawful pressure comes from employees, you should discipline them; if it comes from an outside agency, such as a customer, you should consider reporting the circumstances to the relevant commission.

Employment agencies

When you use an employment agency to recruit employees, it is important to make it clear to the agency that you are an equal opportunity employer and that no discrimination, either by the agency or by your own employees, will be tolerated. The EOC code (in paragraph 42(d)) refers to the importance of giving clear instructions to the agency where you are taking advantage of the positive action provisions. Where the positive action provisions under the SDA are being used, you should instruct the agency that:

(a) they must tell both men and women about the posts;
(b) they should tell the 'under-represented' sex that applications from them are particularly welcome;
(c) they must not withhold information from one sex in an attempt to encourage applications from the opposite sex.

Similar instructions must be given to the agency when you are using the positive action provisions under the RRA.

Summary

1. The relevant commission can take proceedings in respect of:
   (a) a discriminatory practice;
   (b) unlawful advertising;
   (c) instructions and pressure to discriminate unlawfully.
2. Under the SDA, it is unlawful to publish or cause the publication of an advertisement which gives the impression that you intend to discriminate unlawfully. Under the RRA, it is not an automatic defence to show that the intended racial discrimination itself would be lawful.
3. The word 'advertisement' is very widely defined and even includes internal notices.
4. Instructions and pressure to discriminate are unlawful so long as the discrimination itself would be unlawful. Both Acts cover *instructions* given to subordinates or to persons accustomed to act in accordance with one's instructions; under the SDA, *pressure* to discriminate is unlawful only if accompanied by an inducement or detriment (or promise or threat of one).
5. Great care is required where an advertisement or employment agency is being used to fill a vacancy and one of the GOQ or positive action exceptions is being relied on.

13
Equal Pay and Pensions

The question of racial discrimination in terms of employment has already been referred to in Chapter 10. As explained in that Chapter, the SDA is not concerned at all with complaints by employees about their pay or other contract terms for the payment of money. All these matters are dealt with by the Equal Pay Act and by EC law. Most complaints about contract terms other than those for the payment of money also fall under the EPA rather than the SDA.

Average earnings for women in Great Britain are substantially lower than those for men; this is partly because more women do part-time work and fewer work overtime, but there is also a substantial difference between basic hourly rates of pay. The purpose of the law is to eliminate these disparities so far as they result from traditional or continuing sex discrimination in fixing or negotiating pay and other contract terms. Some progress has been made towards this end, but mainly in the few years after the Equal Pay Act came into force at the end of 1975.

The Equal Pay Act

Most complaints under the EPA are made by a woman seeking the same rate of pay as a male colleague, known as the comparator. There are, however, the following variations on this theme:
(a) The complaint can relate to other contract terms, not only the rate of pay.
(b) Sometimes the complainant is a man and the comparator is a woman.
(c) The complainant and the comparator can sometimes be 'in the same employment' even if they do not work at the same establishment.

The effect of a successful complaint is to improve the complainant's rate of pay and other contract terms to match those of the comparator. The adjustment for the future takes place by reason of the 'equality clause' which the EPA inserts into all contracts. Compensation can also be awarded, based on the back pay from two years before the date on which the tribunal application was presented. For example, a woman claims the same rate of pay as a male colleague. They have been working together for more than two years, doing similar work and working the same hours, but he is paid £2,000 a year more than she is. Her complaint, which is decided six months after she presents the tribunal application, is successful.

In this example, the arithmetic for working out the compensation would be as follows:

(a) Compensation can be awarded to reflect the back pay for the six months since the proceedings were started and for the previous two years, a total of two and a half years.
(b) The difference in gross pay for this period, at £2,000 a year, would be £5,000.
(c) If the complainant had received this additional pay, tax would have been deducted at, say, 25 per cent, producing a figure of £1,250 for the tax.
(d) Accordingly, the compensation would be £3,750.

If one of your employees brings a complaint against you under the Equal Pay Act, there are the following matters to be considered:

1. Are the complainant and the comparator (or the comparators, because there can be more than one) 'in the same employment'?
2. Have the two jobs been covered by a job evaluation scheme? If so, the result of this scheme can be conclusive either way (subject to the material factor defence mentioned below).
3. If not, are the two jobs comparable, by reason of being 'like work' (the same or broadly similar) or 'of equal value'?
4. Can you in any event defeat any claim by showing that the difference in pay or contract terms which is complained of is genuinely due to a 'material factor' other than the difference in sex?

The same employment

The complainant and the comparator cannot be said to be 'in the same employment' unless each of them is employed by you or an associated employer. The employers would be associated in the following examples:

(a) You, as an individual, employ one of the employees and the other is employed by a company which you control.
(b) The complainant is employed by a company and the comparator is employed by another company in the same group.

So long as they have the same employer or associated employers, the complainant and the comparator are always 'in the same employment' if they work at the same establishment.

But what if they have the same employer or associated employers but work at different establishments? They will be 'in the same employment' only if there are 'common terms and conditions of employment' at the different establishments, either generally or for employees of the relevant classes. This is a broad test which is easily satisfied following the House of Lords decision in the case of *Leverton v Clwyd County Council*. In that case, a nursery nurse claimed the same rate of pay as male clerical staff employed by the council at different establishments. She and they and the other employees at the relevant establishments were covered by the same collective agreement, set out in a document known as the 'purple book'. However, she worked $32^1/_2$ hours per week and had 70 days' annual holiday; the comparators worked 37 hours a week and had 20 days' annual holiday.

It was ruled that the complainant and the comparators were 'in the same employment'. It was immaterial for this purpose (although very relevant to the material factor defence mentioned below) that they worked longer hours than she did and had less holiday. Lord Bridge said:

> The concept of common terms and conditions of employment observed generally at different establishments necessarily contemplates terms and conditions applicable to a wide range of employees whose individual terms will vary greatly.

Lord Bridge went on to give two examples of cases where an equal pay claim could fail because the complainant and the comparator are not 'in the same employment'. These examples can be summarised as follows:

(a) You have an establishment in London and one in Newcastle. There is no sex inequality in rates of pay at either of the two establishments, but the men and women employed in London enjoy substantially higher rates of pay than those employed in Newcastle. If one of the women in Newcastle could claim the same rate of pay as one of the men in London then 'this would eliminate a differential in earnings which is due not to sex but to geography.'

(b) You have a factory where there is a long-standing collective agreement with a particular union. You take over another company or business which has a factory elsewhere. The previous owner of this other factory had a long-standing collective agreement with a different union and you continue to operate this agreement. The two collective agreements have produced 'quite different structures governing pay and other terms and conditions of employment at the two factories.'

EC Law

For the purpose of the EPA, the complainant and the comparator can be 'in the same employment' only if they are employed at the same time. However, a claim can be brought under EC law on the basis of a comparison between the complainant's pay or other contract terms and those of an immediate predecessor of the other sex. Article 119 of the EC Treaty establishes the principle of equal pay as between men and women for equal work. This Article was relied upon in 1980 in the case of *Macarthy Limited v Smith*.

A stockroom manageress was paid about £500 a year less than her predecessor, who had left the company about four months before her appointment. There was no current employee with whom she could compare her work. Her claim under the Equal Pay Act failed, but her claim under EC law was upheld.

The Definition of Employment

In most equal pay cases, the complainant and the comparator are employees in the conventional sense of the word. However, the EPA, like the SDA, covers employment not only under a contract of service or apprenticeship but also under 'a contract personally to execute any work or labour'. There could, for example, be an equal pay claim in the following circumstances.

You are a manager of an insurance company which sells policies through financial advisers. They are technically self-employed but are not permitted to sell policies for any other company. All the financial advisers have the same basic form of contract, but one of them, a woman, complains that she is entitled to a lower rate of commission than one of the men. He and she are 'in the same employment' for the purposes of this claim under the Equal Pay Act.

Job evaluation

The next step, once it has been established that the complainant and the comparator are 'in the same employment', is to consider whether their two jobs have been covered by the same job evaluation study. If there has been such a study, there are then the following possibilities:

(a) The study has given the same rating to the two jobs.
(b) The study has given them different ratings.

If the two jobs have been given the same rating then the study is conclusive in favour of the complainant, subject only to the 'material factor' defence mentioned below. If, on the other hand, the study has resulted in different ratings for the two jobs, then the study is conclusive against the complainant, subject to the following important conditions:

(a) The study must not be tainted by any direct or indirect sex discrimination.
(b) The jobs of both the complainant and the comparator must have been analysed and evaluated as part of the study.
(c) The study may be invalidated if either job has changed since the study was carried out.

The conditions mentioned in (a) and (b) above were laid down by the Court of Appeal in 1988 in the case of *Bromley v H & J Quick Limited*. The condition in (c) was established in the case of *Dibro Limited v Hore* in 1990. It was also ruled in this case that you may carry out and rely on a job evaluation study even after the proceedings against you have been commenced. One would have thought, however, that the time constraints and other pressures created by the existence of proceedings do not constitute the ideal background for a job evaluation study.

The methods used to carry out a job evaluation study are similar to those mentioned later in this chapter as being used by independent experts appointed to determine whether two jobs are of equal value.

Before either you or the complainant can rely on a job evaluation study, it must have been completed and accepted as being valid both by you and by any other party (usually a union or unions) who have agreed to carry it out. However, it is immaterial that for some reason the study has not been implemented. This principle was laid down by the House of Lords in 1980 in the case of *O'Brien v Sim-Chem Limited*.

Like work and equal value

If the two jobs have not been covered by a job evaluation study, the next two questions to be asked are:

1. Are they 'like work'?
2. If not, are they of 'equal value'?

Like work
For a claim to succeed, it is not necessary for the two jobs to be identical. They need only be the same or broadly similar. If there are differences in the work, they can be ignored if they are things which are not of practical importance in relation to pay and other terms and conditions of employment. It is necessary to look at what actually happens in practice and not at any theoretical differences between the two jobs.

The above rules are set out in the EPA itself. The following two cases illustrate how the rules can work in practice.

In *Capper Pass Limited v Lawton*, in 1976, the complainant worked as a cook for the directors of a company, providing lunch for between 10 and 20 persons per day and working a 40-hour week. The two comparators were men working as assistant chefs, under a head chef. Together they provided 350 meals a day for six sittings in the factory canteen and worked a 45-hour week. It was held that the complainant and the comparators were employed on like work, so that the complainant was entitled to the same hourly rate as the two men.

On the other hand, in *Eaton Limited v Nuttall*, in 1977, the complainant and the comparator were employed as production schedulers by a company making fork-lift trucks. They worked in a centralised department for the control of materials. She looked after 2,400 items up to a value of £2.50; he looked after 1,200 items, the value of which ranged from £5 to £1,000. Although there was little to choose between the two jobs in terms of the work actually carried out, the comparator's job carried greater responsibility, because of the greater value of the items. It was held by the EAT that this aspect of his job could prevent the two jobs being like work, because 'an error by him was likely to have far more serious consequences.'

The two jobs are not prevented from being 'like work' if the comparator, but not the complainant, works overtime or works on the night shift. It was held by the Court of Appeal in the early case of *Shields v E Coomes (Holdings) Limited* that 'the only legitimate way of dealing with night work or for longer hours is by paying a night shift premium or overtime rate assessed at a reasonable figure.'

Equal value
If the two jobs are not 'like work', the claim can nevertheless succeed if they are 'of equal value'.

For this purpose it does not matter if the two jobs are of quite different kinds. In the case of *Leverton*, which has already been mentioned, a nursery nurse was claiming the same rate of pay as male clerical staff. In the case of *Hayward v Cammell Laird Shipbuilders Limited*, a canteen cook succeeded in claiming the same rate of pay as male welders and other craftsmen in the shipyard.

There is an important difference in the procedure between like work and equal value cases. In a like work case, the industrial tribunal hears evidence from both sides and then decides whether it is satisfied that the two jobs are 'like work'. In an equal value case, the industrial tribunal holds a preliminary hearing and then refers the evaluation of the two jobs to an independent expert, unless the claim fails at the preliminary hearing on one of the following grounds:

(a) The complainant and the comparator are not 'in the same employment'.
(b) There is in fact no difference between their pay and other contract terms and conditions.
(c) The two jobs have been given a different rating by a properly carried out and non-discriminatory job evaluation scheme.
(d) The 'material factor' defence mentioned below is dealt with and upheld at the preliminary hearing.
(e) The tribunal is satisfied that there are no reasonable grounds for determining that the work is of equal value, ie the disparity is so obvious that there is no need for the case to go to the independent expert.

When a case is referred to an independent expert, the latter studies the two jobs and measures the demands which each job makes in terms of, for example, skill, mental effort, physical effort, decision making and responsibility. The two jobs are given points under each heading and if the complainant's job carries as many points as the comparator's job, the two jobs are of equal value. It is all like a mini job evaluation study.

The industrial tribunal then meets again to consider the independent expert's report, but this report is not necessarily conclusive. It is common for the parties themselves to appoint their own experts to produce reports. The party who is not satisfied with the independent expert's report will then challenge it at the industrial tribunal hearing on the basis of their own expert's report.

The whole process is very long and complicated. Sometimes a claim is brought by a union on behalf of a very large group of complainants (perhaps running into the hundreds). To reduce the cases to manageable proportions, it is usual to agree that a number of test cases will be heard and that the other cases will depend on the outcome of these test cases.

Can you put an end to an equal value claim at an early stage on the ground that the complainant enjoys the same rate of pay and contract terms and conditions as employees of the other sex who are employed on 'like work'? This question arose in the case of *Pickstone and Others v Freemans plc*. In this case, the company employed men and women as warehouse operatives and they received the same rate of pay. Some of the women claimed the higher rate of pay enjoyed by a male checker warehouse operative. They claimed that their work was of equal value to his.

It was ruled by the House of Lords that the women were entitled to proceed with their complaint. Otherwise, employers could have blocked complaints by large numbers of women simply by employing one token man on the same terms (it was not suggested that this had been done in the actual case). A significant effect of the decision is that if a complaint is successful in these circumstances, there could be a major knock-on effect. For example:

(a) Mrs A is employed on like work with Mr B.
(b) Mrs A wins an equal value claim, in which she claims the higher rate of pay enjoyed by Mr C, who is doing work of equal value.
(c) Mrs A is now paid more than Mr B; he therefore can bring a like work claim to which there will be no answer.

What is the position where the expert's report shows that the complainant's job is not quite as demanding as the comparator's, but that the differential in pay is too great? Is she entitled to have the differential reduced? Or if the report shows that her job is actually 10 per cent *more* demanding than the comparator's? Is she entitled to a 10 per cent higher rate of pay? The answer in both cases is no. The Act operates only to give *equal* pay, etc, for work of at least *equal* value.

The material factor defence

You can still defeat a claim, even if the two jobs have been given the same rating under a job evaluation study, or are like work, or of equal value. You have a defence if you can show that the difference in pay or other contract terms which is complained of is genuinely due to a material factor which is not the difference of sex. In equal value cases, this defence must be raised at the preliminary stage and not after the independent expert has reported; if you wait until then, it is too late.

Before your 'material factor' defence can succeed, you have to prove each of the following three things:

1. That the difference in pay or other contract terms which is complained of is *genuinely due* to the material factor.
2. That the factor is *material*.
3. That the factor relied on does not involve any element of *sex discrimination*.

Genuinely due
In some cases it is possible to trace the development of the current rate of pay and other contract terms, especially where terms have been negotiated through collective bargaining for some years. In other cases, however, differences in pay and other contract terms cannot be explained; they simply exist. In such cases, it is not enough for you to point to some factor which applies to the comparator but not the complainant and to argue that this factor must explain the disparity complained of. You must be able to demonstrate or persuade the tribunal to infer a link of cause and effect between the factor and the disparity.

The principle can be illustrated by the *Hayward* case, which has already been mentioned. This was the case where a female canteen cook was held to be entitled to the same rate of pay as male craftsmen in the shipyard. It was argued by the employers that there was no real disparity because, viewed as a whole, her employment package was as valuable as those of the comparators; although she had a lower rate of pay, she also enjoyed several benefits, such as paid meal breaks, which they did not. This argument was rejected by the House of Lords, who ruled that it was necessary to compare individual terms, such as the rate of pay, and not the employment package as a whole.

However, the House of Lords also considered what would have been the position if the employers had relied on the material factor defence. What if they had argued that the difference in pay complained of was due to the paid meal breaks and other favourable terms enjoyed by the complainant? Lord Mackay doubted whether this factor could be material, even if there were no element of sex discrimination in the negotiation of the terms, and his doubts in this respect were reinforced by the decision of the European Court in the *Barber* case mentioned below. However, he also made it clear that in any event the defence could not succeed unless the lower rate of pay was shown to be the *direct* result of the paid meal breaks and other favourable terms enjoyed by the complainant; there will rarely be cases where this can be shown.

A case where the material factor defence did succeed was that of *Leverton*, which has already been mentioned. Many equal pay claims relate to hourly-paid workers and it is the hourly rate of pay, rather than the weekly or monthly wage, which is at issue. However, *Leverton* concerned salaried workers. The complaint was that the male clerical workers had an annual salary much greater than that of the nursery nurse who brought the complaint. However, she worked five hours a week fewer than they did and had 50 days more annual holiday. Because of this great difference in the number of hours worked, her salary could be translated into a notional hourly rate not significantly different from theirs. It was said by Lord Bridge in the House of Lords that it was accordingly:

> a legitimate, if not a necessary, inference that the difference in their annual salaries is both due to and justified by the difference in the hours they work in the course of a year and has nothing to do with the difference in sex.

It is necessary only to show in broad terms that the disparity in pay or other terms complained of is genuinely due to the factor relied on; it is not necessary to explain the difference in precise arithmetical terms.

Material

It is not enough to show that the disparity is genuinely due to the factor relied on; that factor must also be shown to be material.

In many cases, the material factor relates to what used to be termed the 'personal equation' of the complainant and the comparator. A higher rate of pay could be justified, for example, if the comparator:

(a) is better qualified than the complainant;
(b) has much longer service; or
(c) is on a higher grade under a grading scheme which has been properly and fairly carried out.

The material factor is not, however, limited to personal factors of this kind. In the important case of *Rainey v Greater Glasgow Health Board*, it was decided to start a prosthetic (artificial limb) fitting service in the NHS in Scotland. Men and women joined the service on pay rates determined by the NHS Whitley Council scale; higher rates of pay were necessary to attract experienced prosthetists employed by private contractors. A woman in the former group claimed the same rate of pay (nearly £3,000 a year higher) as a man in the latter group.

It was held by the House of Lords in the above case that the need to offer the higher rates of pay to attract experienced prosthetists was a material factor which the employers were entitled to rely on. There was no element of discrimination. There were men as well as women on the lower rates of pay; there were women as well as men on the higher rates of pay.

It was, though, made clear by the House of Lords that a factor is not material simply because the employer believes it to be material. A factor, to be material, has to be objectively justified. However, the grounds on which it is justified need not be economic; in a non-commercial organisation, a disparity in pay and other contract terms can be objectively justified on grounds of administrative efficiency.

The *Leverton* case has established that the hours of work can be a material factor in the case of salaried employees. Can they also be a factor when the claim is about the rate of pay of an hourly-paid worker?

Overtime working and shift working are both material factors which can justify a reasonable percentage uplift to arrive at overtime rates of pay and a shift premium; but can a disparity in basic rates of pay be justified where the complainant works *part time* and the comparator works full time?

If you have a higher basic rate of pay for full-time workers than part-time workers, you will need to produce an objective justification for this disparity if faced with an equal pay claim by one of the part-time workers. It is not enough to show that you have always had a lower rate of pay for part-time workers and that you are not intending to discriminate on grounds of sex. An old case where an objective justification was made out was that of *Handley v H Mono Limited* in 1978.

The complainant was a machinist, claiming the same rate of pay as male full-time workers. She worked two-thirds of the normal working week of 40 hours. When she was not working, her machine was idle. She received a lower hourly rate of pay than the full-time workers (of both sexes); if she had wished to increase her working week to 40 hours, the company would have allowed her to do so and would then have paid her at the higher rate.

It was held by the EAT that the difference in the hours worked was a material factor, but Mr Justice Slynn said:

> It is clear that this variation in pay would only be justified in a case where the difference in hours is a substantial one, and where there are special factors such as those relied on here, eg the utilisation of the equipment, the advanced receipt of higher [overtime] rates and the fact that 40-hour workers are treated alike be they men or women.

If part-time workers have a lower rate of pay than full-time workers or are excluded from other benefits enjoyed by the full-time workers, then there may also be a claim under Article 119 of the EC Treaty, unless the different treatment can be objectively justified. This principle was established by the leading European case of *Bilka-Kaufhaus v Von Hartz*. In this case a former employee complained about not receiving a pension which would have been payable if more of her service had been full-time rather than part-time. It was ruled by the European Court of Justice that the question to be considered was whether the rule excluding part-time workers (the majority of whom were women) was based on objectively justified factors unrelated to any discrimination on the ground of sex. It was stated by the House of Lords in *Rainey* (mentioned earlier in this chapter) that the requirement of objective justification is broadly the same whether the case involves:

(a) a claim under Article 119;
(b) the material factor defence to a claim under the EPA; or
(c) the justification of a requirement or condition in a claim of indirect discrimination (Chapter 3).

No sex discrimination
You cannot hope to succeed in a material factor defence if it is tainted by sex discrimination. This principle is expressly stated in the Act itself and has been emphasised by the courts on several occasions, for example by the House of Lords in *Hayward*.

A material factor defence would not succeed in the following examples:

(a) The complainant has a lower grade than that she would have had if she were a man; her early years of service were not counted because of past sex discrimination.

(b) The material factor on which you rely is that the pay rates for the two jobs have been freely negotiated through separate collective bargaining structures. However, women are not fairly represented in the collective bargaining arrangements. Moreover, excessive weight is given to the physical demands of the work done by the comparator and other men. They are paid more for lifting a few heavy weights each day and otherwise doing undemanding work; the complainant and other women are paid less, even though their work is intensive and demands considerable mental, as well as physical, effort.

Pensions

Although the law requires equal access to pension schemes, the EPA, like the SDA, does not cover pensions or lump sums paid on death, retirement or dismissal. It would have been surprising if Parliament had required equal pension ages under occupational pension schemes, having regard to the discrimination in pension ages under the state retirement scheme.

This exception was blown out of the water, however, by the decision of the European Court in the case of *Barber v Guardian Royal Exchange Assurance Group* in 1990. This case has already been mentioned, in Chapter 10, because the court ruled that redundancy and severance and other lump sum payments were to be regarded as pay within Article 119. The main issue in the case, however, was whether an immediate pension should have been paid.

The facts of the case, which are well known, can be outlined as follows. Under a contractual severance scheme, women who were made redundant at the age of 50 or more were entitled to an immediate pension; men qualified only if they were at least 55 when made redundant. Mr Barber was made redundant at the age of 52. While he received a greater lump sum payment than that which would have been paid to him if he had been a woman aged 52, he did not qualify for the immediate pension which he would have received if he had been a woman of that age. He would in fact have had to wait until he was 62 before any pension was payable to him; the extra lump sum payment was only partial compensation for the deferment of his pension.

Mr Barber had no claim under UK law, because of the exclusions contained in the SDA and the EPA. However, it was ruled by the European Court that a pension counts as pay and that he had been entitled, under Article 119 of the EC Treaty, to receive the immediate pension which would have been paid to him if he had been a woman of 52.

Furthermore, it was immaterial that the lump sum payment made to Mr Barber was greater than that which would have been made to a woman of 52. Each term of the severance scheme has to be looked at separately. Mr Barber was entitled to the immediate pension; a woman of 52 who had been made redundant could have claimed a lump sum payment calculated on the same basis as that made to Mr Barber.

The effect of the Barber case

The implications of the decision in *Barber* were potentially revolutionary. For example:

(a) Most occupational pension schemes had different pension ages for men and women, commonly 65 for men and 60 for women.
(b) These differences were reflected in most contractual and discretionary severance schemes, so that, for example, employees became entitled to an immediate pension if made redundant at the age of 60 or more for men but 55 or more for women.
(c) It was common for pension schemes to discriminate in other respects *against* women, both in the amount of pension payable and in the more favourable treatment given to dependants of male pensioners.

If the law had required all the effects of past inequality in these matters to be made good, the cost to the pensions industry and to employers would have been phenomenal. Accordingly, the European Court decided that the direct effect of Article 119 of the Treaty may not be relied upon (except by those who had already started proceedings) 'in order to claim entitlement to a pension with effect from a date prior to that of this judgment' (17 May 1990).

The difficulty is to determine exactly what the European Court meant by these words. There are at least the following possibilities:

1. With effect from 17 May 1990, the pensions and other benefits payable to former employees and their dependants under occupational pension schemes must be increased so far as necessary to match those which would have been payable if the employee had been of the other sex, irrespective of the date when the employee retired.
2. Employees who retire on or after 17 May 1990, and their dependants, are entitled to have their pensions and other benefits increased where necessary to match those which would have been payable if the employee had been of the other sex.
3. With effect from 17 May 1990, employers must change the basis

on which they fund their pension schemes, so that the benefits accrued in the future for employees and their dependants will be unaffected by the sex of the employee.

Until the ruling in *Barber* has been clarified in future cases, it is simply impossible to state which of the above approaches will be adopted or even to rule out some other possibility. If the true interpretation of *Barber* were to be that in (2) or particularly (1) above, then the cost to employers of providing improved pensions and other benefits would be very substantial. Pensions are paid out of funds accumulated over many years; if the contributions were too low, because they were made on legal assumptions which have been proved to be wrong, than the money has to be found to make good the shortfall in the fund. It is hoped that the law will be clarified by the *Coloroll* and other cases to be heard by the European Court during 1993.

Practical advice

There are two questions to be considered:

1. If you have a pension scheme, what steps should you take, particularly while the full implications of the *Barber* case remain to be resolved?
2. What steps should you take to prepare for the possibility of equal pay claims; and what should you do if a claim is made?

Pensions after Barber

Until the legal position has been clarified, few employers are likely to do anything to enhance the payments to employees who retired before 17 May 1990 and their dependants.

What of the expectations of existing employees and the payments to employees who have retired on or after 17 May 1990, or their dependants? The counsel of perfection is to arrange with the trustees to upgrade all benefits to the extent necessary to achieve full equality and to make the necessary contributions to the fund for that purpose. If your pension scheme has pension ages of 60 for women and 65 for men, this policy would involve:

(a) reducing the pension age for men to 60;
(b) giving enhanced benefits to men who are already over the age of 60, based on their service since that age.

For most employers, however, there are two objections to this policy, as follows:

(a) They cannot afford the extra funding for the scheme.
(b) It may turn out that the law requires less of them than this.

Accordingly, most employers fall into one of three groups:

(a) Those who are preening themselves on having already achieved equality in pension provision, long before *Barber*.
(b) Those who are adopting a 'wait and see' policy.
(c) Those who are removing differences in treatment as between men and women by downgrading to the lowest common denominator, for example by increasing the pension age of female employees, not reducing that of male employees.

It may be possible for employers who adopt the last mentioned policy to avoid wrongful or unfair dismissal complaints, so long as they give sufficient notice of termination of existing contracts and so long as there has first of all been adequate consultation. However, employers who adopt this approach could well face a successful challenge under the EPA or the EC Treaty; it is the policy of both the Act and the Treaty to achieve equality in an upwards, not a downwards direction. The question is likely to be determined by the European Court in one of the cases to be heard during 1993.

Equal pay

If an equal pay claim is brought against you, there are several disadvantages from your point of view. For example:

(a) Claims can be very expensive and time consuming.
(b) Where a claim is successful, the pay of your employees is being changed in a way over which you have no direct control.
(c) Equal value claims can have a significant knock-on effect, by reason of the decision in *Pickstone*, which was mentioned earlier in this chapter.

Avoiding claims — job evaluation

The most important step which you can take in order to minimise the risk of equal pay claims is to have a full job evaluation study carried out and put the study into effect. In *Leverton*, Lord Bridge said that:

> an employer's most effective safeguard against oppressive equal value claims is to initiate his own comprehensive job evaluation study under s.1(5) [of the EPA] which, if properly carried out, will afford him complete protection.

If the study gives different values to two jobs, then it will not be possible for the holder of either job to bring an equal pay claim naming the holder of the other job as comparator. However, you should note that Lord Bridge used the words 'if properly carried out'. The study will not give you a defence unless it is carried out on a proper and analytical basis, without any element of sex discrimination.

A job evaluation study is a sophisticated exercise and it is usual for expert consultants to be used. There should be consultation with any union recognised at the relevant establishment.

You should also note that job evaluation is not a cheap option; putting a study into effect will almost inevitably increase your overall wages bill. However, the study does enable you to approach matters in a comprehensive and orderly way, and in one over which you have some control.

The material factor defence

You may decide not to have a job evaluation study carried out, or you may wish to have different pay rates for jobs given the same value by the study, for example if you have a grading scheme based on skill or length of service.

In such circumstances, you should take the following steps:

1. Identify disparities in pay and other contract terms in cases where men and women are doing jobs which could be held to be like work or work of equal value.
2. Try to find out, if you do not know it, the reason for the disparity.
3. Consider whether the reason is one which objectively justifies the disparity.
4. Consider whether the disparity is partly the result of sex discrimination.
5. Move as quickly as possible to the elimination of all disparities which are inexplicable, not capable of objective justification or partly caused by sex discrimination.

Dealing with claims

If faced with an equal value claim, do not treat the preliminary hearing as a mere formality. In particular, you *must* raise any material factor defence at this stage; do not wait until after the matter has been referred to the independent expert.

If the matter goes to an independent expert and you wish to be able to challenge the report, then you will need to appoint your own expert as well.

If you are faced with a large number of similar claims (and a large number of comparators), try to reduce costs by agreeing on a small number of test cases. There will have to be one or more preliminary hearings for this purpose.

Remember that any victimisation of a complainant or witness will be dealt with under the SDA in the same way as direct discrimination. The matter is covered by the definition of victimisation even if the person victimised has only threatened to bring a complaint or if you suspect that he or she intends to bring a complaint.

Summary

1. A complaint can be made by an employee of either sex; complaints can relate to other contract terms and conditions as well as the rate of pay.
2. The complainant and the comparator must be 'in the same employment'.

3. An equal pay claim cannot succeed if the two jobs have been given different ratings under a job evaluation study which has been carried out properly and without discrimination.
4. The complainant must show that the two jobs:
   (a) have been given the same rating by a job evaluation study;
   (b) are 'like work'; or
   (c) are 'of equal value'.
5. A complaint can be defeated if it is shown that the difference in pay or contract terms complained of is:
   (a) genuinely due
   (b) to a factor which is material (viewed objectively) and
   (c) which is not the difference of sex.
6. Benefits under occupational pension schemes are pay within Article 119 of the EC Treaty. This Article can be relied on, in relation to pension entitlement, only with effect from 17 May 1990, but the precise effect of this limitation has still to be determined.

14
Discrimination Outside the Employment Field

If you are an employer, it is likely that you will also have customers, clients, patients, students or other purchasers or recipients of goods, facilities or services from you. With very few exceptions, you must ensure that there is no racial or sex discrimination in the way in which goods, facilities or services are provided to the public or any section of the public. It makes no difference whether you are a commercial organisation, receiving payment, or a Government department or local authority providing a facility or service for which no direct charge is imposed.

With one exception, the definition of discrimination is the same both in and outside the employment field. The only exception is that marriage discrimination is covered only in the employment field.

This chapter deals briefly with the following matters:
1. The extent and common examples of the duty not to discriminate.
2. General and specific exceptions.
3. The legal rights which the law also gives to you.
4. Practical advice.

Extent and common examples

Both the RRA and the SDA cover discrimination in relation to:
(a) the sale, renting and management of land and premises, and licences for the transfer of tenancies;
(b) entry into schools, universities and colleges and the treatment of pupils and students;
(c) the provision of other goods, facilities or services to the public or any section of the public, whether for payment or not.

The law also covers discriminatory advertisements and instructions and pressure to discriminate.

Territorial extent

The law covers acts of discrimination in relation to land and premises and educational establishments in Great Britain. The law also covers acts of discrimination in relation to goods, facilities or services provided in Great Britain and on most British ships, aircraft and hovercraft. Facilities for travel outside Great Britain are covered when they are provided by a travel agent or travel company in Great Britain or on a British ship, aircraft or hovercraft.

Racial discrimination

The following used to be some of the most common examples of discrimination against ethnic minority men and women in Great Britain:
(a) When seeking lodgings or a house or flat to rent, they were falsely told that there was no accommodation available.
(b) They were turned away from dance-halls and even public houses, and found it difficult to obtain membership of social and sporting clubs.
(c) Local authorities, in deciding on priorities for council-owned accommodation, would take into account nationality and length of residence in Great Britain.

Sex discrimination

The following were some of the most common examples of sex discrimination:
(a) Women had great difficulty in obtaining credit, whether from banks, building societies, hire purchase companies or stores.
(b) Even where credit was not refused altogether, women had to provide a male guarantor.
(c) The income of a woman was disregarded, or given little weight, when she and her husband applied for a mortgage advance, even when she earned more than he did.
(d) Women faced similar discrimination when trying to obtain tenancies of shops and other business premises.
(e) There was discrimination at schools against girls wishing to take technical subjects and boys wishing to take domestic science.

Indirect discrimination

All the above examples are cases of direct racial and sex discrimination. The following is an example of indirect discrimination.

Your store refuses credit to residents of a particular district, because of a high rate of default in the past. This district has a much higher than average ethnic minority population. Your policy involves indirect racial discrimination and is unlawful. You should make decisions on the income and personal circumstances of each individual applicant for credit.

The case of *Mandla v Lee*, mentioned below, is another example of indirect discrimination, this time in the field of education.

Motive irrelevant

The examples of discrimination given above are now far less common than they were in the two decades before and a few years after the current discrimination laws came into force (in the mid-1970s). There has been a considerable change of attitudes on the part of local authorities, major financial institutions, manufacturers and retailers, and other public and private sector organisations.

Discrimination is also unlawful, however, if it takes place as a result of some benevolent motive, unless it is covered by one of the exceptions mentioned later in this chapter. For example:

(a) Your bank, conscious of the difficulties experienced by many women in obtaining business finance, offers favourable lending terms to women starting a business; a man going into business for the first time has to pay more. This direct sex discrimination is unlawful.

(b) You are director of housing of a local authority. On one particular estate, nearly all the tenants are of Asian origin. You take the view that it would be in the interests of good race relations to have a more balanced racial mix on the estate. Accordingly, when a couple of Asian origin apply for a house on the estate, their application is refused and they are offered a tenancy on another estate; the vacant house which they wished to occupy is instead offered to a white couple who had wished to live on another estate. The direct racial discrimination against both couples is unlawful, however good your motive.

Unintentional discrimination

It has already been explained, in Chapter 2, that an act can fall within the definition of direct discrimination even if you had not intended to discriminate. This principle was clearly established by the case of *James v Eastleigh Borough Council*. This was the case where a man of 61 had to pay to use the local swimming pool; if he had been a woman of 61 he would have been a pensioner and would therefore have been allowed in free.

A similar approach had been adopted by the House of Lords in the earlier case of *R v Birmingham City Council, ex parte Equal Opportunities Commission*. In Birmingham, there were eight selective secondary schools, all single-sex. However, five of them were for boys and only three for girls. This meant that there were many more places for boys than for girls and that girls needed to reach a higher standard than boys in order to be sure of obtaining a place. The officers of the council recommended a number of possible options to remove this discrimination against girls, but there was no easy answer and the matter was deferred so that further options could be investigated.

It was held by the House of Lords that there had been direct sex discrimination by the council in carrying out its functions as local education authority. It was immaterial that there was no intention or motive on the part of the council to discriminate; it was sufficient that, because of their sex, girls received less favourable treatment than boys.

This case and *James v Eastleigh* had important implications for employment cases, as explained in Chapters 2 and 4. Another important case which dealt with discrimination outside the employment field but which had implications for employers as well was *Mandla v Lee*, the indirect discrimination case involving a young Sikh schoolboy, which was referred to in Chapter 3.

General exceptions

The general exceptions referred to in Chapter 7 also apply to discrimination outside the employment field. These are the exceptions relating to charitable benefits, sport, statutory discrimination, national security and, under the SDA, communal accommodation.

The following are examples in the education field of the exceptions relating to charitable benefits and sport:

(a) A 19th century benefactor endowed a scholarship for girls born in Wales. The trustees are entitled to comply with the terms of the trust, so that boys, wherever born, and girls not born in Wales can be denied the opportunity of competing for the scholarship. The trustees (or the governing body) can apply to the Secretary of State for Education for the trust to be modified to enable boys to benefit, so long as the application is made either more than 25 years after the creation of the trust or with the written consent of the donor or his personal representatives. Any restrictions on grounds of colour (for example to *white* girls born in Wales) must be disregarded in any event.

(b) There may be discrimination in the selection of sports teams or participation in sporting events, 'where the physical strength, stamina or physique of the average woman puts her at a disadvantage to the average man'. Accordingly, girls may lawfully be excluded from the boys' football team and boys may lawfully be excluded from the girls' hockey team. It could be unlawful, however, for a school to refuse to allow boys to play hockey against other boys or girls to play football against other girls, where there is a genuine desire to do so on the part of the students involved.

The exception in the SDA for statutory discrimination is wider than it is for discrimination in the employment field. It is, for example, lawful for clerks in the DSS to discriminate by paying pensions to women at the age of 60 but not paying men until they reach the age of 65; they are protected because this discrimination is necessary for them to comply with legislation which was in force when the SDA was passed.

The extent to which the law permits positive action in providing vocational training has already been explained in Chapter 8. So long as the statistical conditions are complied with, local authorities, educational establishments and others can lawfully discriminate under these provisions.

Employers can also, of course, take advantage of the positive action exceptions when they provide work experience or other training. At the same time you should bear in mind that discrimination not covered by the exception could be unlawful. For example, you arrange with a local school to provide work experience to a number of the students. In doing so you are providing a service to a section of the public. It is immaterial that you receive no payment for doing so. If you insist that you will only allow girls to gain work experience on secretarial work and only allow boys to gain work experience on the shop floor, this sex discrimination is unlawful.

The 'special needs' exception under the RRA, which is also explained in Chapter 8, also applies outside the employment field. A local authority or school can, for example, lawfully provide special language classes for the ethnic minorities.

There is also, in the SDA only, a general exception relating to insurance. This exception relates to any kind of annuity, life assurance policy, accident insurance policy or similar matter involving the assessment of risk. Under Section 45 of the SDA, discrimination is permitted:

(a)   if it is effected by reference to actuarial or other data;
(b)   if this data comes from a source on which it is reasonable to rely; and
(c)   if the discrimination is reasonable having regard to the data and any other relevant factors.

The above exception means that, for example, a man may have to pay a higher premium than a woman of the same age for life assurance, because actuarial data shows that she is likely to live longer; on the other hand, and for the same reason, she may have to pay more for a pension or annuity.

Both in and outside the employment field, the definition of direct discrimination excludes special treatment for women in connection with pregnancy or child birth. Men can have no complaint on the ground that they cannot qualify for social security benefits and special medical treatment which are received only by pregnant women.

Specific exceptions

There are specific provisions in the legislation under which discrimination is occasionally permitted in:

1. The disposal or management of land and premises.
2. Admission to educational establishments and the treatment of pupils or students.

3. The provision of other goods, facilities or services to the public or a section of the public.

Land and premises

Both the SDA and the RRA contain exceptions of very limited importance permitting discrimination in the sale or letting of premises by an owner-occupier. The reason why this exception is unimportant in practice is that it does not apply if the services of an estate agent are used and it does not apply either if any advertisement is published. The definition of advertisement includes not only newspaper advertisements, but even a board in the garden or a notice in the window.

There is also an exception for letting (or selling) part of a building for residential purposes, so long as the following conditions are complied with:

(a) The building must also be occupied by the landlord or a near relative of the landlord.
(b) The building must not normally provide residential accommodation for more than three households (including that of the landlord or his near relative).
(c) The building must include accommodation (other than storage or access) which is shared by the different households occupying it.

There is also a provision permitting discrimination when taking in lodgers, so long as there are not more than six lodgers in all and so long as they will be sharing accommodation (other than storage or access) with the household of the person agreeing to take them in (or a near relative of that person).

Education

The SDA permits any school or college or other educational establishment to be run as a 'single-sex establishment'. This status is enjoyed if an establishment admits pupils or students of one sex only. The single-sex status is also retained in the following circumstances:

(a) If there are pupils of the opposite sex whose admission is exceptional.
(b) If pupils of the opposite sex are admitted in comparatively small numbers for particular courses or classes.

Where an establishment takes both boarders and day pupils, the latter may be disregarded for the purpose of ascertaining whether sex discrimination in the admission of boarders is lawful.

There has, of course, been a trend for single-sex educational establishments to become co-educational. It is possible for the body responsible for an establishment to apply for a 'transitional exemption order' so that the conversion can take place in stages. Local education authorities apply to the Secretary of State; applications in the private sector go to the EOC.

Under the RRA, special provision may be made for students who are not ordinarily resident in Great Britain and who intend to leave the country after their period of education or training.

Goods, facilities and services

The SDA contains a special provision relating to services. A person such as a tailor or a dressmaker who provides a skilled service to customers who are normally all of the same sex cannot be compelled to exercise his or her skill in a *different* way for customers of the opposite sex.

Although both the RRA and the SDA generally apply to the provision of goods, facilities or services on British ships, aircraft and hovercraft, there is an exception when the vessel enters the jurisdiction of some other country. Any act of discrimination which is necessary for the purpose of complying with that country's laws is permitted.

Both Acts also contain a special provision permitting discrimination in the provision of grants, loans, credit, finance and other banking and insurance facilities for an overseas venture, or in connection with risks arising outside Great Britain.

Clubs and associations

There is an important distinction between the RRA and the SDA in the way in which clubs and associations are treated.

Under the RRA, it is unlawful for any club or association with 25 or more members to discriminate against an applicant for membership, either by not accepting his application or in the terms on which membership is offered. It is also unlawful for such a club or association to discriminate against members or associate members.

There is an exception for associations which genuinely have as their main object the provision of the benefits of membership to persons of a particular racial group defined otherwise than by reference to colour. For example, an association for West Indians may lawfully exclude any applicant for membership who is not of West Indian origin. However, it would not be lawful to exclude an applicant of West Indian origin because he or she has a white skin.

The SDA has a very wide exception for voluntary bodies. Single-sex voluntary bodies which are permitted to practise sex discrimination range from small local clubs and societies to national and international organisations, such as Rotary, the Women's Institute, the Boy Scouts and the Girl Guides.

The SDA also permits political parties and affiliated organisations to make special provision for persons of either sex (for instance by having a separate women's branch).

A club or association which is carried on for profit (which applies to many social or sporting clubs) may discriminate on grounds of sex if the club or association is genuinely private. If, for example, a social club run on commercial lines were to give membership automatically to every man who applied, then discrimination in turning down applications from women would be unlawful. If, on the other hand, there is a genuine admission and selection procedure, then sex discrimination is permitted.

Responsibility for agents and employees

If one of your employees or an agent discriminates, the rules are the same as those which apply in the employment field.

You are fully responsible for any discrimination by an employee acting in the course of his or her employment, whether or not you knew or approved of the discrimination. The only exception is if you had taken all reasonably practicable steps to prevent the act of discrimination or acts of that kind.

For example, you own a night club. The 'bouncers' turn away a group of young black men, on the ground that they are not suitably dressed, but at the same time allow in a group of young white men who are identically dressed. You will be held accountable for this racial discrimination unless you have taken all reasonably practicable steps to prevent it. You should at least have given explicit instructions to your staff and made it clear that racial discrimination will be dealt with as a serious disciplinary offence.

Similarly, you will be held responsible for any discrimination by your agent acting within the scope of his or her express or implied authority.

Provisions for your benefit

There are several circumstances in which, particularly if you have a small business, you may find yourself in the position of complainant rather than defendant. When you are seeking business premises, applying for business credit or finance, or purchasing goods or services for your business, you are entitled to be treated in a way which does not involve any racial or sex discrimination. For example:

(a) You are of Asian origin and have started a new business. Your application for a business tenancy is turned down because this is your first business venture and you do not have any trade references. However, a white person who applied for the adjoining unit was granted a tenancy, even though this was his first business venture as well. Unless a satisfactory explanation can be given for this difference in treatment, there has been direct racial discrimination against you.

(b) You are a woman, running your own business. A wholesaler refuses to give you his normal credit terms, unless you have your account guaranteed by your husband. This is a clear case of direct sex discrimination.

Practical advice

It is important that you should give clear instructions and, where necessary, training to your staff to ensure that there is no discrimination in the way in which they treat your customers, clients, patients and students. It is particularly important that guidance and training be given to staff who are meeting or speaking to the public on a regular basis, such as:

- receptionists and telephonists;
- shop assistants and sales representatives;
- bank and building society staff;
- estate and travel agency staff;
- transport staff;
- employees at places of entertainment and recreation;
- staff at job centres and benefit offices;
- Inland Revenue staff and customs officials;
- police officers;
- teachers.

Local authorities have particularly comprehensive responsibilities. Many local authorities are:

- major employers;
- responsible for schools and colleges;
- landlords of rented accommodation on a large scale;
- providers of a wide range of facilities and services;
- collectors of local taxes.

The positive approach is to encourage employees who deal with the public not only to avoid discrimination but also to make a favourable impression on the members of the public who have dealings with the organisation, by treating them fairly, efficiently and courteously.

Summary

1. The law forbids racial and sex discrimination in relation to:
    (a) the sale or letting and management of land and premises;
    (b) admission to educational establishments and the treatment of pupils or students;
    (c) the provision of goods, facilities or services to the public or a section of the public, for payment or not.

2. The law relating to the following matters is the same, both in and outside the employment field:
   (a) discriminatory advertisements;
   (b) instructions and pressure to discriminate;
   (c) responsibility for employees and agents.
3. Generally the law applies only to Great Britain, but it also covers discrimination in relation to facilities provided in Great Britain for travel overseas and also discrimination on most British ships, aircraft and hovercraft.
4. The general exceptions are broadly the same as in the employment field, ie statutory discrimination, national security, sport, charitable benefits, special needs (under the RRA) and communal accommodation (under the SDA).
5. There are also specific exceptions, of which the most important are:
   (a) provision for single-sex educational establishments;
   (b) exceptions under the SDA only for voluntary clubs and associations;
   (c) an exception under the SDA only for other clubs and associations which have a genuine admissions procedure;
   (d) an exception under the RRA for clubs and associations which have fewer than 25 members or which exist for the benefit of members of a particular racial group defined otherwise than by reference to colour.

Part II
Legal Procedures

15
Dealing with Complaints by Individuals

If a job applicant or employee complains of discrimination, the complaint will be heard by an industrial tribunal. The rules of procedure are similar to those relating to other tribunal cases, such as complaints of unfair dismissal. Most employers have at least some knowledge of the procedure, which will not therefore be explained in detail. There are special rules for equal value cases.

Anyone complaining of discrimination by you outside the employment field will pursue the matter by way of county court proceedings. There are court rules which apply to all civil cases in the county court. It is likely that you will be legally represented in any such proceedings, and accordingly it is not proposed to spell out the basic rules of procedure.

There are, however, some special or unusual features of discrimination cases, both in and outside the employment field. The matters covered in this chapter are:

1. The questionnaire procedure.
2. The rules for disclosure of documents.
3. Time limits.
4. Compensation.
5. Practical advice.

The questionnaire procedure

Under both the SDA (Section 74) and the RRA (Section 65) there is a procedure under which the complainant can put questions to you. If, for example, a job applicant has been refused an interview and sex discrimination is suspected, the questions could include:

(a) How many men and how many women applied for the job?
(b) How many of each sex were offered interviews?
(c) What, if any, criteria were laid down for the job?
(d) Were a job description and person specification or similar documents prepared? If so please supply a copy.

(e) What were the qualifications and experience of each candidate who was offered an interview?
(f) Why was I refused an interview?
(g) How many similar posts have been filled in the last 12 months?
(h) On each occasion, how many men and how many women applied? How many men and how many women were shortlisted?
(i) How many comparable posts are there in the organisation? How many of them are held by men and how many by women?
(j) Does the organisation have an equal opportunity policy? If so please supply a copy.

These questions may be sent to you before proceedings are commenced. In employment cases they may also be sent to you within 21 days after the commencement of the industrial tribunal proceedings. The time limits can be extended by the industrial tribunal or county court (as the case may be).

You are not obliged to answer the questions. However, the court or tribunal can draw an appropriate inference, including an inference that you have unlawfully discriminated, if you:

(a) omit to reply within a reasonable period and do so deliberately and without reasonable excuse; or
(b) give replies which are evasive or equivocal.

It is important therefore that you should reply promptly and fully to the questions. You must also ensure that the information given is correct and consistent with the evidence which will be given at the hearing. Suppose that in the above example you had overstated the qualifications of one of the shortlisted candidates. At the hearing the tribunal could well draw the inference that you were giving a false reason for having shortlisted this person and were doing so because there had in fact been discrimination.

If the questions include any which are irrelevant or oppressive, you should give all the information which is relevant and which it is reasonably practicable for you to supply and state clearly why you are unable or unwilling to answer the remaining questions. If, for example, you are asked about thousands of previous job applications, you should deal only with the last few and, if practicable, give a summary of the remainder.

There are at least four reasons why you should answer the questionnaire promptly and as fully as possible. They are:

(a) If you do not, the court or tribunal may draw an adverse inference.
(b) If, on the other hand, you have clearly and cogently set out the reason for the treatment complained of, you may thereby influence the court or tribunal in your favour.
(c) The information given may persuade the complainant that there are no grounds for the complaint and that he or she should not proceed.

(d) Even if the complainant is not convinced, any organisation which is proposing to fund or back the complaint, such as the EOC, the CRE or a union, may decide in the light of your reply not to do so.

Documents

Most complaints of discrimination involve a comparison of the complainant's treatment with that of some fellow employee or that of at least one other job applicant. Furthermore, in order for a court or tribunal to establish whether there has been discrimination, it is often necessary for documents relating to the other employee or job applicant to be produced by you. For example:

(a) A black job applicant complains that there has been racial discrimination in not shortlisting him for a job. It will be necessary for the industrial tribunal to look not only at the complainant's own application form but at those of the candidates who were shortlisted.
(b) A woman who was interviewed for a job complains that there was sex discrimination in appointing a man to the post and not appointing her. The relevant documents include the application form and interview notes in respect of the successful candidate.
(c) An employee of Asian origin complains that he has been kept in a low grade, while a white colleague has been promoted. Documents such as annual appraisals relating to both the complainant and the white colleague will be relevant.

The question whether documents of this kind should be disclosed, even though they are confidential to other job applicants and employees, was considered by the House of Lords in 1979 in the case of *Science Research Council v Nassé*). Two principles were laid down:

1. An order should not be made automatically for the disclosure of a confidential document simply because the document is or could be relevant to the proceedings.
2. However, the judge or tribunal chairman should read the document and should order its disclosure, notwithstanding its confidentiality, if disclosure is *necessary* for disposing fairly of the proceedings or to save costs.

Precautions are commonly taken to protect the identity of other job applicants and employees, for example by blanking out their names and addresses and identifying them by means of code letters. Precautions of this kind are important, because generally tribunal and court proceedings take place in public.

Whether or not documents are confidential, you can also resist an application for disclosure if the request which has been made by the complainant would be oppressive towards you because of the large number of documents involved. In the 1979 case of *British Railways*

Board v Natarajan, a member of the management staff complained of racial discrimination in an assessment of his performance and potential which was made in July 1977. He asked the board to disclose the annual appraisals and assessment sheets relating to himself and six colleagues for each of the years 1974, 1975, 1976 and 1977. He also asked for the weekly work diaries and progress report sheets of himself and these six colleagues for the whole of 1977. The EAT adopted the following approach:

(a) The weekly work diaries and progress report sheets were not confidential, but there were many of them and they were of doubtful relevance. Accordingly, only those for the four weeks prior to the date of the assessment were to be disclosed.

(b) The annual appraisals and assessments on the six colleagues were confidential. Those for 1974, 1975 and 1976 were not relevant. However, the appraisals for 1977 could just possibly be relevant. The tribunal chairman should look at them to see if there was any relevant material in them and, if there was such material, order disclosure.

Time limits

The questionnaire procedure and documents have been considered consecutively because there is some relation between them. However, before you even reach the stage of disclosure of documents in the proceedings, there is the question whether the proceedings have been commenced in time. There are very strict time limits in both industrial tribunal cases and county court proceedings.

In employment cases, both the SDA (in Section 76) and the RRA (in Section 68) provide that the tribunal application must be made within three months after the act or omission complained of. This time limit is the same as that which applies in unfair dismissal cases.

In non-employment cases, the time limit is six months from the date of the act or omission complained of. This time limit is very much shorter than the time limit of six years (or three years in personal injury cases) which applies to most county court proceedings.

Both industrial tribunals and county court judges have the power to extend the time limit where it is 'just and equitable' to do so. This is a very broad discretion but it is one which is rarely exercised. The following are examples of cases which could be heard out of time:

(a) The complainant, a job applicant, has only recently found out that the person of the opposite sex who was appointed had inferior qualifications to those of the complainant.

(b) The tribunal application was posted in time but held up in the post.

(c) The complaint is based on a recent change in the law and the matters complained of are still so recent that it would be reasonable for the complaint to proceed.

(d) You are a public sector employer and the complaint is based on your breach of an EC Directive.

There are two main reasons why in general time limits are strictly enforced:

(a) Complaints of discrimination are usually difficult both to prove and to disprove. The more time goes by, the more difficult it is to establish the truth.
(b) Complaints of discrimination can be very sensitive, particularly where a person who is still employed is complaining of such matters as sexual and racial harassment. It is desirable in the interests of employee relations and of the individuals concerned (both the complainant and the alleged harasser) that such complaints be dealt with quickly.

Equal pay

In the case of *Dodd v British Telecom plc*, the view was taken that because of a quirk in the drafting of the Equal Pay Act there is no time limit for claims under that Act. The practical consequences of this decision were mitigated by the fact that the compensation awarded could not cover any back pay for a period of more than two years before the date of the tribunal application. If, therefore, a claim was brought more than two years after the complainant had ceased to be employed by you, no compensation could be awarded.

In the much more recent case of *Etherson v Strathclyde Regional Council* a different approach has been adopted. It was decided that there is a time limit and that complaints must be brought during or within six months after the complainant's employment.

Continuing discrimination

A claim about racial discrimination in relation to rates of pay or other contract terms is to be brought under the RRA, just like any other complaint of racial discrimination. If there is discrimination in the rate of pay or any other contract term, then generally that discrimination will continue so long as the inequality in pay or contract terms remains. The rule, under both the RRA and the SDA, for an act of discrimination extending over a period is that the time limit of three months does not start to run until the continuing discrimination comes to an end.

Continuing discrimination is often alleged in sexual harassment cases, where incidents occur with great frequency over a period of several months. The question in each case is whether a campaign of sexual harassment amounts to a series of separate acts or a single act extending over a period. The question is essentially one of degree.

A further difficult distinction which can arise is that between an act of discrimination extending over a period and a single act which has continuing consequences. The following cases illustrate this distinction.

In *Barclays Bank v Kapur*, bank clerks of Asian origin complained that previous service in Africa was not taken into account for pension purposes. They complained several years after the decision to disallow their earlier service, but it was held by the House of Lords that there was a continuing act of discrimination so long as they were required to work on the less favourable terms relating to their pensionable service. Accordingly, the complaints were not out of time.

Similarly, in *Calder v James Finlay Corporation Limited*, a woman complained of discrimination in excluding her from a mortgage subsidy scheme. Her most recent application to join the scheme had been refused more than three months before her complaint was brought. However, there was continuing discrimination against her so long as the scheme continued to operate in a discriminatory way and so long as she remained employed. Accordingly, her complaint was in time because it had been made within the three months after she left her employment.

On the other hand, in the recent case of *Sougrin v Haringey Health Authority*, a black nurse complained of racial discrimination against her in the course of a regrading exercise. Her complaint was brought more than three months after the grading decision, but it was argued on her behalf that there was continuing discrimination so long as she remained in the lower grade. It was held by the Court of Appeal that the grading decision was a one-off decision with continuing consequences. There was no question of a rule or policy under which black employees were paid less than white employees. Accordingly, the complaint was out of time.

Previous acts of discrimination

Where more than three months have elapsed since an act of discrimination against one of your employees, this does not mean that the act can no longer be relied on in any proceedings. Although a complaint based on that act will probably be ruled out of time, the act may nevertheless be relied on in any industrial tribunal proceedings relating to a subsequent allegation of discrimination. The earlier incident of discrimination may be linked to or part of the essential background to some subsequent unfavourable treatment of the complainant. This principle was established in 1982 in the case of *Din v Carrington Viyella Limited*.

Amending the complaint

Sometimes, where a complaint is made within the three month time limit, the complainant then wishes to amend it by adding additional heads of complaint. For example, the complaint may refer only to unfair dismissal and the complainant may now wish to add a claim of racial or sex discrimination.

Amendments are generally permitted if the new head of complaint is based on the same facts as those set out in the original complaint.

However, leave to amend is far more likely to be refused if the amendment relates to new and unrelated allegations.

Leave can also be given by the tribunal to amend a complaint by adding the name of an additional party. If, for example, there is a racial or sexual harassment complaint against you, then the proceedings may be amended by adding the alleged harasser as an additional respondent.

Preliminary hearing

Where a question of time limits arises in employment cases, the industrial tribunal may well hold a preliminary hearing to determine the point. A hearing of this kind should be distinguished from the other hearings which are sometimes held before the full hearing in employment cases. These other hearings are:

1. An interlocutory hearing, to settle procedural disputes, for example whether some particular document must be disclosed.
2. A pre-hearing assessment, which is a formal hearing (but without evidence being taken) to determine whether the complaint or the answer to it (or any specific contention by either party) has a reasonable prospect of success. If it is found that there is no reasonable prospect of success, then a 'costs warning' can be given to the party in question. The procedure is now adopted far less commonly than it used to be in discrimination cases.
3. The pre-hearing discussion. This is an informal meeting, the purpose of which is to clarify the issues and to resolve such matters as the number of days required for the full hearing.

Compensation

The remedies which can be awarded to a successful complainant in an employment case are:

1. A finding of unlawful discrimination.
2. An order for compensation.
3. A recommendation that action be taken within a specified period to obviate or reduce the adverse effect of the discrimination on the complainant.

An example of a recommendation would be that an unsuccessful job applicant or promotion candidate be automatically shortlisted for the next suitable vacancy. If, without reasonable excuse, you fail to comply with a recommendation, then the complainant can come back for more compensation.

In practice, compensation is the more important remedy. If the complainant has suffered some financial loss as a result of the discrimination, then compensation can be awarded in respect of that loss. Compensation for financial loss usually arises where there is discrimination in not appointing or promoting a person to a job, or discrimination in dismissing an employee.

Loss of opportunity

In complaints relating to job applications and promotion decisions, compensation of a modest amount can be awarded even where it is likely that without any discrimination the complainant would have been unsuccessful. The compensation in these cases is for the complainant's loss of opportunity.

Injury to feelings

Whether or not there has been any financial loss, compensation can also be awarded to a successful complainant for injury to feelings. This head of compensation is for the annoyance, worry, distress or humiliation caused by the discrimination.

Compensation for injury to feelings can be awarded in both employment and non-employment cases. The Court of Appeal, in two cases in 1988, considered the principles on which compensation should be awarded.

In *Alexander v The Home Office*, a black prisoner complained of racial discrimination in not permitting him to work in the prison kitchens. The county court judge awarded compensation of £50 for injury to feelings. The Court of Appeal increased the award to £500. Although the discrimination was aggravated by the way in which the prisoner had been appraised, it was found that he had not suffered any substantial injury to his feelings and it was said in the Court of Appeal that the case 'was not one of the most serious'. Nevertheless, awards:

> should not be minimal, because this would tend to trivialise or diminish respect for the public policy to which the Act gives effect. On the other hand, just because it is impossible to assess the monetary value of injured feelings, awards should be restrained.

In *Noone v North West Thames Regional Health Authority*, there was a finding that there had been racial discrimination against the complainant in dealing with her application for a post as a consultant microbiologist. She had superior qualifications, experience and publications to the successful candidate and no satisfactory explanation was given. The amount of compensation eventually awarded was £3,000. The Court of Appeal said that there had been severe injury to feelings and that an award at the top end of the bracket was appropriate.

The upper limit

The law fixes a maximum amount which can be awarded as compensation in discrimination cases. The principle of limiting the compensation, where a breach of EC law is involved, is currently under challenge, by Mrs Marshall (see page 146)

The maximum is equivalent to that of the compensatory award in unfair dismissal cases. The current limit is £10,000.

Where, however, there is an actual or constructive dismissal, the complainant, if he or she has more than two years' service, can complain of unfair dismissal as well as discrimination. The maximum compensation for the unfair dismissal can be more than £25,000, because there can be a basic award and additional award as well as the compensatory award.

Non-employment cases

There is no limit on the amount of compensation which can be awarded by the county court judge in non-employment cases. Both the SDA (in Section 66) and the RRA (in Section 57) provide that the county court can award whatever remedies would be available in High Court proceedings. These include unlimited damages and an injunction.

Where proceedings are brought in Scotland, they are heard by a sheriff court, not a county court, and the rules of procedure are quite different from those which apply to cases heard in the county court in England and Wales.

Indirect discrimination

As mentioned in earlier chapters, compensation cannot be awarded against you in a case of indirect discrimination (whether in or outside the employment field) if you can show that there was no discriminatory intention behind the treatment complained of.

Practical advice

When you become aware of a complaint of discrimination you should investigate quickly but thoroughly.

If the complaint is not well founded, your prompt and thorough investigation will ensure that the evidence to resist the complaint is collected while it is still fresh. You should then respond fully and consistently to the allegations of discrimination, whether made by way of the questionnaire or in tribunal or court proceedings.

If, on the other hand, your investigations show that there is substance in the complaint, you should offer redress and not insist on fighting the matter out in the industrial tribunal or county court. If you act promptly, you may be able to satisfy the complainant without the need for proceedings. In an employment case, where tribunal proceedings have already been commenced, you should negotiate through an ACAS conciliation officer.

Technical defences

If you are an equal opportunity employer, would it be right for you to rely on a technical defence, particularly the point that the complaint is out of time? If you believe that the allegations made are not justified, there can be no moral objection to reliance on a technical as well as a substantive defence. This is particularly so where delay in commencing proceedings has made it more difficult for you to investigate and find out what happened. Furthermore, since the question is one of jurisdiction, the court or tribunal may well raise the question of time limits even if you do not.

Equal pay cases

Remember that if you are facing an equal value claim you must raise the material factor defence at an early stage, so that it can be considered at the preliminary hearing. If you do not raise the defence until after the independent expert has been appointed, you will be out of time.

Avoiding victimisation

It is important that you should give the clearest possible instructions to managers and other employees that there must be no victimisation as a result of any formal or informal complaint of discrimination. Those entitled to protection from victimisation include witnesses and potential witnesses as well as the complainant.

Furthermore, no pressure of any kind must be used to persuade the complainant not to proceed or the witnesses not to give evidence.

Summary

1. Complaints of discrimination in the employment field are heard by industrial tribunals; non-employment cases go to the county court (or sheriff court in Scotland).
2. The complainant can use the questionnaire procedure to obtain relevant information; an adverse inference can be drawn if the respondent fails to reply or gives evasive answers.
3. The court or tribunal will order the disclosure of relevant documents, including confidential documents which are necessary to the fair disposal of the proceedings.
4. There is a time limit for bringing proceedings. In employment cases the time limit is three months; in non-employment cases the time limit is six months. In both cases the time limit runs from the date of the act complained of (or from the date when continuing discrimination comes to an end).
5. The compensation in non-employment cases is unlimited; there is a limit, currently £10,000, in employment cases. In both cases, the amount awarded can include compensation for injury to feelings.

16
The Role of the Commissions

The Equal Opportunities Commission (EOC) and the Commission for Racial Equality (CRE) are both given several different roles by the SDA and the RRA respectively. They are required to:
(a) work towards the elimination of discrimination;
(b) promote equality of opportunity between men and women generally (in the case of the EOC) and between persons of different racial groups (in the case of the CRE);
(c) promote good race relations (in the case of the CRE);
(d) keep under review the working of the legislation and make proposals for amending it.

It will be seen from the first two of these functions that the commissions have both a negative and a positive role. The negative side is their function of working to prevent unlawful discrimination; the positive side is that of promoting equal opportunity and good race relations.

The positive role

This positive role of the commissions is one which should not be overlooked. Many employers have approached the commissions for information and advice on equal opportunity policies and other matters. The commissions are always ready to respond to an approach of this kind, so far as funding and staffing levels permit. They recognise the importance of encouraging employers to have a positive commitment to equal opportunity.

The EOC has also promoted an Equality Exchange, which equal opportunity employers can join at a modest cost. Having joined, they can receive information from the commission and attend meetings and conferences in order to exchange information and ideas with other equal opportunity employers.

Both commissions have also published a wide range of guidance notes and other documents, some of which are free.

The address and telephone number of the main office of the EOC is:

Equal Opportunities Commission
Overseas House
Quay Street
Manchester M3 3HN
Tel: 061 833 9244

The EOC also has offices in Glasgow and Cardiff.

The address and telephone number of the head office of the CRE is:

Commission for Racial Equality
Elliot House
10–12 Allington Street
London SW1E 5EH
Tel: 071 828 7022

The CRE also has offices in Edinburgh, Manchester, Birmingham, Leeds and Leicester.

The enforcement role

One of the important enforcement functions given to the commissions is that of advising and funding individual complainants. There are also steps which the commissions can take directly against employers and others in order to prevent repeated unlawful acts.

Chapter 12 dealt with proceedings by the commissions in respect of discriminatory practices, unlawful advertisements and instructions and pressure to discriminate unlawfully. Both the RRA (in Section 63) and the SDA (in Section 72) give the relevant commission the power to apply to a county court (or sheriff court in Scotland) for an injunction or order to prevent a further infringement. For example, an advertisement which you place for a job vacancy indicates an intention to discriminate on racial grounds. The CRE brings a tribunal complaint against you and obtains a finding that you have acted unlawfully. You inform the CRE and the tribunal that you intend to continue to place similar advertisements. The tribunal cannot prevent you from doing so, but the CRE can apply to a county court for an injunction. You will then be at risk of being committed to prison for contempt if you persist in defying the law.

There is an important distinction between unlawful acts in the employment field and those outside the employment field. If, for example, you instruct staff to discriminate unlawfully against customers, the finding that you have acted unlawfully and the injunction not to act in a similar way in the future can be obtained in the same county court proceedings; where the act complained of is in the employment field, however, it is necessary for the commission to obtain a finding that you have acted unlawfully from an industrial tribunal, before going to the county court for an injunction.

Persistent discrimination

The same principle applies where one of the commissions wishes to prevent repeated discrimination in the employment field or a repeated infringement of the Equal Pay Act. An application for an injunction must be based either on a non-discrimination notice or on an industrial tribunal finding that you have acted unlawfully. The procedure relating to non-discrimination notices is explained below. Where the application for an injunction is based on a tribunal finding, there are two ways in which this can be obtained, as follows:

(a) as a result of a complaint, of the type considered in Chapter 15, brought by an individual; or
(b) as a result of preliminary action by one of the commissions to obtain a finding that you have acted unlawfully.

Both the SDA (in Section 73) and the RRA (in Section 64) give the relevant commission the power to make a complaint to an industrial tribunal in order to obtain a finding that you have acted unlawfully. Where the complaint is brought by the EOC, the commission can seek a finding that you have infringed either the SDA or the EPA.

Once the finding has been obtained, the commission can then apply to the county court for an injunction if it appears likely that you intend to break the law again.

Formal investigations

As mentioned above, an application for an injunction can also be based on a non-discrimination notice. However, a notice can only be served on you as a result of a formal investigation into your activities. Accordingly, the starting point is to look at the rules which apply to formal investigations.

Formal investigations are of two kinds. There are general investigations, for example into patterns of discrimination in a whole industry. There are also investigations into the activities of a named person (whether an individual, a company or some other organisation). It is only investigations of the latter kind which can lead to a non-discrimination notice.

A commission carrying out a formal investigation has very extensive powers. For example:

(a) The commission can serve notices requiring the attendance of witnesses and production of documents.
(b) If a notice is ignored or defied, the commission can apply to a county court for an order to compel compliance.
(c) It is an offence to alter, suppress, conceal or destroy documents which you have been required to produce.
(d) It is also an offence knowingly or recklessly to give false information.

There are, however, several safeguards for your protection. The following rules must be complied with before a formal investigation can result in a non-discrimination notice against you:

1. The commission cannot launch the investigation unless it has at least a suspicion, albeit on tenuous grounds, that you *may* have discriminated unlawfully (or infringed the EPA).
2. Before starting the investigation, the commission must hold a preliminary inquiry, tell you, as specifically as possible, what unlawful acts it thinks you may have done and give you the opportunity to make representations.
3. The terms of reference of the investigation must also state the belief that you may have done or be doing unlawful acts of a specified kind. If the original terms of reference did not state this, the terms may be amended once the commission has formed its suspicion and carried out the preliminary inquiry.

Non-discrimination notices

If, as a result of a formal investigation, the commission forms the view that you have acted or you are acting unlawfully, a non-discrimination notice may be served on you. The notice may be served because of unlawful discrimination by you or because of a breach of the EPA. It may also be served because of a discriminatory practice, unlawful advertising, or instructions or pressure to discriminate unlawfully.

Before a non-discrimination notice can be served on you, there are the following further steps for your protection:

1. The commission must give you notice that it is minded to issue the notice and must state the grounds on which it contemplates doing so.
2. It must offer you the opportunity to make oral or written representations (or both if you wish) and must allow at least 28 days for this purpose.
3. It must then take account of any representations made.

The commission is not obliged, however, to allow you to cross-examine witnesses. The commission's function, in deciding to issue the notice, is essentially administrative, not judicial. Your chance to challenge the notice and test their evidence will come later, as mentioned below.

If the non-discrimination notice is then served on you, it will require you not to commit similar unlawful acts in the future. There may also be reporting requirements, so that the commission can be satisfied that you have complied with the notice and made any necessary changes to your employment practices or other arrangements.

When a non-discrimination notice is served on you, that is not the end of the matter. You have the right to appeal to an industrial tribunal (or a county court if the notice relates to discrimination outside the employment field). The appeal must be made within six weeks. If it is successful, the industrial tribunal or county court may set aside the notice as a whole, if it is found that you have not in fact acted unlawfully. It may also set aside any particular requirement of the notice (for example where the reporting restrictions are found to be too onerous).

Since you have the right to challenge the non-discrimination notice by appealing against it, you cannot generally seek judicial review of the commission's decision to issue the notice. This principle was established in 1984 in the case of *R v CRE ex parte Westminster City Council*.

The facts of this case were interesting. Jobs as refuse collectors had gone mainly to relatives and friends of the existing staff, all of whom were white. A black road sweeper employed by the council applied for a post as a refuse collector. The assistant director of cleansing, who was personally committed to equal opportunity, offered the post to him. However, the offer was withdrawn, in the interests of industrial relations, because of union pressure. A formal investigation was carried out and a non-discrimination notice served on the council.

Time limits

Under both the RRA (Section 68) and the SDA (Section 76), the relevant commission must commence proceedings within six months in order to obtain a finding that you have acted unlawfully in relation to a discriminatory practice, advertisement, or instruction or pressure to discriminate.

There is also a time limit of six months for preliminary action by one of the commissions in an employment case. If the commission takes the view that you have discriminated unlawfully or (in the case of the EOC) infringed the EPA, then the commission must start proceedings within six months in order to obtain a finding to that effect. There is provision for extending the time limit on the ground that it is 'just and equitable' to do so, but this discretion is not lightly exercised.

An application to a county court (or sheriff court in Scotland) for an injunction must be made within five years after the unlawful act relied upon or within five years after a non-discrimination notice has become final.

Practical advice

You should treat the commissions as sources of advice and information, not as potential enemies. Both commissions take or support enforcement action where necessary, but prefer to see employers adopting and implementing genuine equal opportunity policies.

If you are threatened with a formal investigation, you should take the matter seriously and seek to persuade the relevant commission either that its suspicions are unfounded or that you will take the necessary corrective action. The adverse consequences of a formal investigation and non-discrimination notice include the following:

1. An investigation can be very lengthy and expensive, both for the commission and for the person being investigated.
2. Reports into formal investigations are published and there is also a public register of non-discrimination notices. Where a formal investigation results in a non-discrimination notice, the publicity is not good publicity.
3. In the last resort, a non-discrimination notice can lead to an application for an injunction.

Summary

1. Both the commissions are important sources of information and advice for equal opportunity employers.
2. A formal investigation into the activities of a named person can lead to a non-discrimination notice, but there is a right to appeal within six weeks. In employment cases the appeal must be made to an industrial tribunal; where the notice relates to activities outside the employment field the appeal must be made to a county court (or sheriff court in Scotland).
3. Either commission can apply to a county court (or sheriff court in Scotland) for an injunction to prevent persistent discrimination (or other persistent breaches of the RRA, SDA or EPA). The application must be made within five years after an unlawful act or after a non-discrimination notice has become final.
4. When applying for an injunction, the commissions cannot rely on an unlawful act in the employment field unless it has been the subject of a non-discrimination notice or of a finding by an industrial tribunal. In order to obtain a finding on which to base a subsequent claim for an injunction, the commission can apply to an industrial tribunal within six months after the act has taken place.

Part III
Equal Opportunity Policies

17
Adopting a Policy

The purpose of this chapter is to consider why a policy should be adopted and to outline the essential steps which must be taken in order to formulate the policy and put it into practice. The continuing process of monitoring and reviewing the policy, adapting and improving it, and carrying out new policy initiatives is considered in Chapter 18.

The essential steps to be taken, when adopting the policy, are:

1. Formulating the policy statement.
2. Appointing the individuals and/or department who will be responsible for making sure that the policy is properly and effectively carried out.
3. Telling your employees and job applicants about the policy.
4. Preparing other policy documents, and programmes and procedures.
5. Reviewing all your existing employment practices, to ensure that they are consistent with the policy.
6. Giving instructions and training to managers, supervisors and interviewers (and, where necessary, to other staff).

Before you start taking these essential steps, however, why should you have a policy at all? In what ways will having a policy either keep you out of trouble or bring positive benefits?

Reasons for adopting a policy

The first and most obvious reason for having a policy is that an effective policy will help you to prevent unlawful discrimination from taking place within your organisation. It could also give you a defence if discrimination takes place against your wishes, as already explained in Chapters 5 and 9.

The CRE code (paragraph 1.1) makes the point that the responsibility for providing equal opportunity for job applicants and employees rests primarily with employers. The code recommends that you should adopt, implement and monitor an equal opportunity policy to ensure that there is no unlawful discrimination and that equal opportunity is genuinely available. You are not under any direct obligation to comply with this recommendation, or any other recommendation in either of the codes, but your failure to do so can be taken into account in any industrial tribunal proceedings against you.

If you do little or nothing and there is a successful complaint against you, the direct cost, in terms of compensation, is likely to be small—only a few thousand pounds (although it can be much more when actual or constructive dismissal is involved). However, the cost in terms of management time, the effect on morale and bad publicity can be very much greater.

Positive benefits of a policy

These are the negative reasons for having a policy. There are also positive reasons.

The EOC code (in paragraph 2) makes the point that the chances of success of your organisation will be improved if you seek to develop the abilities of all employees. The code recognises that an initial cost may be involved, but suggests that this should be more than compensated for by better relationships and better use of human resources.

A similar point is made in the CRE code (in paragraph 1.3 of the introduction). An equal opportunity policy is likely to involve some expenditure, at least in staff time and effort. But a coherent and effective programme will help you to make full use of the abilities of your entire workforce.

It is possible to identify the following specific benefits:

(a) If the careers of all your employees are developed to their full potential, there will be a direct benefit to you as well as to the employees concerned.
(b) Eliminating discrimination involves making selection and other personnel decisions objectively and consistently; decisions made in this way are more likely to be efficient and financially beneficial to you.
(c) Fair and non-discriminatory selection of job applicants is likely to ensure a high standard of new employees.
(d) If employees can see that they have equality of opportunity and are being treated fairly, morale throughout the organisation will be enhanced.
(e) Investors, public bodies and customers are attaching increasing importance to ethical issues. A high profile in equal opportunity will be good for the standing of your organisation.
(f) An effective policy, with active participation by all your employees, should work through into the way in which customers or clients are treated and this again will be directly beneficial to you.

Small firms

Both codes recognise that a small firm may have both less need and less ability to carry out the detailed recommendations of the code.

The CRE code (in paragraph 2.2 of the introduction) recognises that in many small firms employers have close contact with their staff and that there will therefore be less need for formality in assessing whether equal opportunity is being achieved. This applies particularly to such matters as the arrangements for monitoring the policy (these are dealt with in Chapter 18). The code adds that it may not be reasonable to expect small firms to have the resources and administrative systems to carry out the code's detailed recommendations. Small firms should, however, ensure that their practices are consistent with the code's general intentions.

The EOC code (in paragraph 3) also recognises that small businesses will require much simpler procedures than organisations with complex structures and that it may not always be reasonable for them to carry out all the code's detailed recommendations. Small firms should, however, ensure that their practices comply with the SDA.

If you employ only a handful of people, this is not a good reason for dispensing with a written policy. A clear policy statement will tell your employees and job applicants where they stand and will also help to focus your mind on the relevant matters. Avoiding discrimination is not simply a matter of common sense; you also need guidance and instruction on interview and selection techniques and on such matters as avoiding indirect discrimination, using the GOQ exceptions with care, preventing sexual harassment, and dealing effectively with complaints.

Formulating the policy

A policy statement can be a few sentences or it can run into many pages. It is impossible to provide a form of wording which will be appropriate to all organisations. Each employer should adopt a policy statement which will be consistent with the style of other personnel documents.

There should be both positive and negative aspects to the policy statement. Every policy should include a positive commitment to equal opportunity for all job applicants and existing employees, and also to fair treatment for all employees. It is easy to overlook the fact that discrimination must be avoided not only in the way in which employees qualify for benefits, such as promotion or training, but also in the way in which they are required to do unpleasant work, disciplined or dismissed.

The negative aspect of the policy is to specify the kinds of discrimination which will not be practised or permitted. A form of words commonly used is that all employees and job applicants will receive equality of opportunity and fair treatment irrespective of their sex, marital status, race, colour, nationality or ethnic or national origins.

Usually, however, policies do not stop at this point. Although the above wording covers the statutory definitions of direct sex, marriage and racial discrimination, most policies also reject discrimination on at least some of the following grounds:

- religion;
- disability;
- sexual orientation;
- age.

There are good reasons for extending your policy to cover at least some of these matters. If you wish to make personnel decisions objectively and efficiently, it makes no more sense to turn a job applicant down on religious grounds than it does on racial grounds. Furthermore, religious discrimination can amount to indirect racial discrimination and age discrimination can amount to indirect racial or sex discrimination, as explained in Chapter 3.

On the other hand, your policy should not promise more than you can deliver. There is no point in stating in your policy that you will give equal opportunity and fair treatment to the disabled, if you then do nothing about it. It is better to start off with a modest policy, which you can then improve, than to adopt a policy which promises far more than can be achieved.

Similarly, the CRE code (in paragraph 1.3(c)) recommends that, as one of your policy aims, you should take advantage of the positive action provisions which were explained in Chapter 8, so long as it is appropriate and lawful for you to do so. However, positive action is not a legal requirement and you should not commit yourself to it unless you really intend to do something about it.

There is little or no point in having separate policies for racial and sex discrimination. The CRE code (in paragraph 1.4 of the introduction) recommends that a concerted policy to eliminate both race and sex discrimination often provides the best approach.

Your policy definition should of course make it clear that indirect discrimination, as well as direct discrimination, is to be eliminated. Indeed it is particularly important that the policy should deal effectively with indirect discrimination, because indirect discrimination is now more prevalent and more difficult to recognise than direct discrimination.

Unions and staff associations

The CRE code (in paragraph 1.4(b)) recommends that the policy's content and implementation should be discussed and, where appropriate, agreed with trade unions or employee representatives.

Similarly, the EOC code (in paragraph 4) states that it is important that measures to eliminate discrimination or promote equality of opportunity should be understood and supported by all employees. You should therefore involve your employees in the policy.

The EOC code goes on to suggest (in paragraph 35(a)) that the policy should be clearly stated and, where appropriate, included in a collective agreement.

Grievance and disciplinary procedures

The policy should make it clear that it is the responsibility of all employees to report any unlawful discrimination, whether they themselves are victims or witnesses. More detailed guidance on the steps to be taken to complain of discrimination should be given in the information sent to all employees, as mentioned below.

It should also be made clear in the policy that unlawful discrimination will be treated as a serious disciplinary offence and indeed as one which could, in a bad case, justify dismissal.

Responsibility for the policy

The CRE code (in paragraph 1.4(a)) recommends that overall responsibility for the policy should be allocated to a member of senior management. The same recommendation is made in the EOC code (paragraph 35(b)).

The reasons for this approach are obvious. The person responsible for the policy needs to be senior enough to ensure that it is carried out. There is a risk of the policy being marginalised if a comparatively junior person is appointed as equal opportunity officer and is given the sole responsibility for seeing that the policy is carried out.

There are, at the same time, risks in giving the whole responsibility for the policy to one or more individuals who already have other important functions. It is by no means unknown for the same individual to be responsible for equal opportunities and also for all other personnel and safety matters. There is a risk in such circumstances that the individual who has been given the responsibility will simply not have the time to do all the detailed work which is necessary to put the policy into effect and then keep it under review.

The ideal solution, if your organisation is large enough, is probably to give the overall responsibility for the policy to a senior officer, such as the personnel director, but also to appoint specialist individuals or departments who will carry out the detailed work and report to the director.

Communicating the policy

Both the codes recognise the importance of telling employees and job applicants about the policy. The EOC code (in paragraph 35(c)) states that the policy should be made known to all employees and, where reasonably practicable, to all job applicants.

The CRE code (in paragraph 1.2) suggests that the policy should be clearly communicated to all employees, for example through notice boards, circulars, contracts of employment or written notifications to individual employees. The code also suggests (in paragraph 1.7) that any literature which you send to job applicants should include a statement that you are an equal opportunity employer. It is also good practice to include a similar statement in job advertisements.

The EOC code (in paragraph 4) goes further and suggests that your employees should be involved in your equal opportunity policy. One way of doing this is to send out regular newsletters and to invite employees to make suggestions for improving the policy.

The information which you give to your employees should explain what they should do if they experience or witness discrimination. In a large organisation, the information given to employees should include the following:

(a) The name or job title of the person to whom a complaint should generally be made in the first instance, such as the complainant's line manager.

(b) The name of another person, such as a senior manager or member of the equal opportunity department, to whom a complaint can be made if the complaint is against the line manager or if the line manager fails to take the complaint seriously.

(c) An assurance that in the first instance a matter may be raised on a confidential and informal basis (although obviously confidentiality cannot be maintained where a complaint is pursued on a formal level).

There may well be different procedures for complaining on the one hand about matters such as sexual and racial harassment, and on the other hand about company rules and policies, such as rules relating to dress and appearance.

The information given to all employees should also make it clear that unlawful discrimination will be treated as a serious disciplinary offence and that employees are expected to report any unlawful act which they witness and not simply stand by and do nothing.

Written programmes and procedures

In order to make your policy work, you will need not only the policy statement itself but also a number of other written programmes and procedures.

One very important aspect of any policy is to ensure that you have fair and efficient selection and promotion procedures. You should have one or more written documents setting out the procedures which will be used for:

- inviting job applications and specifying the information to be given by job applicants, in application forms or CVs;
- shortlisting job applicants and promotion candidates;
- interviewing;
- selecting successful candidates;
- assessing and appraising employees;

- selecting employees for training;
- grading and regrading employees;
- dealing with applications for transfers;
- ensuring that there is no victimisation of employees who have complained of discrimination or other employees who have supported their complaints.

The CRE code refers (in paragraph 4 of the introduction) to the importance of consistent selection procedures and criteria and of selection criteria which are relevant to job requirements. Otherwise, decisions are often too subjective and racial discrimination can easily occur.

Several of the matters to be covered in these documents were dealt with at the end of Chapter 6.

You should also have written procedures for dealing with complaints of discrimination and, in particular, complaints of sexual harassment (Chapter 9); for claiming the benefit of the GOQ exceptions (Chapter 7); for using the positive action provisions (Chapter 8); for responding to requests for part-time working or job sharing, or for extended leave (Chapter 10); and for placing advertisements (Chapter 12).

Your written procedures relating to GOQ and positive action provisions should make it clear that the consent of senior management should be obtained before these exceptions are relied on.

Reviewing existing practices

The CRE code (in paragraph 1.4(e)) recommends that you should examine and regularly review existing procedures and criteria and change them where you find that they are actually or potentially unlawfully discriminatory.

Several examples of practices and procedures which could be unlawful were given at the end of Chapter 3. One or two further examples, in relation to existing employees, were given in Chapter 10.

The EOC code suggests (in paragraph 36) that trade unions should be involved in the review of established procedures to ensure that the procedures are consistent with the law.

Instructions and training

The EOC code makes the point (in paragraph 5) that individual employees at all levels have responsibilities for eliminating discrimination and providing equal opportunity. They must not discriminate or knowingly aid their employers to do so.

The CRE code recommends (in paragraph 1.4(d)) that you should provide training and guidance for supervisory staff and other relevant decision makers, such as personnel and line managers, to ensure that they understand their position in law and under company policy.

The CRE code goes on to recommend (in paragraph 1.14(b)) that staff responsible for shortlisting, interviewing and selecting candidates should be given guidance or training on the following matters:

(a) selection criteria and the need for their consistent application;
(b) the effects which generalised assumptions and prejudices can have on selection decisions;
(c) the possible misunderstandings that can occur in interviews between persons of different cultural backgrounds.

Examples of several common prejudices and assumptions were given at the end of Chapter 2.

There is both a positive and a negative side to the guidance and training which should be given to your employees. From the negative point of view, they must be given sufficient information to recognise discrimination when they see it and made to understand the potential consequences, both for themselves and the organisation, when discrimination takes place. From the positive point of view, they must be made aware of the commitment to equal opportunity and fair treatment, and given the information and training necessary to make decisions objectively, efficiently and consistently.

Managers and supervisors should also be given training in handling some of the difficult situations which can arise, for example:

(a) instructions or pressure from other employees or customers to try to make them discriminate unlawfully;
(b) dealing with complaints of sexual harassment;
(c) taking steps to ensure that complaints of discrimination do not lead to any victimisation, whatever the outcome of the complaint.

Although the most obvious need is to give instructions and training to managers, interviewers and supervisors, the CRE code also recognises that more junior employees may also need instruction and training. In many cases, the first person to speak to a job applicant (or customer or client) is a receptionist, telephonist or gate keeper. The CRE code recommends (in paragraph 1.14(a)) that gate, reception and personnel staff should be instructed not to treat casual or formal applicants from particular racial groups less favourably than others. The instructions should be confirmed in writing. You should obviously also give instructions that the treatment given to job applicants should not be affected by the sex or marital status of the applicant.

Summary

1. An effective equal opportunity policy can bring important practical benefits as well as helping you to meet your legal obligations.

2. The policy statement should identify the kinds of discrimination (direct and indirect) which are to be avoided (including any which are not explicitly unlawful) and should also refer to the positive aspects of the policy.
3. You should consult union or employee representatives on the content and implementation of the policy.
4. Responsibility for implementing the policy must be clearly allocated to one or more individuals or departments.
5. You must find an effective way to tell your employees about their rights and responsibilities under the policy.
6. Many employees, particularly managers, supervisors and interviewers, will require more detailed guidance and training.
7. You will need to back up the policy with a number of written programmes and procedures.
8. You must also review all your existing employment practices and eliminate any which are discriminatory.

18
Making the Policy Work

There is little point in adopting an equal opportunity policy if you are then going to forget all about the policy and leave the policy documents to gather dust. Making the policy work is a continuing process, containing the following essential elements:

1. You need to monitor the working of the policy and take corrective action when it is seen not to be working.
2. All policy documents and other employment policies and practices must be regularly reviewed.
3. The guidance and training given to managers and others at the outset of the policy will have to be provided on a continuing basis and updated where necessary.
4. You should always be alert to new policy initiatives.

Monitoring the policy

If your organisation is a large one, the only way to find out if your policy is working is to record relevant information and to look at the information on a regular basis in order to identify matters which need further investigation and, possibly, corrective action.

The starting point is to record the information which you need in order to classify all your employees and all job applicants into relevant groups, such as men, women, married men, married women and members of various racial groups. You then need to look at the information at regular intervals in order to ask the following questions in relation to each relevant group:

(a) Are members of the group failing to apply for employment or promotion?
(b) Or are they applying in fewer numbers than might be expected?
(c) Are they not being recruited, promoted or selected for training and development?
(d) Or are they being appointed or selected in a significantly lower proportion than their rate of application?
(e) Are they concentrated in certain jobs, shifts, sections or departments?
(f) Are they 'under-represented' in training or in jobs carrying higher pay, status or authority?

(g) Does one particular manager appear to be turning down job applications from them?
(h) Have an unduly large proportion been selected for redundancy?
(i) Have an unduly large proportion been warned, suspended or dismissed on disciplinary grounds?

Questions (a) to (e) are referred to in the EOC code (paragraph 40) and questions (a) to (f) in the CRE code (paragraph 1.41).

You must then look at the information at regular intervals. Take question (a). If, for example, women are not applying for promotion, it could be because they are not aware of the possibilities or because they have not had training opportunities in the past. In either case, positive action is something to be considered, on the principles explained in Chapter 8. On the other hand, the reason may be that the criteria for promotion are indirectly discriminatory against women; in that event, the criteria must be modified immediately except so far as they are justifiable.

The answer to question (g) is particularly important. If the statistics show that some particular manager may be directly discriminating, you should investigate immediately and find out whether the selection decisions which he or she has made can be explained objectively. If not, then either guidance and training or disciplinary action may be called for.

Classification of employees

The classification required for the purposes of the SDA is quite straightforward. You need to know the sex and marital status of all employees and job applicants.

How complicated should the racial classification be? The CRE has published a guidance paper, *A Measure of Equality*. The sub-title is *Monitoring and Achieving Racial Equality in Employment*. The CRE recommends the nine categories used in the 1991 census; White, Black-African, Black-Caribbean, Black-Other, Indian, Pakistani, Bangladeshi, Chinese, Other. As a minimum, you should adopt the five categories used by the Department of Employment in its Labour Force Surveys; White, Afro-Caribbean, Indian, Pakistani/ Bangladeshi and Other. Sometimes a sub-category may be necessary to reflect local conditions (eg where there is a large Irish community).

Obtaining the information

A Measure of Equality recommends that information from existing employees be obtained in one of the following ways:

(a) all employees to be invited to complete a monitoring form;
(b) all employees to be briefly interviewed and invited to state their ethnic origins.

If an employee fails to complete the form, even after a reminder, or will not answer the question, then management should classify the employee and tell the employee what entry is being made. The classification should then be altered, where necessary, in the light of the employee's comments.

It is obviously very important to explain clearly why the information is required. It is good practice for information obtained from job applicants to be given on a detachable or separate part of the application form, so that the information is not seen by the managers who are carrying out the short-listing and selection of candidates. The CRE code (in paragraph 1.36) recommends that you should ensure that information on individuals' ethnic origins is collected for the purpose of monitoring equal opportunity alone and is protected from misuse.

The CRE code (in paragraph 1.35) also recommends that, in order to achieve the full commitment of all concerned, the chosen method of monitoring should be discussed and agreed, where appropriate, with trade union or employee representatives.

Analysis of the information

It is not enough simply to obtain details of the sex, marital status and ethnic origin of employees and job applicants. You also need to be able to analyse the information. The combined effect of the advice given by the CRE code (in paragraph 1.37 and 1.38) and the EOC code (paragraph 39) is as follows:

(a) An initial analysis is required of the ethnic composition of the workforce and of the numbers of men, women, married men and married women. The statistics should be compiled both on an overall basis and by reference to individual branches, departments, plants, sections, shifts, job categories, grades and pay scales.

(b) Further analysis should be carefully carried out at regular intervals so as to show changes in distribution over periods of time.

(c) Where practicable, selection decisions should be analysed. The reasons for selection and rejection should be recorded at each stage of the selection process, such as initial shortlists, selection for interview, final shortlist and actual appointment.

(d) Information should be kept about all complaints of discrimination or of infringement of the equal opportunity policy, and of the way in which the complaints have been dealt with.

(e) Any formal analysis should be readily updated and available to management and trade unions to enable any necessary action to be taken.

Small firms

Both the CRE code (in paragraph 1.34) and the EOC code (in paragraph 38) recognise that in a small firm, with a simple structure, it may be quite possible to assess the distribution of employees from personal knowledge and visual identification.

It is very easy, however, when you rely on these methods, to overlook the need to carry out a regular analysis of the distribution of the workforce and of the success rates of job applicants and promotion candidates from different groups. If, for example, you have no women or black employees in managerial or supervisory positions, you should look back over previous job applications and the way in which they have been dealt with. The analysis may show that there could have been direct or indirect discrimination and that you need to improve your selection procedures.

Reviewing the policy

You need to keep the policy itself, and all related documents, under constant review to ensure that the policy is up to date and effective. If, for example, monitoring shows that direct discrimination may have been taking place in dealing with job applications, you should consider tightening up on your recruitment and selection procedures. The changes to be made could include:

(a) having a more structured system, with job descriptions and person specifications;
(b) using panels, rather than individual managers, for shortlisting, interviewing and selection;
(c) involving a member of the personnel department in all decisions;
(d) requiring the reasons for all decisions to be recorded in writing.

Even when a policy is working well, changes may be needed in order to reflect changes in the law or in good employment practice. For example:

(a) It was only in 1990 that employers became aware that sex discrimination in relation to pensions and redundancy and severance payments was contrary to EC law.
(b) It was only towards the end of 1991 that the EC code on sexual harassment was published.

You must also bear in mind that, with changed circumstances, employment practices which have a discriminatory effect may cease to be justifiable. Similarly, factors which at one time were material as reasons for pay differences between men and women may, with changed circumstances, cease to be valid.

Furthermore, it must never be assumed that the GOQ exception will be available for a job simply because the exception has applied in the past. Each time there is a vacancy to be filled the question needs to be considered afresh in the light of the current circumstances.

Continuing training

It was explained in the last chapter that as part of the implementation of the policy it is essential to give guidance and training to managers, supervisors and interviewers. Furthermore, staff such as receptionists, telephonists and gate keepers need guidance and instructions on the way to deal with job applicants.

You cannot expect the guidance and training given initially to have a permanent effect. Employees should be given further guidance and training on a regular basis. You will also, of course, need to provide training and instruction for new employees who have personnel responsibilities.

Instruction and training is also needed in order to update managers and other employees on changes in the law and in good practice, and in changes to your own policy.

Policy initiatives

If the policy is not to stand still, you should always be ready to explore new methods of improving the policy and of taking initiatives to extend equal opportunity.

It is very important, however, that before embarking on some new initiative, you should assess the resistance to it and also the difficulties to be overcome. If you carry out an initiative which fails, you could set back the whole of the policy and lose support for it. Examples are given in Chapter 19 of several policy initiatives which have been successful, but in each case the success was achieved only as a result of a good deal of planning and hard work.

Consider as an example the provision of greater opportunities for job sharing and part-time work. The experience of some organisations has demonstrated that it is possible even for very senior jobs to be shared effectively, to the benefit of the organisation as well as the individuals concerned. However, experience has also shown that there is widespread hostility to the principle of job sharing, at least in senior positions. If a job sharing scheme is to succeed you must take the following steps:

(a) Make the scheme available to all employees and not only to women.
(b) Ensure that any applicants are fully committed to the scheme and are aware of what is required of them.
(c) Ensure that each pair of potential job sharers can work well together and fully co-operate with each other.
(d) Discuss the proposals fully with the managers and colleagues of the job sharers and (if there is one) the union.
(e) Identify all practical difficulties and make sure that they can be overcome.

A similar hard-headed and objective approach should be followed in relation to all other policy initiatives.

Summary

1. Monitoring is an essential part of the implementation of any policy. You must record the relevant information and do so carefully and sensitively. You must also analyse and use that information when you have it.
2. No policy can be set in stone. You must review it regularly and keep it up to date.
3. Managers, supervisors and interviewers should receive guidance and training on a continuing basis, to reinforce that already received and also to keep their knowledge up to date.
4. Policy initiatives should be non-discriminatory (except where the law expressly permits a limited measure of discrimination) and should be carefully planned and fully discussed.

Some Success Stories

The purpose of this chapter is to give some examples of equal opportunity policies which have been found to work in practice. One or two employers will be taken from each of the following sectors:

- manufacturing (including energy);
- the police;
- financial services;
- communications;
- local authorities.

Most of the employers mentioned will be from the private sector. Many business managers take the view that equal opportunity policies and programmes are luxuries indulged in by local authorities and other public sector employers and cannot be afforded by commercial organisations. The private sector employers mentioned in this chapter have demonstrated that adopting an equal opportunity policy is consistent with running a successful business. Indeed, most of them say that the policy contributes to the efficiency of the organisation and the success of the business. Some of the reasons for this are given at the end of this chapter.

It is right to add that the employers mentioned in this chapter are only a small proportion of the employers who have made equal opportunities a priority and devoted resources to ensuring that the policy is successful. I have approached only a handful of employers and have been able to use the material contributed only by a few of those approached.

Manufacturing industry

Shell UK is a good example of an equal opportunity employer operating in an industry where traditionally most employees were male and white. Like other equal opportunity employers mentioned in this chapter, the company has equal opportunity programmes which go far beyond the legal requirements.

Employees on maternity leave, so long as they have at least two years' service, qualify for six months' maternity pay, half of which is paid in stages after they return. The whole period of maternity leave is counted as pensionable service. Even before these improved benefits were adopted, early in 1991, more than 80 per cent of women taking maternity leave from Shell returned to work; the proportion was higher in the senior jobs.

Maternity leave as such is a benefit which can be enjoyed only by women, but other benefits, although likely to be taken up mainly by women, are available to both sexes. Men as well as women may take up to three career breaks, not totalling more than five years. The employee is kept on contract to the company during the break and the principle is that he or she should return to a position at least at the same level as his or her last job. The employee remains in the pension scheme and several benefits, such as loans from the company and death in service benefit, are unaffected by the career breaks. Statutory rights which would normally be lost by the break in employment are provided on an *ex gratia* basis to staff who return to work. A feature of the scheme is that staff are expected to work or receive training for at least four weeks a year during the break, so as to minimise what could otherwise be a major task of re-training and re-adjustment on returning to work after a long break.

The company also has written procedures and guidance for managers on part-time working, job sharing and home work, which can all be important options for women (and sometimes men) with family responsibilities.

Shell is also prepared to contribute to equal opportunities in circumstances where there is no direct benefit to the company or its existing employees. For example, the HGV drivers employed by the company, who are required to handle hazardous materials, are required to have both a Class One HGV licence and at least three years' driving experience. It was observed that very few ethnic minority workers had had the opportunity to overcome the first of these hurdles, let alone the experience. Accordingly Shell provided funds, facilities and trainers for unemployed people from the ethnic minorities to take a seven-week course at no cost, to enable them to obtain HGV Class One licences. The course included training in handling hazardous products. In consequence, the pool of HGV Class One licence holders has been increased by a number of ethnic minority drivers.

Similarly, the Shell Education Service has published material aimed at encouraging girls to take up scientific studies and the Shell Enterprise Unit has funded and published research into possible solutions for the particular problems which women face when starting their own businesses.

Shell, like other leading equal opportunity employers, also makes a point of telling its employees what it is doing about equal opportunities and underlining the priority given to the subject. The company regularly produces *Shell UK Review*, a large and glossy business and social report. In the first issue of 1992, the eight highlights from 1991 included not only major new commercial projects but also the improvements in the maternity policy and the driver-training scheme for ethnic minority workers.

It is a feature not only of Shell's policy but also of most successful policies that there are benefits for all employees, of both sexes and all ethnic groups, and that the policy is clearly set out and well communicated to employees.

National Power is another employer which clearly demonstrates both these qualities, for example in its Childcare Charter. The document is attractively presented and easy to follow and begins with the following words:

> National Power recognises that male and female employees have to combine and balance caring for families with responsibilities at work. This Childcare Charter provides a number of options to ease childcare arrangements...Assistance is also offered to employees who are adopting children. Our objective is to provide solutions that can best meet individual needs.

The initiatives which are described in the booklet and which are open to both male and female employees include flexitime, job share, career breaks and childcare allowances. The latter take the form of vouchers to be used towards the cost of childcare. There is also a Retainer Scheme, so that employees who decide to leave for family reasons can be kept in touch with job opportunities with National Power.

The point that employees of both sexes can benefit from good equal opportunity policies is also illustrated by Hotpoint. In 1992 12 women working in the factory at Llandudno Junction started a 30-week in-house 'Women Mean Business' course, designed to qualify them for positions as team-leaders. At the same time there is a technical leader development scheme in the company for young high-fliers of both sexes, and one of the current successes is a young man who started as a plumber but whose leadership potential was identified and who became a team-leader in production engineering at a very young age.

The police

Police forces throughout the country are major employers, with a tradition of employing mainly white male officers, and are also high-profile providers of services to the public.

The Police Staff College at Bramshill has a dual role as a training organisation for the police and as an employer. The former role is now particularly important because it has been the policy since 1988 for attendance at Bramshill to be part of the career structure of all senior police officers.

There are three levels of command courses, ranging from the junior command course for newly promoted chief inspectors to the senior command course for superintendents and chief superintendents. The junior command course includes two days and the senior command course four days specifically dedicated to equal opportunities.

There is also a short course programme, which includes:
(a) Five-day courses on equal opportunities for officers and civilian staff.
(b) A ten-day course, 'Police and Visible Minorities', for operational commanders and their deputies (and sometimes also community liaison officers). Although the main focus of the course is on ethnic minorities, the current course includes sessions on gender and disability.

The accelerated promotion course is for high potential officers in the ranks of sergeant and inspector. It includes sessions on sensitivity and awareness, and sexism and racism are confronted.

The college also has an equal opportunities policy statement and grievance procedure for its own employees. The assistant commandant, who has assistant chief constable rank, is a woman and there is a black member of the academic staff. The college has a high-powered equal opportunities group to examine equal opportunity issues and to make policy recommendations.

The issue of equal opportunities for the disabled has not been neglected. A programme of proposed alterations includes the designation of routes through the campus which will be accessible to wheelchairs and the installation of unisex toilet facilities and a chair lift.

The college's equal opportunities vision statement ends with the following words: 'We are determined to live and work in a place where equality and fairness are a way of life'.

If equal opportunity policies are to be effective throughout the police, attitudes such as these need to be effectively communicated to and adopted by officers at all levels in individual forces. The Greater Manchester Police is an example of a force which has adopted attractive methods of communication. There is a well-presented management handbook on equal opportunities and a particularly important measure which has been adopted is that of the equal opportunities newsletter. Initially the newsletter was sent to management teams but it is now aimed at all staff. The newsletter is short and makes its points effectively by using examples. The August 1992 newsletter gives the example of an officer in another force who went to an industrial tribunal to complain of racial abuse and of inaccurate appraisal reports. He received compensation of £20,000 and the newsletter makes the point that 'it can be an individual officer who has to pay a tribunal award, not the force'.

The newsletter also describes the following case:

> In another force, a sergeant who made sexist remarks and jokes at a female officer was dismissed from the service following a discipline hearing into the complaints. The female officer was strongly supported by colleagues and senior officers when she complained. (At the time of writing, the decision is subject to appeal).

Having described these actual cases, the newsletter then makes the point that 'any racist or sexist behaviour, discrimination or language cannot be tolerated. It is unprofessional, unacceptable and can lead to dismissal'.

Financial services

Midland Bank has two attractive and well-presented guides on equal opportunities, one for managers and one for all employees.

In common with other major equal opportunity employers, the bank has taken policy initiatives specifically designed to meet the needs of women, ethnic minorities and the disabled, and has also adopted schemes which can be for the benefit of all employees. The latter schemes include career break schemes, job sharing and currently 115 nurseries, with approximately 900 subsidised childcare places.

Schemes designed specifically for women employees include training courses for women managers to develop their skills and career potential, a personal development programme for women below manager level, the establishment of women's networks and extended maternity leave.

The bank offers up to 30 paid summer placements to second year undergraduates from ethnic minorities and a one-day training course has been established to help enterprise managers build links and maximise business opportunities with their local ethnic minority community. There is also a pilot scheme to develop ways of using the multilingual skills of staff to communicate with ethnic minority customers.

Several internal publications are now available in braille/large print/audio cassette, access for the disabled is to be provided in all new and refurbished premises, facilities for disabled people are available at two training centres run by the bank and disability awareness training is available for employees.

Allied Dunbar has an unusual and effective way of demonstrating both its commitment to equal opportunities and the success of their policy. Its booklet on equal opportunities includes photographs, names and biographical details of employees who have benefited from the policy. These employees include a blind man who joined the company as a programmer and who has become a programming manager; a senior secretary who was recruited at the age of 41 with two dependent children, high blood pressure and no recent secretarial experience; and a black woman employed as a solicitor since she qualified several years ago.

Communications

The Independent Television Association has a policy of allowing employees (of both sexes) to work part time, wherever practicable, in order to meet their particular circumstances. A number of female employees have taken advantage of this scheme and returned on a part-time basis following maternity leave. At least one female member of staff has been provided with a fax machine at home to assist her in fulfilling her domestic and work obligations.

Measures specifically designed to improve opportunities for women include sending employees on personal effectiveness courses for women.

The BBC was a pioneer so far as equal opportunities for women are concerned. Initiatives taken for ethnic minority workers include:

(a) Running a series of pre-selection courses for people of Asian and Afro-Caribbean origin (eg television production).
(b) Advertising a selection of jobs in the ethnic press.
(c) Open evenings at regional centres for Asian and Afro-Caribbean communities, to give them a clearer impression of the types of jobs available and experience required.

The BBC has also recognised the importance of effective communications by introducing regular newsletters on equal opportunities and giving the policy regular publicity in its own staff magazine, *Ariel*.

Local authorities

Gloucestershire County Council is one of many local authorities which has detailed and sophisticated policies and programmes to achieve equal opportunity. A less common feature is that some work has been done to measure the impact of the policy.

The steps taken include:

(a) A career break scheme which is offered to all staff under clear criteria and guidelines. The scheme has enabled individuals to gain qualifications, to care for children and to travel with a measure of security and support for returning, so that both the council and the individual gain greatly under the policy. In one case a member of staff took up the scheme to be able to care for her dying husband.
(b) The council has 182 job sharers and the 91 posts involved are at a range of grades. The majority, but not all, of the job sharers are female. While some employers require the staff involved to prove that job sharing will work, the presumption at Gloucestershire is that job sharing will be allowed unless there are insuperable practical difficulties in any particular case. The scheme allows women to retain high-level jobs while working part time and enables the council to retain skilled people who may wish to return to full-time employment at a later date. In one case, a member of staff used the scheme to develop her own business, while keeping her job on a part-time basis for security.
(c) The childcare allowance scheme was introduced to aid retention and recruitment and offers weekly support towards the cost of childcare. A county nursery has also been set up. The object is

to enable employees with young children to remain at or return to work, helping the council to retain trained and skilled staff.
(d) The social services department has joined with a local college to run the Diploma in Social Work, with funded positions for trainees, and has targeted minority groups for training. It is also proposed to introduce a pre-employment positive action package in the surveyors' department to train ethnic minority workers to enable them to apply for technician positions.
(e) Work placements have been provided for disabled people to enable them to gain experience and apply for employment. The council also supports sheltered placements for disabled people and has 180 places in industrial workshops for registered, severely disabled people. These workshops make a profit of over £1 million each year.

For some years the council has run an Effective Career Development for Women programme. A study has been carried out to test the impact of the courses on the participants. The tentative conclusions are that women who have participated are rather more likely to remain with the county council than comparable women who have not taken part in the programme (82.4 per cent as against 75.8 per cent over the period considered). The study also showed that 21.2 per cent of the respondents had been influenced to change jobs, 22.4 per cent to make changes for the better in their working life and 29.4 per cent to undertake further training or education.

General conclusions

I have received a great deal of information and assistance, not only from the handful of employers mentioned in this chapter but also from the many others who have written to me (and who are listed in the acknowledgements at the beginning of this book). All these employers state that the equal opportunity policies which they have adopted are being retained and developed, and that the resources committed to the policies have been more than justified. Employees are recruited objectively and efficiently; individuals are encouraged and helped to develop their potential; interruptions to a career and the balancing of work and domestic responsibilities are catered for; employee loyalty and morale are enhanced.

The main features of successful policies, in both public and private sectors, include:

(a) Clearly-written and comprehensive policies.
(b) Training and awareness programmes, and clear procedures, for managers.
(c) Some degree of positive action, in order to offer encouragement and training to women, ethnic minority workers and the disabled.
(d) Improved maternity schemes.

(e) Other schemes, such as career breaks, job share and childcare, which are taken up mainly by women but which are available to employees of both sexes.
(f) Using newsletters to tell managers and other employees about the policy and how it is working in practice.

Appendix 1

Key provisions of the Race Relations Act 1976 and the Sex Discrimination Act 1975 (as amended)

Race Relations Act

PART I

Definitions of discrimination

1. Racial discrimination

(1) A person discriminates against another in any circumstances relevant for the purposes of any provision of this Act if:

    (a) on racial grounds he treats that other less favourably than he treats or would treat other persons; or

    (b) he applies to that other a requirement or conditon which he applies or would apply equally to persons not of the same racial group as that other but—

        (i) which is such that the proportion of persons of the same racial group as that other who can comply with it is considerably smaller than the proportion of persons not of that racial group who can comply with it; and

        (ii) which he cannot show to be justifiable irrespective of the colour, race, nationality or ethnic or national origins of the person to whom it is applied; and

        (iii) which is to the detriment of that other because he cannot comply with it.

(2) It is hereby declared that, for the purposes of this Act, segregating a person from other persons on racial grounds is treating him less favourably than they are treated.

2. Discrimination by way of victimisation

(1) A person ("the discriminator") discriminates against another person ("the person victimised") in any circumstances relevant for the purposes of any provision of this Act if he treats the person victimised less favourably than in those circumstances he treats or would treat other persons, and does so by reason that the person victimised has—

    (a) brought proceedings against the discriminator or any other person under this Act; or

    (b) given evidence or information in connection with proceedings brought by any person against the discriminator or any other person under this Act; or

    (c) otherwise done anything under or by reference to this Act in relation to the discriminator or any other person; or

    (d) alleged that the discriminator or any other person has committed an act which (whether or not the allegation so states) would amount to a contravention of this Act,

or by reason that the discriminator knows that the person victimised intends to do any of those things, or suspects that the person victimised has done, or intends to do, any of them.

(2) Subsection (1) does not apply to treatment of a person by reason of any allegation made by him if the allegation was false and not made in good faith.

3. Meaning of "racial grounds", "racial group", etc.

(1) In this Act, unless the context otherwise requires—"racial grounds" means any of the following grounds, namely colour, race, nationality or ethnic or national origins; "racial group" means a group of persons defined by reference to colour, race, nationality or ethnic or national origins, and references to a person's racial group refer to any racial group into which he falls.

(2) The fact that a racial group comprises two or more distinct racial groups does not prevent it from constituting a particular racial group for the purposes of this Act.

(3) In this Act—

    (a) references to discrimination refer to any discrimination falling within section 1 or 2; and

    (b) references to racial discrimination refer to any discrimination falling within section 1,

and related expressions shall be construed accordingly.

(4) A comparison of the case of a person of a particular racial group with that of a person not of that group under section 1(1) must be such that the relevant circumstances in the one case are the same, or not materially different, in the other.

PART II

Main duties of employers

4. Discrimination against applicants and employees

(1) It is unlawful for a person, in relation to employment by him at an establishment in Great Britain, to discriminate against another—

 (a) in the arrangements he makes for the purpose of determining who should be offered that employment; or

 (b) in the terms on which he offers him that employment; or

 (c) by refusing or deliberately omitting to offer him that employment.

(2) It is unlawful for a person, in the case of a person employed by him at an establishment in Great Britain, to discriminate against that employee—

 (a) in the terms of employment which he affords him; or

 (b) in the way he affords him access to opportunities for promotion, transfer or training, or to any other benefits, facilities or services, or by refusing or deliberately omitting to afford him access to them; or

 (c) by dismissing him, or subjecting him to any other detriment.

(3) Except in relation to discrimination falling within section 2, subsections (1) and (2) do not apply to employment for the purposes of a private household.

PART II (continued)

GOQs

5. Exceptions for genuine occupational qualifications

(1) In relation to racial discrimination—

 (a) section 4(1)(a) or (c) does not apply to any employment where being of a particular racial group is a genuine occupational qualification for the job; and

 (b) section 4(2)(b) does not apply to opportunities for promotion or transfer to, or training for, such employment.

(2) Being of a particular racial group is a genuine occupational qualification for a job only where—

 (a) the job involves participation in a dramatic performance or other entertainment in a capacity for which a person of that racial group is required for reasons of authenticity; or

 (b) the job involves participation as an artist's or photographic model in the production of a work of art, visual image or sequence of visual images for which a person of that racial group is required for reasons of authenticity; or

(c) the job involves working in a place where food or drink is (for payment or not) provided to and consumed by members of the public or a section of the public in a particular setting for which, in that job, a person of that racial group is required for reasons of authenticity; or

(d) the holder of the job provides persons of that racial group with personal services promoting their welfare, and those services can most effectively be provided by a person of that racial group.

(3) Subsection (2) applies where some only of the duties of the job fall within paragraphs (a), (b), (c) or (d) as well as where all of them do.

(4) Paragraph (a), (b), (c) or (d) of subsection (2) does not apply in relation to the filling of a vacancy at a time when the employer already has employees of the racial group in question—

(a) who are capable of carrying out the duties falling within that paragraph; and

(b) whom it would be reasonable to employ on those duties; and

(c) whose numbers are sufficient to meet the employer's likely requirements in respect of those duties without undue inconvenience.

PART IV

Responsibility for employees

32. Liability of employers and principals

(1) Anything done by a person in the course of his employment shall be treated for the purposes of this Act (except as regards offences thereunder) as done by his employer as well as by him, whether or not it was done with the employer's knowledge or approval.

(2) Anything done by a person as agent for another person with the authority (whether express or implied, and whether precedent or subsequent) of that other person shall be treated for the purposes of this Act (except as regards offences thereunder) as done by that other person as well as by him.

(3) In proceedings brought under this Act against any person in respect of an act alleged to have been done by an employee of his it shall be a defence for that person to prove that he took such steps as were reasonably practicable to prevent the employee from doing that act, or from doing in the course of his employment acts of that description.

PART VI

Positive action

35. Special needs of racial groups in regard to education, training or welfare

Nothing in Parts II to IV shall render unlawful any act done in affording persons of a particular racial group access to facilities or services to meet the special needs of persons of that group in regard to their education, training or welfare, or any ancillary benefits.

38. Other discriminatory training etc

(1) Nothing in Parts II to IV shall render unlawful any act done by an employer in relation to particular work in his employment at a particular establishment in Great Britain, being an act done in or in connection with—

(a) affording only those of his employees working at that establishment who are of a particular racial group access to facilities for training which would help to fit them for that work; or

(b) encouraging only persons of a particular racial group to take advantage of opportunities for doing that work at that establishment,

where any of the conditions in subsection (2) was satisfied at any time within the twelve months immediately preceding the doing of the act.

(2) Those conditions are—

(a) that there are no persons of the racial group in question among those doing that work at that establishment; or

(b) that the proportion of persons of that group among those doing that work at that establishment is small in comparison with the proportion of persons of that group—

(i) among all those employed by that employer there; or

(ii) among the population of the area from which that employer normally recruits persons for work in his employment at that establishment.

Sex Discrimination Act

PART I

Definitions of discrimination

1. Sex discrimination against women

(1) A person discriminates against a woman in any circumstances relevant for the purposes of any provision of this Act if—
   (a) on the ground of her sex he treats her less favourably than he treats or would treat a man; or
   (b) he applies to her a requirement or condition which he applies or would apply equally to a man but—
      (i) which is such that the proportion of women who can comply with it is considerably smaller than the proportion of men who can comply with it, and
      (ii) which he cannot show to be justifiable irrespective of the sex of the person to whom it is applied, and
      (iii) which is to her detriment because she cannot comply with it.
(2) If a person treats or would treat a man differently according to the man's marital status, his treatment of a woman is for the purposes of subsection (1)(a) to be compared to his treatment of a man having the like marital status.

2. Sex discrimination against men

(1) Section 1, and the provisions of Parts II and III relating to sex discrimination against women, are to be read as applying equally to the treatment of men, and for that purpose shall have effect with such modifications as are requisite.
(2) In the application of subsection (1) no account shall be taken of special treatment afforded to women in connection with pregnancy or childbirth.

NOTE: The reference to Part II is to Part II of the SDA, which contains Sections 6 to 21 of the Act and creates the obligations in the employment field. Part III of the Act creates obligations outside the employment field.

3. Discrimination against married persons in employment field

(1) A person discriminates against a married person of either sex in any circumstances relevant for the purposes of any provision of Part II if—
   (a) on the ground of his or her marital status he treats that person less favourably than he treats or would treat an unmarried person of the same sex, or
   (b) he applies to that person a requirement or condition which he applies or would apply equally to an unmarried person but—
      (i) which is such that the proportion of married persons who can comply with it is considerably smaller than the

proportion of unmarried persons of the same sex who can comply with it, and
- (ii) which he cannot show to be justifiable irrespective of the marital status of the person to whom it is applied, and
- (iii) which is to that person's detriment because he cannot comply with it.

(2) For the purposes of subsection (1), a provision of Part II framed with reference to discrimination against women shall be treated as applying equally to the treatment of men, and for that purpose shall have effect with such modifications as are requisite.

4. Discrimination by way of victimisation

(1) A person ("the discriminator") discriminates against another person ("the person victimised") in any circumstances relevant for the purposes of any provision of this Act if he treats the person victimised less favourably than in those circumstances he treats or would treat other persons, and does so by reason that the person victimised has—

- (a) brought proceedings against the discriminator or any other person under this Act or the Equal Pay Act 1970, or
- (b) given evidence or information in connection with proceedings brought by any person against the discriminator or any other person under this Act or the Equal Pay Act 1970, or
- (c) otherwise done anything under or by reference to this Act or the Equal Pay Act 1970 in relation to the discriminator or any other person, or
- (d) alleged that the discriminator or any other person has committed an act which (whether or not the allegation so states) would amount to a contravention of this Act or give rise to a claim under the Equal Pay Act 1970,

or by reason that the discriminator knows the person victimised intends to do any of those things, or suspects the person victimised has done, or intends to do, any of them.

(2) Subsection (1) does not apply to treatment of a person by reason of any allegation made by him if the allegation was false and not made in good faith.

(3) For the purposes of subsection (1), a provision of Part II or III framed with reference to discrimination against women shall be treated as applying equally to the treatment of men and for that purpose shall have effect with such modifications as are requisite.

5. Interpretation

(1) In this Act—

(a) references to discrimination refer to any discrimination falling within sections 1 to 4; and
(b) references to sex discrimination refer to any discrimination falling within section 1 or 2,

and related expressions shall be construed accordingly.

(2) In this Act—

"woman" includes a female of any age, and
"man" includes a male of any age.

(3) A comparison of the cases of persons of different sex or marital status under section 1(1) or 3(1) must be such that the relevant circumstances in the one case are the same, or not materially different, in the other.

PART II

Main duties of employers

6. Discrimination against applicants and employees

(1) It is unlawful for a person, in relation to employment by him at an establishment in Great Britain, to discriminate against a woman—

(a) in the arrangements he makes for the purpose of determining who should be offered that employment, or
(b) in the terms on which he offers her that employment, or
(c) by refusing or deliberately omitting to offer her that employment.

(2) It is unlawful for a person, in the case of a woman employed by him at an establishment in Great Britain, to discriminate against her—

(a) in the way he affords her access to opportunities for promotion, transfer or training, or to any other benefits, facilities or services, or by refusing or deliberately omitting to afford her access to them, or
(b) by dismissing her, or subjecting her to any other detriment

(3) [repealed]

(4) Subsections (1)(b) and (2) do not apply to provision in relation to death or retirement except in so far as, in their application to provision in relation to retirement, they render it unlawful for a person to discriminate against a woman—

(a) in such of the terms on which he offers her employment as make provision in relation to the way in which he will afford her access to opportunities for promotion, transfer or training or as provide for her dismissal or demotion; or
(b) in the way he affords her access to opportunities for promo-

tion, transfer or training or by refusing or deliberately omitting to afford her access to any such opportunities; or
  (c) by dismissing her or subjecting her to any detriment which results in her dismissal or consists in or involves her demotion.

(5) Subject to section 8(3), subsection (1)(b) does not apply to any provision for the payment of money which, if the woman in question were given the employment, would be included (directly or otherwise) in the contract under which she was employed.

(6) Subsection (2) does not apply to benefits consisting of the payment of money when the provision of those benefits is regulated by the woman's contract of employment.

(7) [covers cases where a person has dual status as employee and customer.]

PART II (continued)

GOQs

7. Exception where sex is a genuine occupational qualification

(1) In relation to sex discrimination—
  (a) section 6(1)(a) or (c) does not apply to any employment where being a man is a genuine occupational qualification for the job, and
  (b) section 6(2)(a) does not apply to opportunities for promotion or transfer to, or training for, such employment.

(2) Being a man is a genuine occupational qualification for a job only where—
  (a) the essential nature of the job calls for a man for reasons of physiology (excluding physical strength or stamina) or, in dramatic performances or other entertainment, for reasons of authenticity, so that the essential nature of the job would be materially different if carried out by a woman; or
  (b) the job needs to be held by a man to preserve decency or privacy because—
    (i) it is likely to involve physical contact with men in circumstances where they might reasonably object to its being carried out by a woman, or
    (ii) the holder of the job is likely to do his work in circumstances where men might reasonably object to the presence of a woman because they are in a state of undress or are using sanitary facilities; or
  (ba) the job is likely to involve the holder of the job doing his work, or living, in a private home and needs to be held by a

man because objection might reasonably be taken to allowing to a woman—

    (i) the degree of physical or social contact with a person living in the home, or

    (ii) the knowledge of intimate details of such a person's life, which is likely, because of the nature or circumstances of the job or of the home, to be allowed to, or available to, the holder of the job; or

(c) the nature or location of the establishment makes it impracticable for the holder of the job to live elsewhere than in premises provided by the employer, and—

    (i) the only such premises which are available for persons holding that kind of job are lived in, or normally lived in, by men and are not equipped with separate sleeping accommodation for women and sanitary facilities which could be used by women in privacy from men, and

    (ii) it is not reasonable to expect the employer either to equip those premises with such accommodation and facilities or to provide other premises for women; or

(d) the nature of the establishment, or of the part of it within which the work is done, requires the job to be held by a man because—

    (i) it is, or is part of, a hospital, prison or other establishment for persons requiring special care, supervision or attention, and

    (ii) those persons are all men (disregarding any woman whose presence is exceptional), and

    (iii) it is reasonable, having regard to the essential character of the establishment or that part, that the job should not be held by a woman; or

(e) the holder of the job provides individuals with personal services promoting their welfare or education, or similar personal services, and those services can most effectively be provided by a man, or

(f) [repealed]

(g) the job needs to be held by a man because it is likely to involve the performance of duties outside the United Kingdom in a country whose laws or customs are such that the duties could not, or could not effectively, be performed by a woman, or

(h) the job is one of two to be held by a married couple.

(3) Subsection (2) applies where some only of the duties of the job fall within paragraphs (a) to (g) as well as where all of them do.

(4) Paragraph (a), (b), (c), (d), (e), (f) or (g) of subsection (2) does

not apply in relation to the filling of a vacancy at a time when the employer already has male employees—

(a) who are capable of carrying out the duties falling within that paragraph, and
(b) whom it would be reasonable to employ on those duties, and
(c) whose numbers are sufficient to meet the employer's likely requirements in respect of those duties without undue inconvenience.

NOTE: By reason of Section 2(1) of the SDA, the above provisions also apply with "man" altered to "woman" and "woman" altered to "man".

PART IV

Responsibility for employees

41. Liability of employers and principals

(1) Anything done by a person in the course of his employment shall be treated for the purposes of this Act as done by his employer as well as by him, whether or not it was done with the employer's knowledge or approval.

(2) Anything done by a person as agent for another person with the authority (whether express or implied, and whether precedent or subsequent) of that other person shall be treated for the purposes of this Act as done by that other person as well as by him.

(3) In proceedings brought under this Act against any person in respect of an act alleged to have been done by an employee of his it shall be a defence for that person to prove that he took such steps as were reasonably practicable to prevent the employee from doing that act, or from doing in the course of his employment acts of that description.

PART V

Positive action

48. Other discriminatory training etc

(1) Nothing in Parts II to IV shall render unlawful any act done by an employer in relation to particular work in his employment, being an act done in, or in connection with,

(a) affording his female employees only, or his male employees only, access to facilities for training which would help to fit them for that work, or
(b) encouraging women only, or men only, to take advantage of opportunities for doing that work,

where at any time within the twelve months immediately preceding the doing of the act there were no persons of the sex in question among those doing that work or the number of persons of that sex doing the work was comparatively small.

Note: The Part numbers, in the above extracts, refer to the Part numbers in the Acts themselves.

Appendix 2

The Institute of Personnel Management Code

1 Why an IPM code?

The IPM has produced and issued statements and guidelines on discrimination and equal opportunities since 1969. It has taken part in the consultations when the Commission for Racial Equality (CRE) and the Equal Opportunities Commission (EOC) were preparing their own 'statutory' codes. It has done its utmost to inform personnel managers about the widespread and serious unfair discrimination which exists.

Yet investigation shows that a considerable and unacceptable level of racial discrimination in employment still exists and that sex discrimination is dwindling only very slowly. The regrettable results are increasingly apparent in disillusionment among ethnic minorities and women, in social unrest and, most important in the employment context, *in the misuse and/or waste of human resources.*

As the professional body concerned with the most effective use of human resources at work, the Institute has a role and responsibility to promote good and fair practices in personnel management and to influence members to ensure that the most effective use is made of *all* human resources.

Personnel managers have a special leading role in combating discrimination. While they can use the sex and racial discrimination laws and the EOC and CRE codes, it seems desirable for an IPM Code to reinforce the major laws and the 'statutory' codes with interpretations, emphases and additions specially relevant to the roles of personnel managers.

The aim of the IPM Code is:

- to bring together and update in summarized form the many recommendations on discrimination made by the Institute over the years
- to publish and distribute these recommendations as part of a campaign to inform members and employers of the continuing need

to review, develop and improve personnel policies and practices designed to combat discrimination at work.

The Code covers sex and racial discrimination in employment but also includes sections on two other kinds of discrimination — on grounds of age and against people with disabilities. The Code does not specifically include religion although it is recognized that religious discrimination is a major issue (and is covered by the law) in Northern Ireland. Northern Ireland readers will therefore need to add this factor when applying the Code.

The IPM hopes that employers and personnel managers will apply the Code in their organizations for two sound and practical reasons:

1. The policies recommended should ensure compliance with the 'statutory' codes and thereby help in cases of alleged discrimination before industrial tribunals.
2. They should promote an environment which enables the organization to tap the widest possible sources of talent.

It is also hoped that the Code will act as a very public indication of the IPM's stand against discrimination and will energise any personnel managers who have done little or nothing about discrimination on the grounds that they have "no problems here"—a common, but usually mistaken, view.

2 The law

The three main Acts, in Great Britain, on discrimination are:

- The Equal Pay Act 1970 (as amended).
- The Sex Discrimination Act 1975 (as amended).
- The Race Relations Act 1976.

This Code is mainly concerned with the employment aspects of the latter two.

Rehabilitation of offenders

Naturally, employers will have regard to the provisions of the Rehabilitation of Offenders Act 1974 and not discriminate against or dismiss the applications of candidates with spent convictions. The Act has implications for the design of application forms and interview methods. Guides to the Act are available, published by HMSO.

The Sex Discrimination Act (SDA) renders unlawful two kinds of discrimination on the grounds of sex and marriage. These are

1. *direct discrimination*—where a person treats a woman less favourably than he would a man on the ground of her sex or a married person less favourably than an unmarried person of the same sex on the ground of marital status. The SDA also applies to a man who is treated less favourably than a woman;

2. *indirect discrimination* — where an *unjustifiable* requirement or condition is applied equally to both sexes but has a disproportionately adverse effect on one sex because the proportion of one sex which can comply with it is considerably smaller than the proportion of the other sex which can comply with it. The inability to comply must also have a "detrimental" effect, such as not being promoted or selected. Examples of indirect discrimination may include:

- applying an unjustifiable age barrier
- promoting according to seniority
- applying a mobility clause as a condition for appointing management trainees
- rigidly insisting on certain education qualifications which may not be essential to performance of the job.

This does not mean that, for example, **all** age barriers or mobility clauses would be discriminatory but that employers should examine such requirements and assess how essential they really are.

The Race Relations Act (RRA) renders unlawful both direct and indirect discrimination on the grounds of colour, race, nationality or ethnic or national origins. The indirect discrimination clauses are broadly similar to those in the SDA (*see above*).

The CRE and EOC Codes

These are:

1. The Code of Practice for the elimination of racial discrimination and the promotion of quality of opportunity in employment issued by the CRE.
2. The Code of Practice for the elimination of discrimination on the grounds of sex and marriage and the promotion of equality of opportunity in employment issued by the EOC.

The codes are recommendations and guidance on how to avoid racial and sex discrimination in employment. They contain advice on the policies that are needed to prevent discrimination in such matters as the recruitment and treatment of employees. They also suggest positive steps to promote equal opportunity.

The codes do not have the force of law but they are approved by Parliament and their provisions will be taken into account by industrial tribunals in considering relevant cases.

People with disabilities

No laws exist in the UK on discrimination against people with disabilities similar to those against women and minorities.

However, the laws relating to the employment of people with disabilities are as follows:

The Disabled Persons (Employment) Acts 1944 and *1958* place a duty on employers (with 20 or more staff) to employ a *quota* of registered people with disabilities. The quota is currently three per cent of total staff. If this quota is not reached, an employer may not recruit persons who are not registered as disabled unless he obtains a permit from the MSC. Employers who are subject to the quota are required to keep certain specified employment records for inspection by the MSC.

Registration as a person with disabilities is *voluntary*. Those eligible to register are those who, because of injury, disease or congenital deformity, are substantially handicapped in obtaining or keeping employment of a kind which would otherwise be suited to their age, experience and qualifications.

The Companies (Directors' Report) (Employment of Disabled Persons) Regulations (1980) place a duty on employers (with 250 or more staff) to give a statement in the directors' reports setting out how their policy has operated in the previous financial year towards the recruitment, training, career development and promotion of people with disabilities including the retention of employees who develop a disability after being employed.

These regulations cover all people with disabilities, whether registered or not.

3 Avoiding unfair discrimination

Equal opportunity programmes

These are not required by law but experience has shown that they are necessary if progress is to be made against discrimination. They are an essential part of good management and their benefits include the following:

- they are an effective tool in getting all employees to know the organization's policy on discrimination and what is expected of them
- they form the basis for monitoring, by setting the standards of conduct which monitoring can and should "audit"
- they can provide useful evidence in cases of alleged discrimination. This applies especially to allegations against an individual, since the employer is required by the law to show that he has taken all such steps as were reasonably practicable to prevent the employee from breaking the law
- they conform with the recommendations of the EOC and CRE codes which may be taken into account by industrial tribunals
- they can enhance the organization's image as a forward-looking and progressive employer.

The IPM recommends that personnel managers should promote the publication and adoption of positive* equal opportunity programmes in their organizations. These should have the following characteristics:

- they should cover discrimination on grounds of sex, race, age and disability (and, certainly in Northern Ireland, religion). The IPM recognizes that the causes of discrimination are different for these groups with varying emphases upon prejudice and physiological/psychological differences. Each kind of discrimination must be considered separately
- they should be based upon a policy statement issued and publicly supported by top management
- they should be 'put over', from the highest level, to those in key management posts and especially to those with major roles in recruitment and development decisions
- they should be publicised continuously by every channel of communication, eg house journals, discussion groups, works committees and briefing groups—and, of course, by all managers and supervisors to their subordinates
- they should not be imposed from above but should be produced in consultation between personnel departments, line management, trade union and employee representatives.

A policy statement alone or statements such as "we are an equal opportunity employer" will achieve little or nothing. They must be supported by action, by training and by publicity.

Above all, the working of the programme must be audited—by monitoring (see below).

Monitoring

The need

It is common management experience that it is necessary to check whether the organization's policies are being carried out. This is just as true of equal opportunity policies as of all others. Indeed the Institute does not regard equal opportunities monitoring as separate from the monitoring of other kinds of personnel activities but as part of the whole necessary range of monitoring which should be carried out in an organization.

However in the area of equal opportunities, where prejudices are often strong, even if unconscious, it is particularly likely that individuals 'down the line', will flout the official policies, even to the extent of breaking the law.

To prevent this, the employer needs to know what is going on, what

---

* *This does not imply 'reverse discrimination' which is opposed by the IPM*

decisions are being made and how different groups, men and women, white and ethnic minorities are being treated.
To do this, monitoring is essential and the Institute strongly recommends it.

The object of monitoring is to check that, at every point where decisions are made about individuals—their engagement, promotion, training, treatment, remuneration, hours and other conditions—there are no signs that

1. prejudices about sex, ethnic origin, age or disability are influencing decisions
2. indirect discrimination, eg in the form of non-essential age limits or qualifications criteria, or word of mouth recruitment, is having an adverse impact on women, ethnic minorities, people with disabilities or older workers.

The data

Monitoring is possible only if the necessary data (sex, ethnic origin, age and disability, if any) are recorded. This usually requires only the addition of one or two items to existing records and this presents little technical difficulty with either manual or computerized records.

Recording sex, age and disability normally raises no difficulty. Recording ethnic origin, however, is still the subject of controversy although less so than in the past. Nevertheless since it is essential for auditing purposes, the IPM recommends that ethnic monitoring should be carried out. It is, however, vital to explain to applicants and others who are asked to state ethnic origin that this will be used to protect their interests and ensure that they are fairly assessed and treated.

Perhaps the most important process to monitor is selection and recruitment where prejudices or indirect discrimination can easily influence short-listing and interviewing. But also, such matters as the proportions of women and of ethnic minorities at different levels in the organization are matters which should be regularly checked. For example, women and minorities may be concentrated in lower levels suggesting that there may be unfair discrimination policies/practices in selection for promotion.

The figures alone cannot establish that unfair discrimination is occurring. They can only draw attention to situations which suggest a *prima facie* case for further investigation. This may or may not establish that some apparent disproportion has good valid reasons, other than sex, ethnic origin or age.

The IPM does not recommend quotas (which are illegal except for the registered disabled) and opposes any ideas of lower standards for women or for minority groups. However, when there is serious under representation of a particular sex or ethnic group, possibly as a result of previous discrimination, it sees no harm in setting appropriate targets as a short term remedial measure, *but with no lowering of standards*, if these can be shown to be reasonably necessary for efficient functioning.

The recruitment process

This is the most important area to monitor. If women and ethnic minorities or people with disabilities are not applying or being selected for jobs (in proportion to their presence in the appropriate labour market) the question has to be asked: "Why?". Is it due to factors beyond the employer's control or because the recruitment procedure in some way 'indirectly' discriminates against women, people with disabilities or ethnic minorities or both?

The following steps will help to guard against unfair discrimination in recruitment.

- Have clear, concisely written and up to date job descriptions. Ensure that job titles are not sex biased and are accurate.

- Avoid over inflated or unnecessary job criteria in person specifications. Even in times of high unemployment, when it is practicable to raise the level of qualifications demanded, they should still not exceed the real needs of the job.

- Check that job requirements are really *necessary* to do the job and are not a reflection of traditional practices which may be operating to the disadvantage of women, minorities, people with disabilities or older people.

- Guard against sex/race stereotyping, particularly in illustrations in advertisements and recruitment literature. Where illustrations show a group of people, it may be sensible policy to show a mixed group in terms of race and sex. Such a policy is particularly recommended in literature aimed at school leavers or university graduates.

- Consider adopting equal opportunity slogans such as "we are an equal opportunities employer" or "we welcome applicants regardless of race, ethnic origin, sex, disability, age etc." but only if the statements can be backed up by practice.

- Methods of recruitment exist other than advertisements, eg headhunters, selection consultants, employment agencies, direct recruitment from schools and colleges and, word of mouth. Whichever is chosen, take care to ensure that the method is fair to all potential applicants and does not effectively screen out minorities or members of one sex. In particular the "word of mouth" approach can be discriminatory since it will tend to perpetuate a workforce from the same sources as at present.

The interview

It must be recognized that the interview as a predictive device is an extremely fallible instrument, highly susceptible to interviewer bias and stereotyped perceptions.

To reduce the effects of interviewer bias and to improve the general standard of interviewing, organizations should

- provide training in interviewing for all those who have to conduct selection interviews. Such training should cover interviewing techniques, practice interviews, legal aspects with particular reference to discrimination law, and known areas of recruiter bias other than those covered by law, eg age
- ensure that *only trained interviewers* conduct preliminary selection interviews
- wherever possible provide interview training for line managers.

During the interview

- care should be taken to avoid questions which could be construed as discriminatory, eg questions to young female applicants about marriage plans or, worse, family planning plans. However, an interviewer is entitled to discuss with the applicant any domestic or personal circumstances which might have an adverse impact on effective performance of the job but this should be done *without making assumptions based on the sex of the applicant*
- clear notes or records of the interview should be made and retained.

Training and promotion

Women and minorities are barred from some jobs because they lack the necessary training. Often this is because, through direct or indirect discrimination, they have been excluded from training schemes. As part of the audit process organizations are therefore recommended to:

- check that women and minorities are being trained and developed by participating in appropriate training courses either internal or external and by other development activities such as planned experience, coaching, and encouragement towards self development
- be prepared to take late entrants into training schemes. There are common assumptions about age limits for training which can operate against women and minorities
- examine selection criteria for training and promotion opportunities to ensure they do not indirectly discriminate against women or minorities
- consider using the positive training provisions for women and ethnic minorities (s.48 of the SDA and s.38 of the RRA) where women or minorities are seriously under-represented in particular jobs.

Just as much care, if not more, should be taken over selection for promotion as for initial selection. Organizations should therefore:

- pay more attention to improving their procedures for performance review and assessment of potential. In particular they need to tackle the problems of unequal standards of appraisers and of monitoring how rating scales are used

- guard against perpetuating the effects of past discriminatory policies in selection for promotion where these continue to operate to the detriment of women or of minority groups
- not presume that women or minorities do not want promotion. Their reluctance to come forward may be due to an unwillingness, based on past observations, to subject themselves to probable unfair rejection.

Victimization and harassment

Employers should treat seriously all complaints of discrimination, victimization or harassment. These should be dealt with under the organization's internal grievance procedures and should be thoroughly investigated. It is appreciated that allegations of sexual harassment may prove particularly difficult to investigate in the almost certain absence of witnesses. It will be up to the employer, on the basis of the facts, to decide whether or not such allegations have substance. It should be made clear that any acts of discrimination, harassment etc. by individual employees will be viewed as serious offences under the organization's disciplinary procedure.

4 People with disabilities

The Institute is committed to positive policies to ensure a fairer share of employment opportunities for all people with disabilities.

However, it doubts the value of the quota system (see section 2) for several reasons:

1. It aims to protect only the registered disabled.
2. Employers have difficulty in meeting the quota because so many people with disabilities do not register (and object to registering).
3. It is almost impossible to enforce.

The Institute's view on the quota system should not be seen as showing a negative attitude. Rather the Institute favours a far more positive approach to the employment of people with disabilities, and, in particular, supports the recommendations of the MSC's *Code of Good Practice on the Employment of Disabled People*. It recognizes however that *some* jobs/operations/sites do not offer suitable or safe employment for people with certain disabilities. It will always be necessary to assess the abilities/disabilities of particular individuals for particular jobs but with an open mind.

As a start personnel departments should consider the following immediate areas for action.

- Write or rewrite policy statements on the employment of people with disabilities, both for new and existing employees and those injured at work.
- Obtain the commitment of senior management to the employment of people with disabilities.
- Train line managers not to assume that all people with disabilities are unemployable but to recognize specific handicaps, if any, of different illnesses and disabilities. Train them in how to deal with and help employees with specific disabilities.
- If possible, carry out a review of the employment levels of all people with disabilities and not just registered disabled.
- Implement and maintain a system to monitor organizational practice to ensure that the aims of the organization's policy are being met.

5 Age discrimination*

The problems of sex and racial discrimination are well known, if not resolved. There is, however, another area of discrimination which has received little media attention but which is causing growing concern to the Institute. This is age discrimination which tends to operate across a wide range of ages but is particularly likely to affect people in their 40s and 50s.

The Institute recognizes that prevailing attitudes about youth unemployment and trends in some industries towards early retirement may be important influences on current recruitment policies and manpower planning.

But the Institute believes that, for most jobs, automatically excluding entire age groups is wasteful for organizations as well as damaging to individuals.

In some instances it may be justifiable to have an age limit, eg in graduate trainee schemes or apprenticeships, and necessary to have a sensible organization 'age profile' for manpower and succession planning purposes. But often there is no justification for ignoring a pool of talent and experience purely on the grounds of age.

As with other areas of discrimination, attitudes about age based on stereotyping, transmission of received wisdom and generalization can affect many personnel decisions, but particularly decisions in recruitment, selection and training.

The Institute therefore recommends that

- *as a general rule* age should not be used as a primary discriminator in recruitment, selection, promotion and training decisions

---

* *Age discrimination is not subject to any UK legislation*

- where age bars are used, the questions should be asked "are they necessary and why?"
- organizations should consider incorporating in their equal opportunity statements their commitment not to discriminate arbitrarily on grounds of age
- more should be done by organizations to provide counselling in career development and to encourage self development for both younger and older employees
- those responsible for in-house training and retraining programmes should recognize that older workers can still acquire and retain new knowledge and skills.

6 The personnel manager's special role

The personnel manager will, usually, need to lead, persuade and convince. His/her ability to do this successfully will depend, as always, largely upon personal characteristics. But the task will be easier if the personnel manager clearly possesses greater expertise in this field than others in the organization. This can be ensured in various ways.

First, the personnel manager should study and master the three basic Acts (see Section 2 above). Discriminatory suggestions and comments by fellow managers can, and should, be countered by quoting the sections of the Acts which make them unlawful.

Secondly, it is invaluable to know of the important cases on various issues of principle which have been decided. Decisions of the EAT, Court of Appeal and House of Lords are the most important. Only specialists can know these cases in detail but it is valuable to know, broadly, what the cases were about so as to be able to consult them when relevant.

Thirdly, familiarity with the two 'statutory' codes (EOC and CRE) is essential since it is much more persuasive to quote principles approved by Parliament than to appear to be expressing personal opinions.

Lastly, the personnel manager should know where to go for information and advice. Here, the major sources are the employment departments of the EOC and CRE, the Race Relations Employment Advisory Services of the Department of Employment and the Information and Advisory Services of the IPM, and, for the people with disabilities, the MSC's Disablement Advisory Service through local job centres. In particular, practical advice on collecting and analysing the data for monitoring purposes can be obtained from the CRE and EOC.

APPENDIX 2 261

The IPM is keen to receive comments about the content and operation of the EO Code. These should be sent to:

Professional Adviser, Equal Opportunities
Institute of Personnel Management
IPM House
Camp Road
Wimbledon
London SW19 4UX
Tel: 081 946 9100 Telex 947203
Fax: 081 947 2570

Note: Where the code refers to the MSC, you should now read the Employment Service.

Appendix 3

Extracts from EC Law

Part 1

Extracts from the Equal Treatment Directive

Article 2

1. For the purposes of the following provisions, the principle of equal treatment shall mean that there shall be no discrimination whatsoever on grounds of sex either directly or indirectly by reference in particular to marital or family status.
2. This Directive shall be without prejudice to the right of Member States to exclude from its field of application those occupational activities and, where appropriate, the training leading thereto, for which, by reason of their nature or the context in which they are carried out, the sex of the worker constitutes a determining factor.

Article 3

1. Application of the princple of equal treatment means that there shall be no discrimination whatsoever on grounds of sex in the conditions, including selection criteria, for access to all jobs or posts, whatever the sector or branch of activity, and to all levels of the occupational hierarchy.

Article 5

1. Application of the principle of equal treatment with regard to working conditions, including the conditions governing dismissal, means that men and women shall be guaranteed the same conditions without discrimination on grounds of sex.

Part 2

Article 119 of the Treaty of Rome

Each Member State shall during the first stage ensure and subsequently maintain the application of the principle that men and women should receive equal pay for equal work.

For the purpose of this Article, 'pay' means the ordinary basic or minimum wage or salary and any other consideration, whether in cash or in kind, which the worker receives, directly or indirectly, in respect of his employment from his employer.

Equal pay without discrimination based on sex means:

(a) that pay for the same work at piece rates shall be calculated on the basis of the same unit of measurement;
(b) that pay for work at time rates shall be the same for the same job.

Further Reading

The EOC and CRE Codes of Practice are essential reading. The IPM Equal Opportunities Code is reproduced in this book, but you should consider buying copies of this Code (and of the EOC and CRE Codes) for all personnel and other managers.

EOC Publications

The Code of Practice
Guidelines for Equal Opportunities Employers
Fair and Efficient Selection
Avoiding Sex Bias in Selection Testing—Guidance for Employers
A Guide for Employers to the Sex Discrimination Acts 1975 and 1986

EOC publications are available at varied prices, all under £2.00. You should telephone the Communications Unit on 061 833 9244.

CRE Publications

The Code of Practice
A Measure of Equality: Monitoring and achieving racial equality in employment
Are Employers complying? The Code of Practice in Employment
Equal Opportunity in Employment: A guide for employers
Indirect Discrimination in Employment: A practical guide
Positive Action and Equal Opportunity in Employment
Psychometric Tests and Racial Equality
Racial Discrimination and Grievance Procedures: A Practical Guide for Employers

CRE publications are distributed by Lavis Marketing, 73 Lime Walk, Headington, Oxford OX3 7AD (0865 67575).

The Institute of Personnel Management

The IPM Equal Opportunities Code
IPM Statement on Harassment at Work

IPM Recruitment Code
IPM Statement on Age and Employment

Single copies are available free of charge (with an SAE). The current price for bulk quantities is 25p each.

Copies should be ordered from the Institute of Personnel Management, IPM House, Camp Road, Wimbledon, London SW19 4UX (081 946 9100)

The Employment Service

Code of Good Practice on the Employment of Disabled People (free of charge from the Employment Service Disabilities Services Branch, Courtwood House, c/o Rockingham House, 123 West Street, Sheffield, S1 4ER (0742 739190)
Sexual Harassment in the Workplace: A guide for employers
Sexual Harassment in the Workplace: The facts employees should know

Both the above publications are available from Cambertown Limited, Employment Department, Goldthorpe Industrial Estate, Goldthorpe, Rotherham S63 9BL

Industrial Relations Services

Industrial Relations Law Reports
Equal Opportunities Review

To subscribe to the above publications you should write to the IRS at 18-20 Highbury Place, London N5 1QP or telephone 071 354 5858. Issue 41 of the *Equal Opportunities Review* (January/February 1992) includes the EC Recommendations and Code on sexual harassment.

Table of cases

Alexander v The Home Office (1988) IRLR 190   p204
Aziz v Trinity Street Taxis Ltd (1988) IRLR 204   p61-2, 63
Balgobin v London Borough of Tower Hamlets
  (1987) IRLR 401   p132, 133
Barber v Guardian Royal Exchange Assurance Group
  (1990) IRLR 240   p147-8, 175, 178-9, 180
Barclays Bank PLC v James (EAT only) (1990) IRLR 90   p86
Barclays Bank PLC v Kapur (1991) IRLR 136   p202
Bick v Royal West of England Residential School for the Deaf
  (1976) IRLR 326   p37
Bilka-kaufhaus GmbH v Weber von Hartz (1986) IRLR 317   p177
BL Cars Ltd v Brown (1983) IRLR 193   p144
Bracebridge Engineering Limited v Darby (1990)
  IRLR 3   p131-2, 133, 148
Briggs v North Eastern Education and Library Board (1990)
  IRLR 181   p51, 52
British Railways Board v Natarajan (1979) IRLR 45   p199-200
Bromley v H & J Quick Limited (1988) IRLR 249   p171

Calder v James Finlay Corporation (1989) IRLR 55   p202
Capper Pass Limited v Lawton (1976) IRLR 366   p172
Clarke v Eley (IMI) Kynoch Ltd (1982) IRLR 482   p147, 150
Clymo v London Borough of Wandsworth (1989) IRLR 241   p51, 52
Coleman v Skyrail Oceanics Limited (1981) IRLR 398   p37
Cornelius v University College of Swansea (1987)
  IRLR 141   p61, 63, 64, 65

Dekker v VJV-Centrum (1991) IRLR 27   p155
De Souza v The Automobile Association (1986) IRLR 103   p128
Dibro Limited v Hore (1990) IRLR 129   p171
Din v Carrington Viyella Limited (1982) IRLR 281   p202
Dodd v British Telecom PLC (1988) IRLR 16   p201

Eaton Limited v Nuttall (1977) IRLR 71   p172
Etam PLC v Rowan (1989) IRLR 150   p108
Etherson v Strathclyde Regional Council (1992) IRLR 392   p201

Garland v British Rail Engineering Limited (1982) IRLR 257   p148
Gill and Another v El Vinos Co. Ltd (1983) IRLR 206   p144

Greater Manchester Police Authority v Lea (1990)
IRLR 372 p49, 53
Grimaldi v Fonds des Maladies Professionelles (1990)
IRLR 400 p132

Hampson v Department of Education & Science
(Court of Appeal) (1989) IRLR 69 p47, 48-9
Hampson v Department of Education & Science (House of Lords)
(1990) IRLR 302 p47, 99-100
Handley v H Mono Limited (1978) IRLR 534 p177
Hayes v Malleable Working Men's Club and Institute
(1985) IRLR 367 p153
Hayward v Cammell Laird Shipbuilders Limited (1988)
IRLR 257 p173, 175, 178
Hertz v Aldi (1991) IRLR 31 p155
Home Office v Holmes (1984) IRLR 299 p47, 51, 52

James v Eastleigh Borough Council (1990) IRLR 288
p35, 36, 62-3, 88, 155, 186, 187
Jeremiah v Ministry of Defence (1979) IRLR 436 p143
Jones v University of Manchester (Not yet reported) p50, 52

Kirby v Manpower Services Commission (1980) IRLR 229 p61, 63

Leverton v Clwyd County Council (1989) IRLR 28
p169-70, 173, 175-6, 181
London Borough of Ealing v Race Relations Board (1972)
1 All ER 105 p31
London Borough of Lambeth v CRE (1990) IRLR 231 p106, 112

Macarthys Limited v Smith (1980) IRLR 210 p170
Mandla v Lee (1983) IRLR 209 p47, 185, 187
Marshall v Southampton and South West Hampshire Area Health
Authority (1986) IRLR 140 p69, 146
McConomy v Croft Inns Limited (1992) IRLR 561 p145
Mirror Group Newspapers Limited v Gunning (1986) IRLR 27 p70

Noone v North West Thames Regional Health Authority (1988)
IRLR 195 p90, 204

O'Brien v Sim-Chem Limited (1980) IRLR 373 p172
Orphanos v Queen Mary College (1985) IRLR 349 p46
Owen and Briggs v James (1982) IRLR 502 p33, 81

Peake v Automotive Products Limited (1977)
IRLR 365 p143-4, 145
Perera v Civil Service Commission (1982) IRLR 147 p50-51
Perera v Civil Service Commission (1983) IRLR 166 p48, 53
Pickstone and Others v Freemans PLC (1988) IRLR 357 p174, 181
Price v Civil Service Commission (1977) IRLR 291 p55, 92

Quinnen v Hovells (1984) IRLR 227 p70

R v Birimingham City Council ex parte Equal Opportunities
   Commission (1989) IRLR 173   p186-7
R v CRE Parte Westminster City Council (1985) IRLR 426   p211
R v Secretary of State for Defence and others ex parte Julie Lane
   (not yet reported)   p101
R v Secretary of State for Defence and others ex parte Leslie Leale
   (not yet reported)   p101
Rainey v Greater Glasgow Health Board (1987) IRLR 26   p176

Saunders v Richmond-upon-Thames Borough Council (1977)
   IRLR 362   p82
Schmidt v Austicks Bookshops Limited (1977) IRLR 360   p144-5
Science Research Council v Nassé (1979) IRLR 465   p199
Shields v E Coomes (Holdings) Limited (1978) IRLR 263   p173
Simon v Brimham Associates (1987) IRLR 307   p82-3
Sisley v Britannia Security Systems Limted (1983) IRLR 404   p108
Snowball v Gardner Merchant Limited (1987) IRLR 397   p129
Sougrin v Haringey Health Authority (1992) IRLR 416   p202
Steel v The Post Office (1977) IRLR 288   p36
Strathclyde Regional Council v Porcelli (1986) IRLR 134
                                                     p130-1, 133

Tottenham Green Under Fives' Centre v Marshall (1989) IRLR 147
                                                          p106
Turley v Allders Department Stores Ltd (1980) IRLR 4   p153

Webb v EMO Air Cargo (UK) Limited (1993) IRLR 27   p155-6, 159
West Midlands Passenger Transport Executive v Singh (1988)
   IRLR 186   p91, 93
Wileman v Minilec Engineering Limited (1988) IRLR 144   p129-30
Wylie v Dee & Co (Menswear) Limited (1978) IRLR 103   p107

Zarczynska v Levy (1978) IRLR 532   p164

Note: With one exception, all the references are to the Industrial
   Relations Law Reports, although many of the cases are also
   reported in other Law Reports.

Index

administrative convenience 145
advertisements 23, 56, 73, 121, 161–3, 165–6
age discrimination 20, 27, 50–1, 55, 254, 257, 259–60
aircraft 11, 74, 185
Allied Dunbar 234
amendments, of complaints 202-3
appeals 26
application forms 57, 226
appraisals 54, 85, 94
armed forces 101
arrangements for filling vacancies 79, 163
Article 119 of EC Treaty 25, 101, 141, 147–8, 157, 170, 177, 178–9
assessments 54
assistance with claims 26, 27, 208
associated employers 169
associations 190–1
assumptions 92
authenticity, GOQ 105
automatic discrimination approach in pregnancy claims 154–6

back pay 168–9
beards, and indirect discrimination 47, 56–7
benefits 142–3, 148–9
BBC 235
'but for' test 35–6, 62–3

can comply, meaning of 47
career breaks 125
charitable benefits 102, 187
childcare 121, 124
chivalry 34–5, 145
Church of England 72
civil liability for discrimination 25
civil service 101
clothing rules 56–7, 144–5
clubs 22, 185, 190–1
codes of practice, status of 27

collective bargaining, as a facility 142–3
colour 31, 102
common terms and conditions, in equal pay cases 169–70
Commission for Racial Equality, role of 26–7, 34, 207–8
commissioners, appointment of 71
communal accommodation 103–4
communication 122, 123, 150
company cars 142, 149, 156
company directors 71, 76
comparable man approach, in pregnancy claims 153–4
comparator, meaning of 168
compensation
    and indirect discrimination 16, 52
    for injured feelings 146, 204
    for loss of opportunity 204
    in equal pay cases 168–9
    maximum amount of 26, 204–5
complaints system, in harassment cases 135–7
compulsory retirement age 24–5, 97, 146
conditions, in indirect discrimination claims, meaning of 47-8
considerably, meaning of 50
constructive dismissal 148, 205
continuing discrimination 201–2
contract terms 140–1, 148–9
contract workers 70, 73, 104
costs 26
course of employment, meaning of 76, 131–2
county courts, and industrial tribunals 25–6
Court of Appeal, appeals to 26
credit 185–6
crime, discrimination not a 25, 162
Crown employment 69
cultural backgrounds, different 150

decency, as GOQ 107–8
dependants 179–80
detrimental treatment 129, 143
de minimis 143–4
direct marriage discrimination, definition of 29–30, 243–4
direct racial discrimination, definition of 31, 238–9
direct sex discrimination, definition of 29, 243
Directives, EC, status of 24–5, 69, 71, 101, 201
disabled persons, discrimination against 25, 27, 252–3, 254, 258–9
disciplinary action, discrimination in 145, 150
disciplinary offence, discrimination as 136, 137–8
discouraging questions 82–3
discriminatory attitude 88
discriminatory motive 33
discriminatory practice 160–1
discriminatory tests 84
dismissal 145–8
documents, disclosure of 90, 199–200
domestic employment, see private household
downgrading 150
dress requirements 56–7, 144–5

earrings 145
educational establishments 184–5, 189–90
educational qualifications, as indirect discrimination 54–5
employees, discrimination by 23, 77
employers, discrimination against 15, 23, 191
employment, definition of 69–70, 171
employment agencies 55–6, 122, 166–7
Employment Appeal Tribunal, appeals to 26
English, command of, as requirement 57
Equal Opportunities Commission, role of 26–7, 34, 207–8
Equal Opportunities policies
 comunicating the policy 219–20, 254
 consultations 218, 254
 disciplinary procedure 219

formulating the policy 38, 217–9, 254
grievance procedure 219, 258
importance of 27–8, 215–6, 253
instructions and training 221–2, 228
and see guidance, instructions and training
monitoring 93, 224–7, 254–6
policy initiatives 228–9
responsibility for 219
reviewing existing practices 221
reviewing the policy 227–8
written programmes and procedures 201–1
equal value 173–4
Equal Value Regulations 24
equality clause 168
Equality Exchange 207
Equality for Women (White Paper) 22, 23, 107
Equal Treatment Directive 101, 146, 155
European Community law 11, 24, 26, 101, 111
EC Code on harassment at work 127, 132–9
European Court of Justice, references to 26
ethnic origins 18, 31
experience, requirement of 54, 165

facilities 142–3, 148–9, 184, 190
false reasons 89, 92
financial penalties, as victimisation 63–4
flexible approach, to avoid indirect discrimination 53, 56
flexible hours 125
flexible selection 123–4
formal investigations 27, 71–2, 209–210

gender-based criterion 155–6
Genuine Occupational Qualifications
 general principles 104–5, 110-111, 240–1, 246–8
 and advertisements 162
Gloucestershire County Council 235–6
goods 184, 190
grading 85, 94, 176
Greater Manchester Police 233–4
grievance procedure 142, 149, 258

guidance for managers 41, 52–3, 64–5, 76–7, 93, 166, 192, 221–2, 228
gypsies, as ethnic group 47

hair, requirements relating to 145
harassment, definition of 128–132
health and safety 98–9, 152, 156
hostile approach 89
Hotpoint 232
hours of work, as indirect discrimination 56
House of Lords, appeals to 26
housing 22, 189
hovercraft 74, 185
hypothetical comparisons 16, 32–3, 80–1

immigration control 100
incitement to racial hatred 21
independent expert 173–4, 182
Independent Television Association 234–5
indirect marriage discrimination, definition of 44–5, 243–4
indirect racial discrimination, definition of 45–6, 238
indirect sex discrimination, definition of 44–5, 243
inducements to discriminate 163–4
industrial tribunals and county courts 25–6
injuctions 208
injured feelings, compensation for 146, 153
IPM Code 27, 250–61
instruction, for managers and supervisors 41, 64–5, 76–7, 93, 138–9, 148, 166, 192, 221–2, 228
instructions to discriminate 163–4, 166
insurance 188
interlocutory hearing 203
interviews 82–4, 89, 94–5, 256–7
interview notes 89
investigating complaints 136–7, 205, 258

Jews, as ethnic group 47
job applications, discrimination relating to 79–80, 240, 245
job descriptions 93, 161, 256
job evaluation 171–2, 181
job sharing 51, 125

judges 71
Justices of the Peace 71
justifiable, meaning of 48–9, 53, 177

knock-on effect 174

language requirements 57
language training 122, 123
leave, arrangements for 124, 149
legal aid, not available 26
like work, meaning of 172–3
lists of applicants 94
local authorities 120, 188
long hair, rules relating to 145
lookism 20

marriage discrimination
  definition of 29–30, 243–4
  employment field only 19, 29, 45
marriage plans 37–8
married couples 37, 110
managers, training for 93, 135, 138–9
material factor defence 174–8, 182, 205
maternity leave 119, 124, 156–7, 158
men, discrimination against 29, 243
Midland Bank 234
Ministers of the Crown 71
Ministers of Religion 72
misconduct dismissals 146
misplaced benevolence 35, 112, 186
mobility requirements 16, 19, 57–8
monitoring 93, 224–7, 254–6

nationality 18, 31, 103
national origins 18, 31
National Power 232
national security 100–1
newsletters 220
night-shift 56, 97, 172–3
non-discrimination notice 72, 209, 210–11
Northern Ireland 11, 19, 251, 254
Northern Ireland Courts, decisions of 51–2
nurseries 124

objective comparison 90
objective criteria 93–4
occupational pension schemes 179–81
offences 162, 209

offensive questions 82–3
offers, job 86–7
official discrimination 100–1
oil platforms 11, 72, 109
omissions, to offer employment 80
open discrimination 87–8
overseas duties, as GOQ 110
overseas employment 74–5, 162
overseas, qualifications obtained 55, 165
overseas, skills to be used 115–6
overseas, workers recruited 115–6
overtime 172, 176–7

pandering to prejudice 34, 110
part-time work 51, 120–21, 124, 125, 149, 158
part-time workers
  equal pay 177
  indirect discrimination against 58, 149, 177
partners 70–1, 76, 104
passenger cases 52
past discrimination 202
paternity leave 120, 124
pending complaints, treatment of employee 65–6
pensions, claim under EC law 178–81, 187
pension age 97
pensionable service 156
performance appraisal 54, 94
persistent discrimination 209
personal equation 176
personal services, as GOQ 105–7
physical requirements, and indirect discrimination 58
physiology, as GOQ 105
police officers 72
Police Staff College 232–3
policy statement, on harassment 134–5
political discrimination 17–18
political parties 190
'pools', definition of 50
positive action
  advertisements and, 162, 166
  employment agencies and, 167
  encouragement to apply for work 113–4, 121–2, 242, 248–9
  local authorities and 188
  non-discriminatory steps 120–1, 122–5

overseas, provision for workers from 115–6
pregnant workers, provision for 119–20
  special needs 117–8, 118–9, 188
  training for employees 114–5, 121–2, 242, 248–9, 257
  training for non-employees 116–7
  vocational training by others 188
  work experience 188
positive discrimination 106, 112
prayer times 56, 125
preferences, as opposed to requirements and conditions 48
pregnancy
  dismissals on the ground of 152–6
  health and safety cases 98–9, 152, 156
  other discriminatory treatment 156–8
  special provision on account of 119–120
Pregnant Workers Directive 99, 154, 157
pre-hearing assessment 203
pre-hearing discussion 203
prejudice 21, 22, 33, 39–41, 82, 92
preliminary hearing 203
premises 184, 189
pressure to discriminate 23, 34, 41–2, 163–5, 166
previous acts 202
prison officers 72
privacy, as GOQ 107–8
private households 23, 73, 97, 108–9
promotion arrangements, discrimination in 84–5, 93–5, 257
protected act, in definition of victimisation 62
protective laws 97
public sector employers 69, 111, 201

questionnaire procedure 90, 197–9
questions at interview 82–3, 88–9, 94–5, 156
quotas 25, 112, 255–6

Racial Discrimination (White Paper) 112, 161–2
racial grounds, meaning of 31–2, 38, 239

racial group, meaning of 46–7 239
racial harassment 139
racial provocation 150
racial segregation 32, 144, 238
reasonably practicable steps,
  defence of 27–8, 76–7, 132–3, 191
recruitment arrangements 81, 93–5
recommendations, EC, status of
  132–3
recommendations by tribunals 203
redundancy payments 147–8, 150
redundancy selection 147, 150,
  157–8
Rehabilitation of Offenders Act 251
religious discrimination 11, 19–20,
  251, 254
religious holidays 56, 125
remote sites, GOQ exception 109
requirement, meaning of 47–8
residential areas, indirect
  discrimination and 55–6, 57
residential courses 57, 86, 124
residential requirements 57, 103,
  165, 185
responsibility for employees 27–8,
  75–7, 132–3 191, 241, 248
retirement age 97
reverse discrimination 112, 121
right to return to work 157–8

sailors 74
same employment, meaning of 168,
  169–70
sarees, and indirect discrimination
  56
schools 184
Scotland 11, 31
selection arrangements 81, 94
selection criteria 93, 256–7
selection tests 54
self-employed workers 69–70, 171
seniority, requirements relating to
  54
services 142–3, 148–9, 184, 190
sexual connotations, of certain
  terms 161
sexual orientation 18, 20
Shell UK 230–2
shifts 56, 176–7
ships 11, 74, 109, 185
shortlisting 81–2, 94
short-time working 150
Sikhs, as ethnic group 19, 47, 56–7

single sex establishments, as GOQ
  109–110
single sex schools 56, 189–90
small businesses 23, 97, 216–7,
  226–7
special needs, domestic and family
  responsibilities 117–8
special needs, of ethnic minorities
  118–9, 188, 242
sport 102–3, 162, 187
stamina 105
statistical evidence 50–1, 91
statutory discrimination 98–100,
  162, 187
statutory offices 71
stereotyping 256
strength 105
supervisors, training for 135
support system, in harassment
  cases 135–6

tenancies 184
terms of employment 140–1, 148,
  168
terms offered 86–7
territorial extent 11, 184–5
tests 54, 84
threats 163–4
time limits 25, 200–2, 205
training
  as a facility 85–6
  for managers and supervisors 76,
    93, 122, 135, 138–9, 192,
    221–2, 228
  see also positive action
trade unions, recruitment through
  55–6
Trade Union Reform and
  Employment Rights Bill 27, 99,
  152, 154, 156–7
transfers, as a facility 84–5
trivial complaints 143–4
trousers, and indirect
  discrimination 47, 56
turbans, and indirect
  discrimination 47, 56

unfair dismissal 146, 153, 154–5,
  157–8, 205
uniforms, requirements relating to
  56–7
unintentional discrimination 35–6,
  186–7
universities 184

unmarried persons, discrimination against 30–1

victimisation
  defination of 60, 239, 244
  for disobeying instructions 164
  importance of avoiding 206
  in equal pay claims 182
  private households and 73
voluntary bodies 190

Wales 11, 31
White Papers, *see Equality for Women* and *Racial Discrimination*
whole job, the, and indirect discrimination 51
word of mouth, as method of recruitment 55, 56, 256
work permits 100